'People hate being made to think, above all upon fundamental problems.'
Edith Hamilton, *The Greek Way,* W.W. Norton, New York, 1930.

Globalization's Limits

Conflicting National Interests in Trade and Finance

DIMITRIS N. CHORAFAS
Member, New York Academy of Sciences

Gower Applied Business Research
Our programme provides leaders, practitioners, scholars and researchers with thought provoking, cutting edge books that combine conceptual insights, interdisciplinary rigour and practical relevance in key areas of business and management.

Published by
Gower Publishing Limited
Wey Court East
Union Road
Farnham
Surrey, GU9 7PT
England

Ashgate Publishing Company
Suite 420
101 Cherry Street
Burlington,
VT 05401-4405
USA

www.gowerpublishing.com

British Library Cataloguing in Publication Data
Chorafas, Dimitris N.
  Globalization's limits : conflicting national interests in
  trade and finance
  1. Globalization 2. International finance 3. International trade
  4. Foreign trade regulation 5. European Union
  countries – Commerce 6. European Union countries – Economic
  conditions
  I. Title
  337

  ISBN: 978-0-566-08885-8

Library of Congress Cataloging-in-Publication Data
Chorafas, Dimitris N.
  Globalization's limits : conflicting national interests in trade and finance / by Dimitris Chorafas.
     p. cm.
  Includes index.
  ISBN 978-0-566-08885-8
  1. International economic integration. 2. Free trade. 3. Globalization. 4. International finance. I. Title.

  HF1418.5.C483 2009
  332.042--dc22

2008052668

Mixed Sources
Product group from well-managed
forests and other controlled sources
www.fsc.org Cert no. SA-COC-1565
© 1996 Forest Stewardship Council
FSC

Printed and bound in Great Britain by
MPG Books Ltd, Bodmin, Cornwall.

Contents

List of Figures

List of Tables

Acknowledgements

I am indebted to a long list of knowledgeable people for their contribution to the research which made this book feasible – including their input and constructive criticism during the manuscript's preparation.

Let me take this opportunity to thank Martin West for suggesting the project, Gillian Steadman for seeing it all the way to publication and Pat FitzGerald for the editing work. To Eva-Maria Binder goes the credit for compiling the research results, typing the text and for the artwork and index.

Dr Dimitris N. Chorafas
Valmer, France and Vitznau, Switzerland

Introduction

Globalization is both a process and a state of mind. Global markets open greater perspectives than those that are regional or local in terms of labour, raw materials, agricultural produce, manufactured goods and services. Success in global trade, however, requires cost control, flexibility, adaptation, price competitiveness and marketing skills. Countries and companies that don't meet this challenge may be hurt by globalization.

This book shows that globalization has limits and, like any other process, when such limits are exceeded it may turn from friend to foe. The text has been written for professionals and for the academic market – not necessarily for specialists but for people who want to know why globalization has encountered rough weather.

Is this adversity an anomaly or the new course of things?

Which are the main worries now emerging, and why?

Are globalization's woes an aftereffect of focusing too much on trade, with too little consideration of the way in which it affects the people and the economy of western countries?

One of the generally amiable idiosyncrasies of globalization is that it promotes specialization of labour and by extension brings together the different cultures of outsourcers and insourcers. Better trade than make war. But at the same time the globalized world's uncertainties destabilize both common people and decision-makers in a way reminiscent of Goethe's 'Faust' where, frustrated by the constraints on his learning, the hero makes a pact with the devil.

Treaties like the different 'rounds' of the World Trade Organization (WTO) don't close the uncertainties gap. People often fail to appreciate that it is much easier to launch a treaty than to subsequently control the execution of its clauses. This leads to deception and friction even if, theoretically at least, the results are supposed to be beneficial to every counterparty.

World trade, Foreign Direct Investments (FDIs) and the growing globalization of finance are given credit for greater prosperity. But is it truly so? Development is an activity that implies movement towards some goal, and plenty of evidence suggests this goal of prosperity for all continues to move further away. Running a globalized economy is a lot about judgement and understanding people with diverse objectives and contradictions.

A growing supply of low-cost goods first served to control inflation, then destabilized the economies to which they have been massively exported. Globalization's limits take the form of dislocation of jobs, loss of competitiveness, huge current account deficits, budgetary overruns and more. Precisely because we have closely approached, and sometimes exceeded, these limits we came gradually to recognize that globalization includes unsuspected inconvenient facts and some unwanted consequences.

A first taste of globalization's limits came in the 1980s when American politicians became extremely concerned that the Japanese were buying up their country. The crash of the Japanese economy in 1990–1991 did away with that fear. As François La Rochefoucauld, the French writer and moralist, said: 'It is not enough for you to succeed; others must fail.' Japan obliged.

Post-mortem, a small group of economists, industrialists and politicians came forward with the suggestion that due consideration should always be given to the fact that, just like science, globalization has no morals (more precisely, science is amoral not immoral). The party who is better organized, knows what it wants, has a longer perspective and possesses financial staying power, wins.

That's exactly how one must look at China's $1.4 trillion in foreign exchange reserves, over and above the fact that the country is on its way to monopolizing the world's low-cost goods manufacturing. It's no secret that 80 per cent of the world's toys are made in China and 75 per cent of Chinese exports to the United States are consumer goods. Has the Asian colossus gone overboard?

One way of answering this query is that, with a considerable amount of success, China has copied the industrialization blueprint of nineteenth-century Germany. The British had Sheffield, the Germans Solingen; Solingen produced the same things Sheffield did but much more cheaply. What the Chinese government has probably failed to notice in Germany's book is that this led straight into World War I.

One reason why both the broader globalization and the more regional one of the European Union (which this book takes as a case study) have hit their limits is that they were both concerned with parts of the problem rather than with the whole picture. Here exactly lies the weakness, and even the danger, of globalization's current status: the WTO and its member states have been enthusiastically discussing the parts, but none has paused as frequently as it should to ask whether these parts make a viable system.

Heads of state and their trade representatives have looked at some of the things that constitute regionalization and globalization and apparently contribute towards economic development. But they have not taken the time to support their judgement through critical inquiry about whether each one of these parts makes a positive or negative contribution to the whole, as well as where the *limits* may lie.

* * *

While the concepts of globalization, the World Trade Organization and its rounds, the ever-expanding (in membership) European Union and the tsunami of derivative financial instruments might look good on paper, in practice each one of them brings along its own risks and, with them, an inordinate number of worries. One of these worries is that globalization has given the challengers an advantage over the incumbents.

This is the message of Part I, in its examination of the status of America, China and the European Union in the world market and in its projection of the most likely evolution of this triangular relationship in coming years. While in the past countries in the process of development were satisfied with some sort of symbolic modernization, China is engaged in monument building of a manufacturing industry – as means of solidifying its existence. The economic crisis of 2007–2009 has put the breaks on this expansion but it is far from being sure that it reverses gears.

Chapter 1 examines globalization's prerequisites and consequences, including the challenges posed by emerging markets. The text looks at the ability of China and India to have an impact beyond their borders, including contrarians' opinions and their reasons. It also pays attention to globalization's impact on the middle class, the great stabilizer of a modern economy.

It has been a deliberate choice to include references to and statistics from the middle of this decade. This provides the reader with a better perspective on recent developments and their likely evolution.

Study the past, Confucius said, if you would define the future.

The text also highlights one of the crucial issues that Japan and China have been chasing: the enforcement of a clause of racial equality. Japan sought but did not obtain it, though it fought on the side of western allies in World War I. With Asia rising in industrial and financial might, racial equality is by now old news but, as Chapter 2 notes, Japan, South Korea and China have been leveraging their resources to a level that looks unsustainable, which is bad for them but also negative to racial equality because it feeds nationalistic reactions.

While Asia's industrial and economic might is on the rise, Europe has entered a phase of *déclinisme*. Chapter 3 looks for the reasons by examining the European Union's place in globalization and its aftereffect. Italy and textiles are taken as examples of a country and an industry that have lost their bearings due to Asian competition.

When, in the years that immediately followed World War II, the General Agreement on Tariffs and Trade (GATT) set out to establish open borders and eventually one global market, many expressed scepticism over whether it would be possible to return to the free trade principles of the late nineteenth century. As Chapter 4 documents, this goal has been reached, but three recent happenings may turn back the clock:

- rising economic nationalism;

- the global banking and financial crisis; and

- the unexpected consequence of massive cost/effectiveness, which devastates high labour cost markets.

The theme of Part II is *financial globalization*, which proceeds by leaps and bounds and washes away basic concepts of finance such as the rules of creditworthiness. Ironically, if the Doha Round had succeeded in 2006, the 2007 crisis of US subprimes would have been delayed by another couple of years. Subsequently, its sweeping effects on credit, banking, liquidity and market confidence would have hit the whole globe in a more vicious way than the present crisis has.

Economists with contrarian opinions have been suggesting for some time that the globalization of financial markets had the effect that even formerly well-managed banks were converted to speculators. The lowering of credit standards, followed by securitization of loans and slicing and dicing of debt on a massive scale, has proved to be a dangerous business – particularly when based on much laxer credit standards than central banks would like.

To the question 'Has the globalization of finance done something big?' the answer is 'Yes' and the documentation is provided by the Sovereign Wealth Funds (SWFs) which are heavily investing in (and might eventually control) a number of global companies, most particularly big banks. Chapter 5 takes an investigative attitude towards SWFs – a hot political issue which will, most likely, be passionately discussed over the next few years.

A growing number of heads of state are looking at other countries' SWFs as the Trojan horse of state capitalism, which should be subjected to limits. Only a few are saying that, in the last analysis, by acquiring equity (and rescuing) American and European financial institutions, Asian and Middle Eastern creditors have found a way to get back money they have loaned to the West; specifically to those countries with large current account deficits.

Chapter 6 addresses another major change presently taking place in the globalized financial market, namely, that the world's best known financial centres are no more all-western. Hong Kong and Shanghai are well-established, while Mumbai and Dubai are upcoming. It is not unlikely that all four will overtake some western financial centres because of the rapidly increasing economic power in their hinterland – which rebalances capital markets and securities trading in Asia's favour.

This shift in the world's industrial, commercial and financial dynamics has an evident impact on monetary policy in the global economy. Chapter 7 documents that the basic metrics of money supply – M1 and M3 – have escaped the control of western central banks. In 2006 and 2007 both Russia and China increased their and the world's money supply by leaps and bounds. This fed both inland and global inflation, proving that the absence of limits to globalization can have unwanted consequences.

China provides a good example of how far the banking industry can be destroyed due to inattention to credit risk. Chapter 8 documents that in the early years of the twenty-first century, Chinese banks were sinking under the weight of non-performing loans. Western banks lectured the Chinese on the need to be alert to credit risk while themselves failing to do so, and in 2007–2009 they fell in the deep hole of the subprimes debacle.

As the last chapter of the book addressing the US–China relationship in financial, industrial, trade and other matters, Chapter 8 also focuses on the proactive question of whether America and China look at one another as antagonists or allies. Theoretically it seems as if they are heading for a confrontation, but *realpolitik* obliges them both to follow a much more pragmatic approach.

Part III looks at the European Union, and more particularly at Euroland, as a laboratory of globalization that has delivered mixed results. Is the EU's financial integration successful, or at least on course? Have different big ticket projects, like the Lisbon Agenda and MiFID (Markets in Financial Instruments Directive), succeeded? Has economic nationalism among its member states been kept under lock and key? Most importantly, who is in charge of the EU's fortunes?; of Euroland's?

In a nutshell, the answer is that both the European Commission and the European Parliament are impotent because of their lack of authority over member states, their limited stature and the fact that they work by inverse delegation – which precludes a leadership position. Also, for the reason that managing the chiefs of state of the EU's 27 members is like herding cats. As for the euro, it is a currency without a country.

Questions of Euroland's priorities and courses of action are only partly answered by statistics on budget deficits, current account red ink and lag in productivity. Therefore, the text pays attention to the impact national interests have on EU decisions and the fact that member states' contributions to the common good are sadly overestimated.

Chapter 9 explains why financial integration in the European Union might be a goal, but it is not a fact. The Lisbon Agenda and European Commission's Action Plan, which have gone nowhere, as well as Market in Financial Instruments Directive which went into effect rather recently, can best be interpreted as miscalibrations. There is always a big difference between what is thought to work and what actually works under the principle of horse trading and compromise.

Chapter 10 looks at the euro, and aims to answer the question: 'Is it a blessing or a curse for the EU economy?' After providing a brief insight into the birth of the European Monetary Union (EMU) and the political ploys behind it, the text concentrates on the challenges posed by a single currency, including the likelihood that one of Euroland's countries rushes to the exit. The consequences have been revealed through a simulation by Standard & Poor's.

The book concludes with Chapter 11, whose subject is Euroland's missed opportunities. The text explains why, from the start, a political union would have been Europe's best bet. As it now stands, each of the member countries has its own agenda – and together they are permanently confronted by a clash between *dirigisme* and a liberal economy. Without a political union the goals and plans of EU's member states are diverging; and everybody is exploiting to their advantage Euroland's Stability and Growth Pact which was thought to establish:

- limits to budget deficits; and

- a sense of member state accountability.

The most enlightened economists have taught that practically all societies have the capacity for growth, but if established institutions hold a country to its past then it is necessary to change them. That's what the management of change is all about. Instead, at different degrees in EU countries, nineteenth-century socialist theories still provide the guiding light and politicians fail to appreciate that short-term stimulus is a long-term error.

PART I

UNITED STATES, EUROPE, CHINA AND THE WORLD MARKET

1

Globalization in Motion

1. China Enforces the Racial Equality Clause

Without having necessarily planned for it, China, India, Brazil, South Korea and other emerging countries have enforced a clause asked for by Japan (then a western ally) at World War I's end – which America, Britain and France had refused. This was Japan's proposal for a *Racial Equality Clause* in the League of Nations Covenant, which was initially nothing more than a non-discrimination provision approving the principle of:

- equality of nations; and

- just treatment of their nationals.

In 1918, the Japanese had been asking for a statement by their allies containing a general declaration, not for concrete measures. In the League of Nations' Commission, 11 out of the 16 countries which were represented voted for the amendment, but Britain and America abstained and chairman President Wilson ruled that in the absence of unanimity the amendment was lost.[1] That episode created the impression that Japan:

- was good enough to be asked for help in the war effort;

- but not good enough to be recognized as equal by the western allies.

A few decades later, rising from the ashes of WW II, Japan has demonstrated that Treaty clauses are meaningless because discipline and hard work are the best means to attain world status. China did the same in the 1990s, after a civil

---

1   David Stevenson, *1914–1918: The History of the First World War*, Penguin Books, London, 2004.

war which created unprecedented devastation and nearly half a century of
Communist rule. Indeed, China's industrial leap forward resembles many of the
events that took place at the end of the nineteenth century when Germany:

- challenged British dominance of world trade in manufacturing; and

- encroached on Britain's home market, which eventually led to
  World War I.

Due to nearly two decades of a vibrant economy, China is fast evolving into
a king-sized consumer/producer society, exceeding everything that the west
has so far seen. Most importantly, for the first time in the country's history
this development has created a middle class of 450 million people, roughly a
third of its population. China's current share of *global consumption* stands at: 40
per cent for coal; 32 per cent, iron ore; 28 per cent, steel; 22 per cent, copper; 20
per cent, aluminum; 11 per cent, nickel; and about 8 per cent for oil. In coal, iron
ore, steel, copper, aluminum and nickel China is the world's no. 1 consumer; in
oil, it is the world's no. 2 after the US.

Correspondingly, the percentage of total copper demand that goes to America
has decreased from 31 per cent in 1960 to 15 per cent in 2005 and with the 2007
real-estate crisis it has dropped even lower. In steel, this share has fallen from 35
per cent in 1960 to 12 per cent in 2005.[2] This is an impressive downsizing and its
consequences will evidently impact on the US economy in years to come.

Measured by the share of exports *plus* imports in Gross Domestic Product
(GDP), China's *trade openness* increased from 27 per cent in 1990 to over 70 per cent
in 2007, with a particularly steep acceleration following the country's accession
to the World Trade Organization in 2001. In terms of global trade, since 2006:

- Chinese openness is significantly higher than in many advanced
  economies and emerging markets;[3] and

- processing trade[4] – an area where technology transfer plays a major
  role – accounts for up to 44 per cent of Chinese trade, according to
  official statistics.

---

2   Merrill Lynch, 12 September 2006.
3   ECB Monthly Bulletin, January 2007.
4   Defined as the processing of imported intermediate goods that become inputs for the production
    of re-exported goods.

It looks as if China has once more decided to reach the heights of the world's gross domestic product which it achieved some centuries ago. Based on the assumption of purchasing power parity, statistics published by *The Economist* are eye-opening. China's share of global GDP was:

- 29 per cent in 1600;

- 23 per cent in 1700;

- 33 per cent in 1820;

- but only 4 per cent in 1950 to 1973;

- bouncing back to 12 per cent in 1998;

- and 16 per cent in 2006.[5]

Critics say that China is well-positioned to conquer the world's markets, in spite of the ongoing economic crisis, thanks to globalization. They also add that today's China is not a traditional capitalistic economy. Rather, it is a sort of government version of capitalism which targets market share in world markets at the expense of profits.

The message behind these statements is that Chinese products are not fairly priced, not only due to local wages, which are very low, but also because many factors that add to the final cost (like health care and pollution control) are simply ignored. At the same time the yuan is an undervalued currency.[6]

While these comments are not undocumented, it is no less true that neither America nor Europe took a long hard look at globalization's aftermath on their own high wages, extraordinary social benefits (by global standards), and rapidly eroding industrial base. To a substantial degree, this oversight is at the origin of the fact that the US and European deficit with China keeps

---

5   *The Economist*, 31 March 2007.
6   In late 2007, Morris Goldstein and Nicholas Lardy, at the Peterson Institute of International Economics, estimated that the yuan was at least 30 per cent to 40 per cent undervalued, despite its gain over the previous two years (*The Economist*, 12 January 2008).

widening while China's industrial base is forcibly overdimensioned to a dangerous level as:

- the west's challenger moves rapidly in more advanced industries where America, Germany and Britain had remained competitive; and

- it is adding, or trying to add, state-of-the-art capacity in electronics, chips, networking, speciality steel, petrochemicals, and automobiles.

Up to a point, this is a replay of the strategy followed by Japan in the 1960s and 1970s, but on a grander scale (see Chapter 2). Part of what China is betting on is that both the US and Europe will become so dependent on its low cost consumer and other goods that resurrecting trade barriers would just raise costs and spark inflation in countries accustomed to Chinese exports. This would do away with globalization's dividend of keeping inflation tamed, which has profited America and Europe for about two decades.

Within China, the progress of its different provinces in uneven. Economists point to Hong Kong, Macao and greater Pearl River Delta (PRD), an area of southern China encompassing much of Guangdong province, as some of the 'winner' regions.

With a GDP of more than $270 billion, if it were independent PRD would be the world's sixteenth largest economy and tenth largest exporter. (Note that PRD is where the mainland's economic reform and renaissance began in 1979, and it still leads today.) Such a rapid rise in wealth was made possible because of Hong Kong's proximity, which:

- offered access to capital and business know-how; and

- served as source of investments for industries that grew in Guangdong.

Is a rapid market conquest compatible with globalization? Economists (who are paid to worry about the future) now argue that the exploitation of globalization's freedoms has become one-sided. Others add that the debate about a level playing field in global competition is less about technical issues and more about the structure of agricultural and manufacturing resources on a worldwide basis. This is the reason why the issue of *globalization's limits* has to be studied and settled in the most careful way.

2. Global Rebalancing

A growing body of opinion is that globalization, which was favourable to most economies in the 1990s and first six or seven years of the twenty-first century, is now in reverse. The aftereffect of globalization without limits has finally hurt the economies of America, Britain and continental Europe. According to Peter Oppenheimer, of Goldman Sachs, 'the markets are assuming that all of the structural benefits of globalization have been whittled away and will not be repeated'.[7]

That's likely. In the mean time, however, some citizen in emerging countries – and most particularly in India and Russia – have joined the club of the richest men in the world. There was a time the 'top ten' were by large majority American. As Table 1.1 shows, in 2008 only two Americans remained on the list, but four were Indian.

Table 1.1   The ten richest men in the world in 2008

		Country	Sector	€ Billion
1	Warren Buffet	USA	Finance	41.00
2	Carlos Slim and family	Mexico	Telecom	38.00
3	Bill Gates	USA	IT	36.80
4	Lakshmi Mittal	India	Industry	28.55
5	Mukesh Ambani	India	Industry	27.70
6	Anil Ambani	India	Industry	26.65
7	Ingvar Kamprad	Sweden	Furniture	19.65
8	KP Singh	India	Real Estate	19.00
9	Oleg Deripaska	Russia	Industry	17.75
10	Karl Albrecht	Germany	Hard Discount	17.10

As should have been expected, the emergence at the forefront of economic development of countries with over 1 billion citizens unavoidably leads to

---

7   *The Economist,* 25 October 2008.

global rebalancing, which clearly correlates with globalization's limits because it requires redistribution of income (and of growth) not only within but also between countries. Until 2007, America's economic growth was driven by an unsustainable consumer boom but, after the 2007–2009 severe credit and banking crisis, it is supported almost entirely by external demand.

- Without the boost from net exports, real US GDP would have fallen since the third quarter of 2007.

- By contrast, consumer spending in China is now growing faster than exports, with retail sales jumping by 23 per cent in nominal terms in the year to July 2008 and by 16 per cent in real terms.

An interesting statistic with far-reaching implications for global rebalancing is that in 2008 China's exports grew more slowly than America's. Economists forecast that in dollar terms in 2008 China's current account surplus was roughly as large as in 2007 because higher income from its big foreign assets offset the smaller trade surplus. As a share of GDP, however, it shrank. Correspondingly, in 2008 America's overall current account deficit fell to about 5 per cent of GDP (still a lot) from a peak of 6.2 per cent at the end of 2006.

Another interesting trend in twenty-first century global rebalancing has been a noticeably weaker contribution from *capital* as a factor of production, with the reduction being more pronounced in the US than in other industrially advanced areas, like Euroland. According to a study by Deutsche Bundesbank, the main reason for this could have been that capital-linked technological advances, which benefited the American economy in particular, lost momentum.[8]

A third significant reference is labour's contribution to growth. Labour's contribution fell in the US in 2002–2004, but in 2005–2006 it returned to levels equivalent to those of the second half of the 1990s. This turnaround was not observed in connection with the role of capital, showing that the theories of both Adam Smith and Karl Marx might be out of date.

Capital and labour were always vital commodities and the downsizing of the former's role as a factor of production saw to it that greater return on capital can be obtained by highly geared financial operations executed within the *virtual economy* rather than the *real economy* of manufacturing and trade. This has been both a reason and a consequence of the fact that the virtual economy

---

8   Deutsche Bundesbank, Monthly Report, May 2008.

and the real economy progressively came unstuck, particularly so in the west, though the trend can also be observed on a more global scale.

The 2007–2009 credit and banking crisis is an effect of this change towards virtual economy trades (see also Chapters 6 and 7). The banks which bled the most with the subprimes and collateralized mortgage obligations (CDOs) – to the tune of trillions of dollars in red ink, roughly equally divided between American and western European institutions – provide factual evidence for understanding some of the risks in the virtual economy and in bank-to-bank financial plays:

- the highest cross-border banking flows across the US and European Union were between American and British, German and French banks (in that order);[9]

- in contrast to these, the volume of claims and debts characterizing cross-border banking flows between American and Italian, Swedish and Austrian institutions were low profile – though Swedish and Austrian banks had a huge exposure to Eastern Europe.

Subsequently, the need for American, British, German and French financial institutions to prune and restructure their balance sheets in the wake of the July/August 2007 crisis, as well as the entry of Sovereign Wealth Funds (see Chapter 5) into cross-border financial flows as lenders of last resort, is bound to have a profound impact on global rebalancing. It will also support the graduation of developing countries into a class of 'new capitalists', which will have a deeper effect than on the restructuring of supranational political and economic institutions.

Halfway between the end of WWII and the present day, the Group of Seven (G7) was instituted on the premise that among themselves the countries of which it was *de facto* composed were the global arbiters of money, goods and political power.[10] But in the twenty-first century this little group – whose membership partly overlaps with that of the Security Council – no longer controls the high ground of the global economy, an imbalance which has not been corrected with the addition of Russia (the G8).

---

9   Also in terms of British-German cross-border banking.
10   United States, Japan, Britain, Germany, France, Italy and Canada.

What increased most with the G8 was the G7's inefficiency: the G7's original small, purposeful gatherings of the 1970s are no more to be seen. Like many of the UN sessions, current 'summits' are purposeless public relations gatherings which produce mostly lengthy communiqués, photo-opportunities and some minutes of news for evening TV shows. (The Security Council, too, engages in platitudes and suffers loss of authority as Russia was not given a chance to veto Kosovo's independence and the Iranians don't give a penny for UN sanctions.)

If the UN is fading, are these 'summits' an alternative? In an effort to show that the summits' base expanded beyond the G8, Germany in 2007 and Japan in 2008 invited the leaders from five other countries – Brazil, China, India, Mexico and South Africa – along for a brief photo opportunity. The fact is that the handshakes between those who did best in the twentieth century and some potential shapers of the twenty-first do nothing to answer the questions of:

- how the old world order should be adapting to the new;

- whether the United Nations can still show some statesmanship; and

- what is supposed to be the role of the Security Council, which is looking increasingly ineffectual and anachronistic.

The pillars of the immediate WWII supranational economic infrastructure are just as radically challenged. The World Bank, critics say, may still have a role to play, particularly in the poorest countries of Africa and Latin America; but this is not true of the International Monetary Fund (IMF), which over the past six and a half decades has slowly but surely lost its reason for being.

Originally projected as a club of the developed economies, primarily to help one another in the long and difficult time of reconstruction, the IMF has lost its bearings as the world's economic order has radically changed and continues doing so. The forecast is that by 2025 today's emerging economies will represent roughly two thirds of global GDP, or double the developed economies' share, while the economies of some of the countries currently seen as developed may be falling by the wayside.

A couple of years ago Goldman Sachs coined the label BRIC to include in one envelope four major emerging economies: Brazil, Russia, India and China. In May 2008 a new label came up identifying the four laggards among the 15 countries of Euroland: PIGS. It's an acronym of Portugal, Italy, Greece and Spain, of whom one (Italy) is a member of the G8 and another (Spain) aspires to be one of Euroland's guiding lights. As 2008 came to a close the four Euroland members in distress were joined by Ireland, making the anagram PIIGS (Chapter 10).

Analysts say that in the second decade of its history the European Central Bank will be confronted by the fact that the PIIGS quartet (and to a significant extent France) still abide by the inflexible model of a highly structured labour market and look at the Euro's devaluation as their life saver. This holds them back from reaping benefits associated with a globalized economy – while, by contrast, developing nations:

- restructure their economies;

- bet on globalization; and

- exercise monetary and fiscal discipline.

This most significant global rebalancing and repositioning redefines the tasks of WWII vintage supranational institutions, and unsettles the membership of ad-hoc bodies like the Group of 8. China, India, Brazil and possibly also Mexico, South Korea and South Africa, are in the way of having more weight than some of the current G8 members. Should these rising economies be added, making up a new G14, or should the G8 prune itself of its weaker economies? And is there a role for the G8 in the first place?; for the IMF?; the Security Council?; the United Nations?

3. China and India as Large Emerging Countries

If the United Nations organization is taken as reference, *then* a careful analysis will demonstrate that in the majority of cases the economies of its member countries continue to display *emerging market* characteristics.[11] Their levels of development, however, differ widely. It's a fairly safe bet that those at the bottom of a 'best to worst' classification will have:

---

11 The terms 'emerging market' and 'emerging country' are relatively recent. Terms used prior to them have been 'Third World', 'less developed countries' and 'countries in the process of development'.

- a central bank under the thumb of the government and of politicians;

- a currency that is not accepted as legal tender outside the country;

- extensive currency controls, and sometimes different exchange rates for commercial and financial purposes; and

- high inflation which continues unabated, because of large budgetary deficits.[12]

China, India, Russia and Brazil are no longer in this class, although the first three do suffer from high inflation. All four countries are more than a classical emerging market, but less than a fully developed one. The prospects for their future economic stability are good; but they are largely dependent upon the effectiveness of economic measures taken by their government, as well as on legal, regulatory and political developments which should always accompany financial emergence.

China and India are betting on an increasingly better-educated hard-working population, low wages, massive manufacturing and/or perspectives opened by insourcing (Chapter 2). Thanks to globalization, over the last decades they have both leapfrogged many other emerging countries in their race to economic development and eventual financial might – sharing some, but only some, common characteristics. Apart the fact that each features a population of one billion or more, they have:

- global interests;

- up to a point complementary trade;

- a great hunger for natural resources; and

- benefits derived from salutary effects of brisk competition, in which both education and restrained wages are competitive advantages.

For the short to medium term, China and India constitute first class examples for other emerging nations on how to take the future in their own hands.

---

12 Also, a police force in the pocket of the local dictator or oligarch, as well as corrupt judiciary and plenty of nepotism – themes which are not part of the present book.

Self-sustainable policies are not just the better way to eradicate poverty – they are the only way. Without self-sustenance, economic results will be half-baked and graduation to the class of a developed nation will be put in jeopardy.

In their favour, China and India have an important ingredient of economic success, particularly when this is examined from a twenty-first century perspective: about 20 per cent of their population consists of smart, driven, educated people who want to become somebody in life and are eager to improve their standard of living. The challenge is managing those people and their careers, while the navigator is still an opaque bureaucracy that is a relic from both countries' socialist years.

In the course of the next three decades, China stands a good chance of matching (and eventually overtaking) the United States, currently the largest economy in the world. *If* gross domestic product (GDP) at market exchange rates for the US is taken as equal to 100, *then* Japan's GDP stands at 38, Germany's at 21 and China's at 19, followed by those of Britain, France, Italy, Canada, Spain, Brazil (in that order). Brazil's GDP would amount to about 6 on a 100 US scale; India to a little less than that.

Statistics, however, are not forever. According to current projections, this classification will radically change less than a third of a century down the line. Economists forecast that by 2040 America's and China's GDP will be roughly equal, though the latter might have a slight edge. *If* each of these economies is counted as 100, *then* they will be followed by India at 41, Japan at 22, Mexico, Russia, Brazil each at 19, Germany at 18, Britain at 17 and France probably at 16. By then Italy, Canada and Spain would have fallen off the radar screen of the top 10 economies.

To reach that status, the large emerging economies will need an unprecedented amount of capital. Today, globalization takes care of this through foreign direct investments (FDIs), but how long will this last? In 2006 by far the top recipient of FDIs was China with 86.5 billion, while Hong Kong was second with $36.5 billion. Adding them together, as should be done in a statistical sense, China benefitted from FDIs to the tune of an eye-popping $123 billion in one year's time. (This is over and above the fact that it flooded the global market with newly printed money; see Part II.)

Exports, insourcing business and FDIs are important to the country benefiting from them not only because they bring in money, but also because they contribute to employment and home-grown skills. This is what emerging economies need to eventually develop their own global industrial giants, as they are in the process of doing (see Chapter 2).

Global companies too play a crucial role. India started developing global companies in the steel industry with Mittal and both in steel and in automobiles with Tata. Buying western firms helps in compressing time scales. In the 1960s Thornton, the man who built the mighty Litton Industries conglomerate, responded to a journalist who questioned the rate of his company's acquisitions: 'We don't buy companies. We buy time.'

The Chinese got into global high tech with Lenovo, arguably their most important technology firm, which rose from obscurity to become the world's third-largest manufacturer of personal computers. The trick has been the acquisition for $1.25 billion in late 2004 of IBM's PC division, which boasted four times Lenovo's own volume of sales. Contrary to Mittal, however, Lenovo lost momentum over the years.

Also impressive by any standard is China's and India's leadership in education; most particularly in technology, as documented by statistics by Morgan Stanley on university students graduating in science and engineering. As Table 1.2 shows, since 2004 every year over 1.2 million engineers and scientists complete their studies at Chinese and Indian universities. This population:

- is almost as big as the combined output of the American, European, and Japanese universities together; and

- represents an amazing increase in the number of graduating Indian and Chinese engineers and scientists compared to a mere dozen years ago.

Critics say that average engineering graduates in China and India come in great numbers, while the truly high quality graduates are much fewer. That no educational system can produce only *prima-donnas* is self-evident; but my experience with Indian and Chinese engineers documents that they are of good standing.

Correctly, the Chinese and Indian governments have channelled funds and directed the attention of students entering university life to the *hard sciences*. This contrasts to the policy of governments and of the young generation in

Table 1.2   University students graduating in science and engineering

	1990/91	2002/04
India	170,000	690,000
China	80,000	530,000
European Union	280,000	470,000
United States	340,000	420,000
Japan	280,000	360,000

the US and EU, where *soft sciences* are the pole of attraction – with the result of having a degree and at the same time being unemployed, particularly so in the EU.

This misdirection of effort and of money earmarked for education in the European Union leads to the silly business that in Germany there are 800,000 jobs that cannot be filled while unemployment stands at millions. For the same reasons, in France 500,000 jobs are asking for applicants while there are also millions unemployed, with plenty of soft sciences university graduates among them. The failure of western economies to produce the scientists and engineers they need to sustain their leadership is theirs and theirs alone.

By contrast, unskilled labor in the west found itself at severe disadvantage as jobs that were previously available moved massively to the east: from Eastern Europe to Asia. This, however, may not be a one-way process – even if between 2005 and 2007 several economists expressed the opinion that the flow of exports from China and the so-called 'Asian tigers' had nowhere else to go but up.

As the global economic and financial crisis gained momentum such projections have turned on their head. In the first quarter of 2009 emerging economies are sinking alongside developed ones. In 2008 emerging stockmarkets fell by more than those in western countries, and some sovereign states like Iceland, Hungary, Latvia and Pakistan went cap in hand to the IMF, while exports waned. Year-on-year:

- Taiwan's exports plunged by 45 per cent over the past year;

- Japan's by 27 per cent;

- South Korea's by 20 per cent;

- Germany's by 12 per cent;

- India's by 10 per cent.

China's exports fell by 17.5 per cent in January 2009 compared to a year earlier (i.e. month-to-month, not year-on-year). At the same time, China's imports tanked by nearly 45 per cent, with severe aftereffects on Taiwan, Japan and South Korea which supply China with many of the components used in its factories.

These statistics evidently have an impact on foreign direct investments. The Institute of International Finance (IFF), a Washington-based big bank lobby and research laboratory, expects that private capital will be subdued in 2009. Only $165 billion will be invested, which is an 80 per cent reduction from 2007. (Already in 2008 some countries like France, Germany and Japan had seen a severe reduction in FDI inflows.)

Altogether, the restraint of capital has significant negative implications for emerging markets; banks are no longer ready to satisfy local private sector credit demands. Such restraint means that growth projections for emerging economies are presently much too optimistic, while at the same time countries with high proportions of foreign claims will be most hurt by protectionist sentiment for capital flows (section 9).

4. Emerging Markets Raise Concerns in OECD Member Nations

As an old adage has it, 'Staying in one place can only make a man grow poor'. This is true not only for people but also for goods and services. For labour, raw materials, agricultural produce, manufactured goods and financial services, global trading opens a greater market perspective than the local or regional market can offer. As the examples of China and India above have shown, the global market:

- helps in expanding business opportunity;

- presents greater potential for growth; and

- provides a landscape for broadening a nation's, as well as a company's, strategic plan.

On the other hand, a product or process which has only advantages has not yet been invented, and therefore globalization should not be examined from a narrow one-sided viewpoint. In a report published on 19 June 2007, the Organization for Economic Cooperation and Development (OECD)[13] said that public mistrust of globalization is founded on legitimate concerns over:

- rising earnings inequality; and

- the falling share of wages in national income.

Thinly veiled behind these bullets are *conflicting national interests* in trade and finance. Carefully, the OECD report added that the threats posed by globalization are frequently overestimated, but the point about 'legitimate concerns' should not be missed. What might the reasons be for these growing concerns?

According to the findings of OECD researchers, globalization is compatible with high employment rates *if*, and only *if*, the right domestic policies are in place. For the majority of states which aim to benefit from globalized trade in commodities and manufactured goods, this *if* is far from being a foregone conclusion. The OECD also said it needed to reassess the impact of freer trade on workers because a wedge had appeared between:

- the rosy analysis put forward by some economists; and

- the much more sceptical view of the general public – a scepticism found to be particularly strong in America and in France.

The OECD moreover conceded that globalization could permanently increase job insecurity for workers by making their employers more vulnerable to external shocks. The way it has been expressed in this study, wages have been shrinking as a proportion of national income in the US, Japan and Europe, perhaps reflecting the weakening bargaining position of workers. (And, I would add, the weakening influence of western nations as well as of Japan

---

13 Paris-based OECD has metamorphosed from the former Marshall Plan; becoming, over the years, the club of richer nations.

in the global financial market, where they have been reduced to just showing their fists.)

One of the ironies of present-day globalization is the shift of global financial power from the American capital markets to the upcoming developing nations and their Sovereign Wealth Funds (SWFs, Chapter 5). A couple of years ago, in mid-2007, Merrill Lynch, the international brokerage house, predicted that 'the main macro-economic risk to the global economy lies in an unexpected curtailment in financing from the global capital providers, China, Middle East and Russia. This could take the form of:

- unexpected tightening;

- discrete currency appreciation;

- a trade war on another event'.[14]

In August 2007, when the Merrill Lynch study was published, these were hypotheses; at the end of 2008 there was plenty of evidence to support the points being made – because of the Western banking industry's self-inflicted wounds. Additionally, in terms of salaries and wages disquieting facts exist. For instance, the gap between the take-home pay of best-and worst-paid workers has significantly increased over the last two decades (1989–2009) in the majority of OECD countries. The law of supply and demand is at play:

- scientists and qualified workers are in demand and hard to find;

- those in the western world who are less skilled are easily replaceable by emerging countries' labour, as companies outsource or relocate to lower their costs.

To appreciate ongoing projections on the shift of the manufacturing base, the reader should remember that, in a matter of half a decade, China's share for textiles in Europe rose exponentially. From 2001 to 2006, it went from 24 per cent to 45 per cent in sectors where quotas were lifted and it continues rising (see Chapter 3 on the effect this had on Italy's textile industry).

It therefore comes as no surprise that with a massive shift in manufacturing facilities and the globalization of labour in steady motion, in the 1989–2009

---

14 Merrill Lynch, *Global Economics*, 17 August 2007.

timeframe the wage share of national income has dropped from 72 per cent to below 60 per cent in Japan and from 62.5 per cent to less than 57 per cent in the European Union, although it drifted only slightly from 62.5 per cent to about 60 per cent in the United States.

This does not mean that globalization is 'bad'; if anything, it is irreversible and will continue being so short of a truly global and devastating trade war or, even worse, World War III. What it means is that the wave of globalization which started in the 1980s has totally lacked:

- an overall strategic plan, with precise objectives;

- an adequate amount of national economic and labor market restructuring; and

- a generally accepted authority which can check and hold *globalization's limits* (the WTO is unfit for this job, see Chapter 4).

Nearly two centuries ago, David Ricardo, one of the influential economists of his time, railed against the doctrine of reinforced national borders by advocating free exchange of goods. Since then, his theory of *comparative advantage* has fed the free trade debate. Ricardo's central argument was that even if one country could produce everything more efficiently than another, which is never the case, it would reap gains from:

- specializing in what it is best at; and

- trading its products with the other nations.

The reference to Ricardo is important because, contrary to what its detractors say, globalization is no late twentieth century development. The globalization of trade is as old as humankind. In more recent times, it started in the mid-nineteenth century, and prior to 1914 and World War I the international community had experienced a rapidly integrating economy. This was reversed in the 1920s as the drive for self-sufficiency – a relic of WWI – worked against globalization, while in 1929–1932 the Great Depression intensified this reversal.

By the beginning of the twenty-first century, however, globalization has become so strongly entrenched that trying to keep out of it would resemble somebody who commits suicide for fear of death. Heads of state like France's Chirac and Spain's Zapatero, who on many occasions took the road to protectionism, should have learned from the example of the Chinese emperor Qianlong. In 1793, China's ruler:

- announced that the economic superpower under his authority had no interest in 'foreign manufactures'; and

- this imperial command set China on the road to two centuries of impoverishment.

History also teaches that globalization typically tends to contract for political reasons much more than for economic ones. Simply put, in countries whose voters are not obviously benefiting from globalization, populist politicians enact measures to 'protect' their constituents. Protectionism can take many forms; it is not limited to trade barriers.

For instance, lately world trade has been tarnished by an increasing number of issues surrounding the quality of goods, from pet food to toys and tyres imported from China. While available evidence suggests that environmental issues and health hazards are not the No. 1 preoccupation of the Chinese, at the same time it is rather odd that few people have questioned the background and quality of China-made goods in the years prior to 2007, when trade relations between the west and China were promoted by finding price bargains for the consumer rather than by care for the consumer's health.

5. Globalization's Prerequisites

What David Ricardo did not say at the time but the last three decades have clearly demonstrated, is that there are prerequisites to an effective globalization. These concern not only the restructuring of national economies, from revamping of labour laws to the establishment of strategic plans, but also lifelong learning, which impacts on the way people get ready for competition. Among personal prerequisites, three are outstanding:

- adaptation;

- flexibility; and

- cultural change.

Globalization's strategic plan and economic guidance is essentially a process of transformation enriched by the weight to make plans succeed. Cultural change is important because, with globalization, all sorts of companies – large, medium and small – as well as individuals, will come under stress as competitive conditions get into higher gear. Market changes affect processes, products and markets, and to survive companies not only need to restructure but also to *reinvent themselves*. This means taking steps beyond those 'most obvious' like:

- revaluing human capital;

- betting on innovation;

- targeting new markets; and

- cutting down the costs of operations to leave a comfortable profit margin.

Along with cultural change, flexibility is necessary because combined with the internet and jet travel globalization greatly increases mobility for individuals and firms, who often find themselves in uncharted territory. Should a company ask for government subsidies? Outsource most or all of its production?[15] Delocalize to take advantage of lower wages? Consolidate to cut overheads?

In March 2008, Michelin, a leading global tyre manufacturer as well as a French industrial star, announced that it was consolidating the smallest of its factories, 16 of them in France and 16 more in other European countries, to gain economies of scale. But it also plans to expand production in Mexico, Brazil, India and China – where the markets grow faster – by 60 per cent in the next few years.

In a globalized economy companies have to learn how to stand on their own two feet without government subsidies. ArcelorMittal, the giant steel company of Lakshmi Mittal, has refused French government aid to keep a factory in the Moselle region open. Aid or no aid, Mittal wants to close a plant that is no longer economic; this has not pleased the French workers who, on 4 April 2008, revolted and tore the director's office to pieces.

---

15 A dangerous step. Olivetti did so under Carlo de Benedetti and in a few years it faded away.

This short-lived revolt dramatizes, in one stroke, globalization's advantage and downside. By integrating their economies into the international business landscape, countries could reap the benefit of access to fast-moving markets. But a recurrent problem is that some national economies (and their people) are not willing or able to adjust to global competition because:

- labour policies are rigid;

- fiscal policies are wanting at best;

- the general public is misinformed; and

- the government will not take the risk of going against the will of labour unions.

According to a 2006 report by Italy's Unioncamere, among companies in all industrial sectors those able to position themselves in the global market and avoid oblivion because of much lower wages abroad have the best chance of surviving the intensified global competition. In the case of Italy (Chapter 3), survivor firms have typically been those medium sized firms who went global, capitalizing on their strengths in:

- innovation;

- product quality; and

- client service.

Finland is an example of an EU member state facing globalization without paranoia, because its firms have succeeded in positioning themselves against global market forces. This is particularly visible in the mobile phone industry. By contrast, in several other EU countries, public opinion, and even the business elite, seem gloomily resigned to being overwhelmed by India and China. The inability to 'get out from under' is the dark face of globalization players.

What can be learned from the case of Finland? For some time the country has been running, proportionally, the biggest fiscal surplus in Euroland.[16] This is the outcome of leadership over the longer haul, not just when the going is easy. By contrast, most other Euroland countries have breached the monetary

---

16 The 15 countries which have adopted the Euro (Part III).

stability rules and fiscal deficit limits, set up before the launch of the single currency, as we will see in Part III. Also impressive is that:

- Finland has managed to have budget surpluses even after it came out of the depths of a recession; and

- while its companies were dealt a severe blow by lost Soviet contracts, they were able to find other markets fast and adapt to them.

By contrast, the people of other European Union countries did not pay enough attention to flexibility, adaptation and cultural change. In early 2006, an interesting incident took place in one of the interminable demonstrations in Paris by young students.[17] A girl in her late teens was heading one of the student groups with a banner '*Non à la globalisation*'. When a reporter asked her why she was against globalization, she answered by citing the usual 'blah-blah' of the uninformed and prejudiced. But the reporter persisted; he wanted to know *if she* goes on holiday in Southeast Asia. The girl said 'Yes. But that's not the same thing'. Really?

- In one sentence this reaction encapsulates the twisted, one-sided way people look at globalization.

- They want to profit from the good things in life it can provide, but they don't want to bear its liabilities.

As Mathieu Kaiser, an economist at BNP Paribas in Paris, was to comment about the students' mini revolt: 'There is a serious fear about the future; a serious fear about what globalization could be bringing in terms of job instability or flexibility.'[18] Most unfortunately, the young generation has not been taught about the need to take personal risk and be proactive. 'Do the work that you like', said Confucius, 'and you will not have to work at all.'

---

17 That demonstration was against the 'youth job contract' (Contrat Première Embauche, CPE), which crystallized all the fears of the French young generation and of the young people's parents about employment and joblessness.

18 *International Herald Tribune*, 31 March 2006.

6. Impact of a Hollowing Economy on the Middle Class

As the classical industrial western jobs have moved away from the old continent, citizens of several European nations have become more pessimistic and inward-looking. In the US, too, this is an issue which sours relations not only with China but also with Mexico. In the aftermath, the proportion of Americans who think their country should be active in the world is the lowest it has been since the early 1990s. Support for international trade and multinational companies is falling while:

- opposition to massive imports and to immigration is gaining momentum; and

- the growing anxiety about globalization is producing a backlash against 'broken borders'.

A November 2007 poll in the United States asked a direct question on perceived benefits from globalization. Among respondents, only 20 per cent of Republicans, and 16 per cent of Democrats answered: 'Yes' to globalization. The silent majority responded 'No' and this speaks volumes about how American citizens now feel about the continuation of current policies, stage-managed in an incompetent way.

Not only formerly free trade politicians but also several economists have noted that globalization and its ideas do not explain the disturbing stagnation in income that much of the middle class is experiencing in western countries. Some even foresee that, should this continue, it might lead to the destruction of the middle class, which is *the* pillar of modern western society.

People showing concern for a wheeling and dealing globalization are by no means anti-free traders or populists making extravagant claims about its negatives. Rather, they are individuals who take stock of the deception *globalization without limits* has brought along, particularly because western countries are unprepared to meet the challenges. Economists and sociologists who are now reevaluating globalization's impact have:

- studied the aftereffects of a massive exploitation of world trade by emerging countries; and

- examined how wideband telecommunications make it possible to handle more jobs offshore, including the outsourcing of professional skills.

The new thinking regarding the dangers presented by globalization is a very important change from what earlier generations believed to be unmitigated, ever-increasing benefits. Beyond the facts of the last few years, existing trends (and estimates based on the assumption of no policy changes) suggest that eventually up to 40 million American service jobs will face competition from workers in India and other low-wage nations.

- This is more than a quarter of the 140 million employed in the US today; and

- it is an altogether dark picture, as many of the newly vulnerable jobs are in professional domains such as research, engineering and accounting.

What these two bullets are describing is turning earlier optimism about the 'global village' on its head. Belatedly, people and governments are discovering that, as always, over-optimism about a linear future is capable of doing more damage than pessimism is – since caution is thrown aside. That is exactly what has caused globalization's drama: over-optimism that things will go right on their own and so letting down the defences which should have stayed in place to assure that:

- cultural change moves at fast pace;

- globalization provides a level field; and

- there are no loopholes which can be enlarged and exploited so that free trade becomes an unfair game.

Sloppy planning and disaster correlate. The less the limits of a process are defined, the deeper will be the drop in confidence and disregard of good sense when the reckoning comes. The west, which has been accusing developing nations of being unprepared, has been caught in its own game.

In a seminal book published half a century ago, Bernard M. Baruch provides an excellent example of preparation needed to be ahead of the curve.[19] He looks at Meyer Guggenheim who, switching out of the lace and embroidery business (a field he did not feel had much of a future), set about to learn the mining enterprise and ordered his seven sons to do likewise. The *Guggenheim principle* goes hand-in-glove with globalization, where technology has given a sense of geographic continuity, with events in the furthermost corner of the world felt all over the globe.

Have we studied the aftereffects of those events, which are unlikely but plausible? Have we analyzed their likely aftereffects? We have not. Instead we have engaged in big ticket superficial political deals based on magic formulas, like 'European Union' and 'NAFTA'. It is largely a reflection of the curious psychology of crowds that politicians, even those who have failed, can exercise great influence just by using words.

A little and mostly superficial knowledge has become the governing rule. There is, however, an old axiom that a little knowledge is a dangerous thing, and this is precisely what lies behind the failure of western nations in positioning themselves against globalization's forces. Politicians who had to leave government twice because of scandals have been assigned the sensitive task of trade negotiators, which talks volumes about their credentials as well as of those who assigned the job to them.

The last two decades have seen a trend whereby in western democracies politicians take decisions that have a massive effect on citizens' futures without bothering to consult them. The European Union's Constitution is a good example because the EU is a miniglobalization, so to speak. Most member states rushed it through parliament, where the ruling party had a majority. In France and Holland, where it was put to test by a referendum, it was rejected by the majority of the people.

Then, the same material of the EU constitution was resurrected by politicians (minus Beethoven's symphony and the flag) and again rushed through parliament without consulting all of the citizenry. A similar story of rush to ratification without popular consultation is true of NAFTA, which tied together two similar economies (US and Canada) with one which is totally different (Mexico) in any measurable dimension.

---

19 Bernard M. Baruch, *Baruch. My Own Story*, Henry Holt, New York, 1957.

In a 2007 interview with the *Financial Times*, then presidential candidate Hillary Clinton (whose husband had signed NAFTA)[20] said she agreed with economist Paul A. Samuelson's argument that traditional notions of comparative advantage may no longer apply. 'The question of whether spreading globalization and information technology are strengthening or hollowing out our middle class may be the most paramount economic issue of our time,' said Gene Sperling, Clinton's chief economic adviser.[21]

The point these references make is not against globalization as such, but against the bad habit of rushing to sign-up on something *without* studying the consequences. Nor is globalization a sort of penicillin for the financial markets as documented by the global credit pandemic of 2008 and 2009. As 2007 came to a close, and the deep wounds opened by the subprimes and credit crunch widened, several economists suggested that it might be better to call the 2008 economic story one of *global slowdown* instead of *global growth*. As 2008 came to a close the risk has been *global depression* rather than slowdown.

7. The Argument Against Free Trade

Bismarck told members of the Japanese imperial family who met him in a state visit to Berlin: 'When large countries pursue their advantage they talk about international law when it suits them, and they use force when it does not.'[22] In a nutshell, Bismarck's dictum describes the founding spirit of colonialism, all the way from the eighteenth century to the twenty-first.

Colonialism continues to exist even if its players, policies, processes, tools and benefits change over time. Today, the driving force of colonialism is the hunger for raw materials, particularly energy and metals. Complex and risky financial instruments sold the world over are also a form of colonialism; while colonialism-in-reverse is practised through the massive migration of jobs.

According to an until recently predominant political opinion, globalization made life better for most Americans and Europeans. The fact that, despite China, the EU's share of world exports rose slightly between 2000 and 2006, while a long list of Chinese exports involve foreign brands made abroad by

20 As well as the repeal of the Glass-Steagall Act, which prepared the ground for the 2007–2009 huge banking crisis.
21 *BusinessWeek*, 11 February 2008.
22 Sterling and Peggy Seagrave, *The Yamamoto Dynasty*, Corgi Books, London, 1999.

European companies was given as proof. Critics say that these arguments don't add up.

- Europe's share of world exports has been all-but stagnating; and

- the fact that firms lower their costs by manufacturing in Asia is a confirmation of job migration, not of an improvement in middle-class conditions.

Critics also add that the argument about compensating the loss of manufacturing jobs by creating service jobs does not stand careful scrutiny because the real economy is in manufacturing and agriculture, while the virtual economy is open to little appreciated risks and reversals. The major credit crisis of 2007–2009 has damaged the standard of living of most Americans while depriving some of them of their homes.

With the crisis in the real estate and the banking industries, the US economy is caught between what may be the biggest asset deflation of our time and an inflation which constrains the purchasing power of households. Faced with the loss of homes and jobs, the middle class is revolting against what it considers to be an overblown globalization. In European countries, too, large segments of the population now say that globalization is bad for them; an attitude which has the power to become a general mood, particularly if unemployment is high.

Appearing on the TV talk show *Porta a Porta* on national television, on 23 October 2007 Giulio Tremonti, Italian Finance Minister and former deputy head of the Chamber of Deputies, called for an end to discussion of petty issues and for addressing 'those issues which are the real concern of the population: food price increases, home mortgage rises, unemployment.' Globalization has taken hope away from families, he added, while suggesting returning to the system 'that gave us secure, stable jobs'.

One may agree or disagree with these statements, but listening to contrarian opinions is like opening the windows to let in fresh air. Two key variables correlate with Tremonti's opinion: jobs at home and global finance,. As he put it: 'Those madmen [the globalizers] introduced uncontrolled capital flows, and competition from low-wage countries [such as] China and India.'

Nor did Giulio Tremonti forget about the odd miniglobalization of the European Union. His position has been that: 'Those madmen have abruptly enlarged the European Union, and now they realize we are having a problem. They used food to produce gasoline, and now food prices are rising … Those idiots, they used to come to us and say: "We have 10 million unemployed? It is the free market…" Now, where is the free market when central banks intervene to rescue endangered banks?'[23]

What Tremonti did not say is that Europe's and America's troubles affect emerging Asia through both commercial and financial channels, even if Asian banks' exposure to the subprime mess is thought to be significantly smaller than that of Western banks. Chinese bank shares tumbled in late January 2008 on reports that they would have to make larger writedowns on their holdings of American subprime securities.

Let's face it. Contrary to what some theorists say, the world economy cannot be decoupled either from the US or from a US hard landing. Once the US demand for imported goods (and hence for massive exports by China and insourcing by India) goes away, developing countries will not have enough internal demand to compensate for the loss. To the contrary, they will be under severe pressure to develop new employment opportunities.

- To avoid rising unemployment, every year China must create 24 million new jobs (2008 projections).

- However, if left to internal demand only, China can create only 10 million jobs. Hence, it is highly dependent on exports.

By contrast, India does not depend on export of manufactured goods as much as China does. But *if* its huge insourcing facilities fail to attract clients from abroad, then its highly educated software engineers will remain idle or they will migrate. India's software and IT services outsourcing originates 66.5 per cent in the US; 15.5 per cent in Britain; and 18.0 per cent in other parts of the world. In addition, year-in and year-out, between 30 per cent and 40 per cent of Indian software and IT services outsourcing is connected to the financial industry – which is ailing these days.

---

23 *Executive Intelligence Review*, 2 November 2007.

8. Globalization's Unexpected Consequences

Contrarian opinions to globalization centre around the notion that it has entered a phase where it no longer just supplies western countries with cheap goods, but creates a large and rising demand for resources with supply constraints in key domains like energy (gas and oil), food, and logistics. Therefore, one of its unexpected consequences has been inflation as commodity prices continue to rise and the period of wage deflation in Western economies is coming to an end, while the inflationary pressures that ravage the Chinese and Russian economies are being exported.

- As Figure 1.1 shows, over a four-year period the price of energy and raw materials has been reaching for the stars.

- Then, as the economic and financial crisis got momentum, the price of commodities sank with the barrel of oil deflating to $33 (WTI) after having hit $145.

Food prices, too, have moved south, but in the longer term they are bound to rise as a result of a triple effect: increase in the world's population, better diet and biofuels. In India the economically weakest part of the population, some 250 million people, has gone from *one* meal per day to *two* meals per day. Similarly, in China people are changing soya milk habits to dairy milk, even if there are not enough cows to fill demand. Another absurdity lies in the fact that 75 per cent of the world's food is shipped with untold consequences for:

- health, because of deficient quality control; and

- pollution, due to intensive transport over global distances.

To a very substantial measure, the pains western societies are now feeling from the aftereffects of globalization without limits are direct result of their own faults. Since the 1980s the body and soul of governments in the US and Europe have been set on expanding globalization while their brains:

- lacked a concrete strategy for the future;

- assigned no priorities to the use of dwindling resources;

- failed to project on likely globalization negatives; and

- showed no interest in positioning themselves against globalization's forces.

For instance, the rise in Chinese imports to the US in recent years (or, for that matter, to France) has been vastly greater than the western country's growth rate and it has been apparently unaffected by variations in that growth. As every good negotiator knows, a good contract should have an *exit clause*. There is no exit clause in the free trade agreements.

Since the time of the General Agreement on Tariffs and Trade (GATT), therefore – the immediate post-World War II years – the Western policy towards what became known as 'globalization' could only advance but had no knowledge of even temporary withdrawal. Yet, successful generals appreciate that a partial withdrawal can very well be a strategic move because it allows to them pause, regroup and think seriously about the next move.

In addition to this, the obsolete rules of the original General Agreement on Tariffs and Trade referred principally to quantities and nature of merchandise products crossing borders, not to miners, manufacturers or just-in-time supply chains. The more recent General Agreement on Trade in Services (GATS) sets rules for both services suppliers who trade internationally and their services traded in four separate modes of supply. But GATS rests on the mistaken hypothesis that:

- trading in goods and services (including finance) will grow forever; and

- there will be no reverses, bottlenecks, disruptions or withdrawals from this process by one or more of its participants.

Nor is there any mention of how the dwindling resources of food and energy should or could be divided, or what kind of environmental protection should take precedence over growth. These are serious failures because, as the planners should have known, thanks to structural and market reforms the more vibrant of emerging economies are growing much faster than available resources allow – over and above the widening gap between their growth rate and that of the sluggish developed world.

The rapidly changing economic and industrial environment unleashed by trade and financial forces has influenced a wide array of developments in emerging economies but left western economies behind because of resistance to *structural reforms*, even if the latter have a decisive role to play in supporting an increase in competitiveness, augmenting the West's growth potential and reducing frictions associated with adjustment.

This failure to manage change has turned global openness in goods, services and labour markets against the globalization's inventors. While developing markets, not just China, industrialized, the west deindustrialized. As a result, positioning the aging population in western countries against the global market forces is more important today than since globalization began.

One does not need to go as far as Joseph Stiglitz, former chief economist of World Bank and currently at Columbia University, who described globalization as a *new system of investment which had gone fundamentally wrong*. Or Naomi Klein, for whom globalization is a *new system of looting and destruction* brought to power by irrational, evil financial and economic circles.[24] This is the wrong appreciation of the problem, not the least reason being that the current challenges are Chinese capitalism and market conquest – not western capitalism. What has happened with globalization during the last decade is that:

- it has hit the limits where national interests in trade and finance converge; and

- it has opened a Pandora's box of risks, many of them with unexpected consequences.

In the 1980s the deindustrialization of western Europe was hailed as the gateway to a knowledge society, but in the intervening years the level of education in western countries has dropped while that of illiteracy has risen. Moreover, it has been finally recognized that the emergence of China and India is a development with systemic implications for the global economy.

Given its huge size and rather well-educated population, China's successful integration into global trade in goods, services and finance has changed the old rules of the game. Measured at market exchange rates, its share of world output rose from around 2 per cent in 1990 to an estimated ±7 per cent in 2008,[25] India's

---

24 Naomi Klein, *The Shock Doctrine. The Rise of Disaster Capitalism*, Metropolitan Books, New York, 2007

25 From the Euroland perspective, China accounted for 10.3 per cent of extra-euro area imports in 2006, more than twice the share of Latin America, which represented 4.7 per cent.

share of world trade in services (but not in goods) has also risen markedly in the last years.

In 2008 Europe's trade deficit with China grew by an estimated €150 billion to €160 billion ($225 billion to $240 billion), on a par with America's record deficit with China in 2006. That is particularly disturbing for Europeans because it means a lot in lost jobs, a process accentuated through stage-managed currency exchange.

- The yuan has been appreciating slowly against the dollar in the past couple of years.

- But it has been declining against the euro, making Chinese imports even cheaper for consumers at the expense of local employment.

Another unexpected consequence has been that the internationalization of finance has emboldened big banks into taking an inordinate amount of exposure off-balance sheet, on the (mistaken) assumption that they can always repackage and sell credit risk while making fat profits. In the aftermath, the subprimes crisis of July/August 2007 cost two million Americans their homes and caused the ruin of some of the better-known names in the financial industry.

Let me conclude this section with a query. Suppose that in the 1960s when the first ideas of globalization hatched out of the multinationals remit, western politicians had asked the American, British, German, French, Italian, Dutch and other western citizens to pay with their houses and their jobs for the glory of free trade four decades down the line. How would they have responded?

9. The Greatest Danger of All is Protectionism

The lesson taught by the 1929–1932 First Great Depression is that the greatest danger of all is a resurgence of protectionism. Superficially this seems to contradict the critique made of globalization in the first eight sections of this chapter. In reality, however, it is further documentation of the need for *limits*. The thesis of this book is for globalization, provided that it is done:

- in an orderly way; and

- within rational limits.

The economic and financial crisis of 2007–2009 has taught some other lessons. When markets panic, the barriers to the free flow of capital and of goods are rising fast. The 'beggar-thy-neighbour' policies which led to the First Great depression are coming back into favour, and politicians look at the road ahead through the rearview mirror.

One of many examples is competitive currency devaluations. In September 2008 Mexico suddenly devalued the peso which, until January 2009, lost about 25 per cent of its value against the dollar. In December 2008 and January 2009 the Russian rouble also lost 25 per cent of its value versus the dollar and it continued sliding. Britain has allowed the pound to drop to 1.44 to the dollar and towards parity against the euro – for the first time ever.

Devaluations are a typical attempt by countries to maintain their edge in exports, but several economists are saying that rampant fiscal stimulus, huge bank and auto manufacturer bailouts, as well as other rescue packages occurring all over the world, are also a version of protectionism.

Since that ballyhooed G20 meeting in Washington on 15 November 2008, five of the participating countries: Russia, India, Indonesia, Brazil and Argentina – have announced their intention to raise tariffs on autos. India has already lifted duties on iron and steel. Brazil and Argentina are putting together a case within Mercosur (Latin America's sort of common market) for boosting external tariffs; and so on. So much for 'global cooperation' and free trade.

'Big 3 Get Lifeline in Bank Rescue Aid' read a headline in the *Wall Street Journal*; 'Treasury Signals Rescue of Carmakers' said an article in the *Financial Times*; 'Treasury Ready to Raid Relief Fund' stated another article. Other headlines have been: 'Carmakers in Asia and Europe Also Look For Help'; 'Japan Responds With Emergency Action Package'; 'Japanese Leader Announces A Sweeping Stimulus Plan'; 'Canada Agrees to Supplement Aid to Auto Industry'. Protectionism has a ball.

In 1929 Willis Hawley and Reed Smoot, two protectionist Republicans in US Congress, sponsored a bill to raise tariffs to the highest levels America had ever seen. The result was a round of reciprocal tariff hikes and a disastrous collapse in international trade. This was precisely the sort of thing heads of state of the G20 sought to avoid when they met in Washington in November 2008, agreeing not to devise new trade barriers as the world economy fizzled.

But in early 2009 one of the first messages from president Barack Obama to his constituency has been 'Buy American'.

Dave Rosenberg, Chief North American Economist of Merrill Lynch and a very sharp analyst, has argued that the US Troubled Assets Relief Program (TARP) is effectively a form of protectionism because the funds associated with it are offered only to US financial services companies. There arealso rumours that American banks that accepted TARP funds might be prohibited from lending outside the US, or at least might find their non-US lending activities curtailed, because, after all, that is US taxpayers' money.

Not to be left behind, in the week of 19 January 2009, Spain's socialist government called on Spaniards to adopt 'patriotic shopping' habits to protect jobs and beat the recession. Miguel Sebastian, the industry minister, said: 'There is something that our citizens can do for their country: bet on Spain, bet on our products, our industry and our services – bet, in short, on ourselves.'[26]

Another socialist, José Luis Rodriguez Zapatero, the Spanish prime minister, praised Sebastian as 'a defender of free trade' (no kidding) and said there would be no restrictions on goods coming from neighbouring Portugal. Yet as Gustavo Matias, economics professor at the Autonomous University of Madrid, has aptly pointed out, since 1959 Spain's economic success has coincided with its abandonment of protectionism – which is in the process of being reversed.

An open quarrel over protectionism and economic nationalism in the European Union turned ill-tempered on 10 February 2009 when the Czech Republic accused Euroland countries of inflicting serious damage on Europe's monetary union. 'The response of the eurozone countries to the financial and economic crisis has deformed the joint project of the Euro more than any other imaginable event,' said Mirek Topolanek, the Czech prime minister, whose country held (at the time) the EU's rotating presidency but which is outside Euroland.

In Germany business leaders accused France of protectionism. 'We are highly alarmed by the state support that has just been announced for the French car industry and by the conditions attached to it,' said Werner Schnappauf, managing director of the BDI federation, on 10 February 2008, 'Subsidies to support domestic industries lead to unacceptable competitive distortions in

---

26 *Financial Times*, 24/25 January 2009.

Europe. We will support all efforts by the chancellor and the new economic minister in their fight against these rising protectionist tendencies.'[27]

Buoyed up by the economic crisis, protectionism is looked at as the 'natural way' in which a political system fights the forces of global competition. Even in normal times no country likes to see its unemployment rise and its wealth deteriorate, but when the economic environment becomes ugly, because of deflating bubbles, the aftereffects tend to exacerbate the pressures of economic nationalism.

- When the economy wanes, governments take on a more populist tone; and

- the ways of government intervention include a whole arsenal – from currency devaluations to trade barriers, special tariffs and direct financial support to home industries.

Yet, heads of state should have the brains to appreciate that *protectionism* has more than one downside. One of the least evident is that supporting industries that have competitive disadvantages versus foreign companies might save jobs in the short term, but it creates significant damage to the economy in the longer run as:

- inefficiencies develop, and

- management quality is allowed to deteriorate.

Good governance is taking leave on the assumption that the government will always be on hand to save the day, no matter which blunders the company does. As an example, competition experts say that American and European politicians who have thrown taxpayers' money wholesale into the self-wounded big banks' coffers have weakened not strengthened these banks.

There is a precedent to keep in mind. By weakening prudential supervision as well as enforcement of antitrust rules, in the 1930s the US economy paid the price of lower growth and higher prices.

- Competition law was in effect suspended in America during the Depression; and

---

27 *Financial Times*, 11 February 2009.

- this resulted in widespread price collusion which prolonged the Depression rather than shortening it.

In a similar way, throughout the world today economic nationalism, massive bank bailouts and random 'stimuli' are not only turning the economic and banking crisis into a political one, but they also repeat the same grave errors of the late 1920s and the 1930s. Governments should expect to reap nothing else than what they have sown; what they have sown are wild seeds and the consequences will be dire.

2

The Rise of Asian Giants

1. A Snapshot of China's Position

In the 1960s and 1970s the busybodies of the State, Treasury, and Agriculture Departments,[1] guessed wrong when they got cold feet about the power of an emerging European Union; and they also misjudged the nature of different problems it might present to America. The challenger to the US is not the EU but China – and China came in from the cold thanks to Henry Kissinger, who did the negotiating which started with ping-pong tournaments in Nixon years.

Changes which have taken place since then provide eye-catching statistics. By 2008 China was already the world's largest mobile-phone market and the second-largest market for personal computers. Its leapfrogging in telecom services became evident in the fourth quarter of 2006, when it already had 430 million mobile phone users versus 120 million in India. A year earlier, at end of 2005, China had around 110 million internet users, compared with 51 million in India. This gap widened over the years.[2]

Other criteria, too, give China a lead. For instance, if credit card ownership is taken as basis for judging the level of development, the way some economists do, then China ranks after Brazil and Russia but way ahead of India.

- In the US, on average, a person has five credit cards;

- Brazil features one credit card per 2.5 people;

- Russia, one card per six people;

---

1 Respectively, State Department, Treasury Department and Department of Agriculture in Washington, DC.
2 *The Economist*, 7 October 2006.

- China, one card per 33 people; and

- India, one card per 64.5 people per credit card, almost twice as many people as China.[3]

On the contrary, one of the domains where the Chinese economy is not at its best is software and Information Technology (IT). According to some estimates, China lags as much as 12 years behind India in IT. The government is not pressing on the accelerator to catch up, in spite of the lead it achieved with Lenovo (Chapter 1). Experts suggest that China is handicapped in software by:

- rather mediocre English language skills;

- poor quality control procedures; and

- a dearth of management talent needed to run complex projects.

But China has a secret weapon up its sleeve: the strategy of overtaking Japan as major exporter to the US market for Wal-Mart type merchandise, using the mainland as manufacturing base and Hong Kong as financial service centre. It is a fairly general opinion that very low labour costs in China, and the country's ability to emulate hardware designed elsewhere, may have a lasting devastating effect on the American economy in regard to employment. China's trade surplus with the US has always been greater than that with the European Union.

- In 1999, trade surplus with America stood at $70 billion and increased steadily until 2006 to about $235 billion, ebbing to $190 billion in 2007.

- With the EU, China's trade surplus has gone from $35 billion in 1999 to over $160 billion in 2006, dropping to $140 billion in 2007 as Western economies faced a severe credit crisis.[4]

In an effort to right the balances somewhat, in December 2006 Hank Paulson, US Treasury secretary, and plenty of other economic officials in the Bush's Administration, met in Beijing in a twice-yearly *strategic economic dialogue*

---

3   *Business Week*, 24 March 2008.
4   *The Economist*, 1 December 2007.

between the two countries. Exchange rate changes, unemployment effects on the American economy because of massive imports from China and other trade issues were reportedly the main themes – but nothing has changed since then.

The irony about a huge current account surplus featured by China is that it brings along its own headaches. A challenge for the Chinese government is that even relatively small changes in the currency mix of its foreign exchange hoard will move markets. Shifting money into euros would push down the dollar and with this China:

- would single-handed inflate the price of commodities; and

- would suffer a significant capital loss on the value of its dollar reserves, which stand at $1.4 trillion.

Because many key commodities are typically denominated in dollars, relative price stability is important to China, which continues facing a hunger for commodities. Price stability is also important at a time when the country is positioning itself as a world power while at the same time trying to improve its people's standard of living – the unlikely feat of hitting two birds with one well-placed stone. China's standard of living is estimated to be about 20 per cent that of western countries; India's is roughly 10 per cent.

According to several economists, China's and the Chinese's perceived increasing confidence in the future is also beginning to affect the way the country behaves in the world, even if the emerging giant still lacks the resources to exert its influence beyond its current search for energy sources in the African continent, which seems to respond positively to China's approach.

China gives priority to exports because it needs foreign exchange, even if it has already plenty of it. At the same time, it uses its big internal market to bring economies of scale that keep low the prices of its products. Rapid growth in exports is also necessary to find employment for new entrants into the labor force. According to some cognizant opinions, *if* annual growth slips below 7 per cent *then* the economy will not generate nearly enough jobs to soak up the:

- millions of young Chinese entering the workforce each year; and

- millions laid off by restructured state enterprises, as well as dispatched agricultural workers from dams and other projects.

Hard work is another Chinese weapon. The country has young workers and managers willing to put in 12-hour days and to work weekends. Comparing that to *déclinisme's*[5] 35-hour week in France, one finds that Chinese labour practices are way ahead of the curve. Nor are Chinese workers retiring at 55 and always asking for more social benefits, as so often happens in the EU.

This is a different way of saying that China's competitive advantages are built on much more than very low wages and unfair trade practices, which is what its critics say. Notice, as well, that some 70 per cent of China's exports now come from private companies and foreign ventures, mainly owned by US, Japanese, Taiwanese, Hong Kong, and German companies (in that order). This makes it difficult to generalize quotas on Chinese exports.

If restrictions are placed on Chinese imports, then many European manufacturers who use China-made semi-finished products will also be hit by the EU or US retaliation against low cost goods. One of the interesting results of the policy to restrain Chinese imports for reasons of unfair competition is that it has pitted retailers against manufacturing firms and the labour unions. Therefore, it comes as no surprise that views on restrictions on imports from Asia diverge widely. As one retail boss puts it: 'They [the manufacturers] see China as a threat and we see China as an opportunity.'[6]

2. Is China Emulating Japan's Rising Sun?

Four economic motors are driving growth and real impact on emerging countries. At the top of the list is the *consumer* who, for the first time in Asia and other countries outside western nations,[7] is borrowing money, spending money and saving less. Some economists equate this with the rise of the middle class in China, India, Brazil and other emerging markets.

The second investment driver is *infrastructure*. All over the developing world there is a pressing need for infrastructure spending. The estimated capital expenditure (capex) of China Mobil in 2007 stood at $13 billion – a huge infrastructural project, which reflects the penetration of mobile services – and which will continue to absorb lots of capital. China's telecoms penetration is

---

5   *Declinisme* is a French word meaning an almost irreversible culture of decline.
6   *The Economist*, 9 December 2002.
7   Among western nations consumers started borrowing in the mid-1920s in America.

300 per cent that of India, and in 2006 its telecom revenue was $83 billion – over 400 per cent more than India's $20 billion.[8]

The third motor driving growth in emerging economies is *capital markets*. Exchanges have begun to have considerable weight, with Shanghai and Hong Kong being the best examples. There is also the beginning of mergers and acquisitions activity and IPO issuance contributing to the creation of a corporate sector. According to some analysts, all these factors will eventually ensure that profitability remains fairly strong, though all emerging markets companies are exposed to:

- internal shocks because of management risk; and

- adversity which may come from western markets.

The fourth driver of all markets, and most particularly those emerging which need restructuring, is *domestic reform*. In China, domestic reform implemented during the 1990s has progressively reduced the weight of the public sector in the economy, and transformed the industrial sector:

- in 1994, 82 per cent of industrial value added was created by the public sector through state- and collectively-owned enterprises;

- by 2008 this share had shrunk to below 40 per cent, whereas the share generated by privately- and foreign-owned enterprises continued to increase.

Productivity improvements have also benefited Chinese enterprises, through trade, technology transfer, foreign direct investment and joint ventures with foreign capital. Conversely, in the twenty-first century productivity improvements in the US and Europe have stalled.

The country's rapid industrialization evidently had inland effects. For instance, it has triggered a massive relocation of labour from rural areas to manufacturing and services. Though roughly 40 per cent of China's labour force is still employed in agriculture, this share has fallen dramatically from almost 71 per cent in 1978. Agriculture's share of nominal GDP has also declined, from 28 per cent in 1978 to about 12 per cent in 2007.

---

8   *Total Telecom Magazine*, July/August 2007.

These are the statistics whose interpretation gives rise to different opinions. According to Goldman Sachs, China will overtake America around 2027 (not around 2040 as mentioned in Chapter 1) and become by far the world's biggest economy by 2050. Some economists, however, believe that China's rising curve will bend.[9]

In early March 2007, in an article in the *Financial Times*,[10] Dr Lawrence Summers, the former president of Harvard University, former Treasury secretary and currently chief economic advisor to President Obama, argued that China was displaying many of Japan's characteristics in the late 1980s, including:

- rapid productivity growth; and

- a heavily regulated financial system that favoured domestic institutions.

By learning from a rather unfortunate history, policymakers on both sides of the Pacific could avoid repeating its mistakes, Summers stated. In the background of this opinion lies the precedent that, in the late 1980s and in early 1990s, the Japanese economic engine overheated and then stalled, leading to a lost decade-and-a-half of deflation and considerable deterioration in Japan's international standing.

This comparison to Japan is no good news for China. As of late 2008 Japan has been officially in recession even if, rare for an industrial country, its financial system is without big toxic assets problems. Major exporters, like Toyota and Sony, and their suppliers have been laying off plenty of workers while consumer sentiment has taken a dive. The shock has come through a sharp slowdown in exports and is a preview of what may well happen to China and India, reversing highly optimistic forecasts about their development.

While there are obvious differences between the two neighbours, such as China's much lower level of development, the similarities are striking and so is the message they bring. The history of Japan's fall to the abyss has yet to be written, but several economists and other knowledgeable observers agree that significant elements include the:

---

9   *The Economist*, 30 June 2007.
10   *Financial Times*, 5 March 2007.

- the stock market bubble;

- real estate and land bubbles; and

- serious problems in the financial system due to leveraging and excesses.

The last-mentioned included huge indebtedness by dubious credit counter-parties, followed by the collapse of aggregate demand as banks stopped extending credit. Japan's recovery has also been impeded by the difficulty of moving from export-led growth to growth supported by domestic demand, particularly at a time when both consumer and business confidence have been lost.

For his part, during the same interview in the *Financial Times*, Dr Barry Eichengreen suggested that there was another example from recent Asian history: that of South Korea. Like China in the first decade of the twenty-first century, Korea in the 1960s and 1970s pursued export-led growth with heavy reliance on foreign capital, but under strong state direction. In the first half of the 1990s, South Korea came under international pressure to:

- liberalize its capital account; and

- move to a more flexible exchange rate.

At the end of 1997, the South Korean economy crashed, proving that financial opening without economic and financial restructuring, as well excessive reliance on consumer electronics and heavy industry, led to an unbalanced economy. A major financial crisis followed.

China, of course, is neither Japan nor South Korea, but this makes matters a little worse not better. While complaining about the Japanese and South Korean governments' policies, the US never took drastic action against its two closer allies in East Asia. Both Japan's rising sun and South Korea's ascendancy fell victim, so to speak, to their own devices and excesses.

The case with China is different in that respect. In 2007, in the US, Democratic Party congressional leaders demanded radical action to contain the economic threat they – rightly or wrongly – perceived from the Asian giant. Delegations of senior American economic officials engaged in dialogues with their Chinese counterparts about the many aspects of the country's economic policies that promote imbalances, warning of unspecified 'congressional demons' who stand ready to act *if* requested changes are not undertaken quickly, including revaluation of the yuan.

In all likelihood, a stronger yuan and higher yields in China than in America would also mean greater inflows of foreign capital. The People's Bank of China (PBOC) would then have to buy even more foreign exchange to hold down the yuan, increasing the hoard of hard currency reserves – as well as the wealth in the coffers of China Investment Corporation, one of the bigger Sovereign Wealth Funds (SWFs, Chapter 5)

The irony is that, according to a growing body of opinion, a stronger Chinese currency would not reduce by much America's trade deficit. It is, indeed, likely that China, not America, has more to gain from setting the yuan free because without a flexible exchange rate there is mounting risk that China's simmering economy will boil over, leading to a repetition of the financial drama in Japan and South Korea.

3. India versus China

To represent the two Asian giants under one label, Jairam Rames, an Indian politician, coined the word *Chindia*. Under that rubric comes 38 per cent of the world's population living in countries which are the heirs of ancient civilizations but until quite recently were desperately poor. *Chindia*, however, is not one bloc. The policies of the two states diverge and their differences in going after the global market are striking.

- China has accumulated capital far faster and achieved a more rapid growth in factor productivity than India;

- investment in infrastructure is significantly higher in China, while India prides itself that its companies conquer the world's basic industries, a case in point being steel.

Some experts find it curious that so many Indian firms are focused heavily on expanding in the west, rather than in developing countries where the operating experience they have gained at home could be more of an advantage. Indian companies respond that their managers are better equipped than

Chinese managers to deal with the developed world and they leave the lesser developed markets to the Chinese.

But China may not be focusing only on low-cost manufacturing for long. On 4 December 2006 the OECD released a study showing that the government had programmed $136 billion to spend on research and development in that year, outpacing Japan's $130 billion and putting itself in second place behind the US. There is no evidence that India spends big money on R&D. Other issues, too, give food for thought:

1.   Why can Beijing push through sweeping free-market reforms while New Delhi cannot?

2.   Why is China so much more open to multinationals than India?

3.   Why do Indian companies have a much deeper pool of managerial talent than Chinese companies?

4.   Why does China have a large current account surplus, while India's economy is characterized by a rising current account deficit?

People with both Indian and Chinese experience suggest that the reason India lies behind China in necessary reforms can be found in the stonewalling of its 10-million-strong civil service, which is the size of a small country. India's unrestructured and unreformed public sector is a huge barrier to:

•   a faster rate of sustainable growth;

•   the ability to improve the lot of India's poor; and

•   infrastructural renewal to set a higher speed for the economy.

All three issues are controversial. Regarding the first two points, some say that today India's poor eat twice per day rather than once only – an improvement. Others insist that the government's development spending fails to reach its intended recipients and this stirs up resentment, causing a backlash. But resentment is not enough of a reason for falling behind in urgently needed infrastructural renewal. So much for query No. 1.

The answer to query No. 2 is that of differences in government choices in terms of priorities. In the wake of the damage created by Mao's Great Leap Forward of the 1950s, and that of the Cultural Revolution (1966–1976), which wiped out a couple of generations of managers, Deng Xiaoping ushered in reforms providing incentives to lure investment by multinationals and by the ethnic Chinese in Hong Kong and Southeast Asia.

This open borders policy was followed by one of lavish favours for foreign investors, especially those bringing high technology or able to help China develop high-priority industries like software and life sciences. Still, it is not easy to erase the memory and effects of the years during which China was inward-looking, which explains why China's bureaucracy is not happy with foreign firms.

In regard to query No. 3, the multinationals are generally credited with the fact India has a better management pool than China. Even during periods of stifling state controls and Indira Gandji's anti-foreign campaigns, which ousted IBM and Coca-Cola in the 1970s, most multinationals did not abandon India. By staying in the country, they trained a significant number of Indian managers.

India's managerial talent received a further major boost from insourcing and outsourcing. In 2002 the six biggest American technology firms with development centres in India had fewer than 10,000 employees in total in the country. In December 2007 their combined Indian workforce exceeded 150,000.[11]

The counterside of this is that India developed a growing talent shortage in spite of the fact that the population of engineers and scientists in Indian universities was in full swing. And thanks to their fluency in English language, Indian graduates became internationalized, the better educated among them learning to switch jobs for career improvement while salaries rise by 10 to 15 per cent a year. The forecast is that, for senior staff, salaries will soon reach western levels.

The response to query No. 4, too, has much to do with national choices. The Chinese government gave first priority to manufacturing for exports, albeit with disregard to environmental issues (see section 7). To the contrary, successive Indian governments have been preoccupied with matters connected to public finances rather than with addressing head-on needed reforms.

---

11   *The Economist*, 15 December 2007.

India's 2008 budget confirmed sad truths about how little headway the government had made in implementing changes during the good years. Not only China but also other big emerging markets have been less complacent, leaving India in an unenviable fiscal shape as the government is:

- short of money for infrastructure;

- reluctant to free banks, pension funds and insurers to serve the market better; and

- unable to improve its record of spending money on low return projects, depriving firms of badly needed competitive advantages in productivity and labour.

Nor has India's banking sector been recently restructured like China's (Chapter 8), or learned a lesson from other banking industry failures. Experts suggest that the reason why, in 2008, the Indian government continued to shy away from overdue reforms of the banking industry is that it needed the bank's goodwill to continue buying bonds to finance the 3.1 per cent deficit of central administration plus state deficits, fertilizer subsidies and fuel subsidies.

Budget deficits and the nature of capital inflows correlate. Big deficits are anathema to foreign direct investments, which are much safer than speculative capital which keeps on coming. According to some estimates, in 2007 about 85 perc ent of India's capital inflows were in the form of debt or portfolio investment and much of which went into and out of the stock market.

By contrast, China's economy looks less risky thanks to a small budget surplus (officially a small budget deficit), its vast current account surplus and its reserves. After running a current account deficit for most of the previous three decades, Brazil also had a surplus for five years, thanks to robust commodity prices. Russia's economy, too, is sheltered by large current account and budget surpluses, thanks to high gas and oil prices. The lack of natural resources with high value in world markets is one of the negatives of India's economy.[12]

Last but not least, business scandals and quality problems related to outsourcing may kill the goose that laid the golden egg. In the week of 5 January 2009 Satyam Computer Services, which was once India's fourth-biggest

---

12 India has some minor oil extraction operations which are of limited worth and are mismanaged.

software and IT services firm, was shaken by a scam perpetrated by its founder, B. Ramalinga Raju and allegedly by his brother.

Raju confessed to cooking Satyam's books for years, and admitted that a $1 billion cash pile did not in fact exist. Some analysts suspect that even after this admission only 50 per cent of the truth is out.[13] As the Satyam scandal has continued to spread, two auditors from PricewaterhouseCoopers have been in police custody trying to explain why they signed off on the insourcing company's cooked books.

- Politicians, too, joined the fray, with the chief minister of Satyam's home trading furious accusations of negligence and worse with his predecessor; and

- On 6 February 2009, the Indian government revealed that its serious fraud office has been investigating no fewer than 325 companies wrapped up in the Satyam scam.[14]

There was further discomfort for India's IT insourcing industry when it emerged that the World Bank had banned Wipro Technologies and Megasoft Consultants from its procurement programme because the firms had provided 'improper benefits to bank staff'. In 2008 Satyam Computer Services was barred from doing business with the World Bank for the same reason. Indians would be well advised to remember that reputation takes decades to build but can be destroyed in a day.

4. Global Firms from Emerging Countries

In 2008, Mittal, Tata, Suzlon, Embraer, Gazprom and plenty of other companies from emerging countries have become almost household names. In the last couple of decades, the origin of multinationals has been changing. We are no longer in the 1960s when de Gaulle's government fretted about IBM, Ford, General Motors, Dow Chemicals and ITT spreading their wings; or the 1980s when the American government got nervous as Japan's Sony bought a Hollywood studio and other Japanese firms invested the big way in Manhattan and Hawaiin real estate.

---

13   *The Economist*, 14 February 2009.
14   *The Economist*, 14 February 2009.

By 2004 the UN Conference on Trade and Development (UNCTAD) already noted that five companies from emerging Asia had made it onto the list of the world's 100 biggest multinationals measured by overseas assets, while more firms from emerging economies found a slot in the top 200. In late 2007, a study by Boston Consulting Group identified 100 companies from emerging markets with total assets in 2006 of $520 billion.

Gone as well is the time when socialists and other leftists condemned the rich North for keeping the poor South in virtual slavery. These days, investment flows increasingly from South to North and South to South. Emerging economies of what used to be called the Third World invest both in the former First World countries and in those which are still less developed. They even take control of rich countries' 'jewels in the crown' (see Chapter 5 on Sovereign Wealth Funds).

In early 2006 Arcelor, a steelmaker of French, Luxembourg and Spanish extraction – Europe's biggest – faced then succumbed to a bid from Mittal, an international steel group largely owned by the family of Lakshmi Mittal. When, in January 2006, the three west European governments heard about it, they first expressed their firm opposition then looked for a white knight and turned to another emerging economy steelmaker, Russia's Severstal, to which they paid a silly premium in millions of euros. Arcelor succumbed to Mittal six months later.[15]

Before Mittal bought Arcelor, Anglo-Dutch steel firm Corus approached Ratan Tata, head of the Tata Group, about joining forces with Tata Steel. Negotiations led to the conclusion that the more efficient way of collaborating would be for the Indian firm to take over Corus. This lead to a bidding war for Corus between Tata Steel and Brazil's CSN group. Tata eventually secured the prize. In 2008, Tata Motors bought Ford England's Jaguar and Rover – for a fraction of the amount Ford had paid for these acquisitions.

Suzlon, an Indian firm that began life as a textile manufacturer but is now among the five leading makers of wind turbines, has acquired England's Hansen (originally a Belgian company) and REpower, a German wind-energy firm – spending over $2 billion on the pair. These are just three examples of

---

15 On 13 February 2008, Arcelor Mittal announced that it had made $19.4 billion, before tax and interest, on sales of $105 billion in 2007, up 27 per cent on the two firms' aggregated profits in the previous year. Mittal's 43 per cent share makes him the world's fifth-richest man, with a fortune of some $38 billion.

how the origin of global companies changes, several coming from emerging economies which are buying businesses in rich countries as well as in poorer ones.

In some industry sectors emerging economies have achieved a leading position. In information technology, the Indian trio of Wipro, Infosys and Tata Consulting Services (TCS) have built an insourcing industry that moved upmarket, became global and gave American IT leaders such as Accenture and IBM a run for their money.

To a significant extent, the automotive supply chain is up for grabs. Not only several European auto manufacturers but also the former Big Three of Detroit – General Motors, Ford and Chrysler – no longer hold dominant positions, having been overtaken as top of the line manufacturers of motor vehicles by the likes of Toyota, Honda and Volkswagen. And many of the US-based auto part providers are struggling to prevent costs, debt, falling output and reduced margins from sinking them forever.

Following the strategy of acquiring relationships with manufacturers, India's Bharat Forge is now the world's second-largest forging company and a leading supplier to the motor industry around the world, tied up with a French firm to get close to PSA Peugeot Citroën. 'We are not really buying factories,' an Indian investor was quoted having said, 'We are buying orders, which we can eventually fulfill with cheaper supplies from India.'[16]

Some experts are, however, worried about disruption in the supply chain in terms of parts from distant countries. Loss of production due to a supplier's failure is, of course, the ultimate nightmare for every original equipment manufacturer (OEM). Anyone who believes it could not happen should think back to 2002, when production of the Land Rover Discovery was on the brink of being halted by the insolvency of chassis frame supplier UPF-Thompson.

UPF's receivers demanded a £45 million ($90 million) payment from Land Rover to secure the engineering firm's survival. Land Rover refused to pay, sparking the supply crisis, but eventually agreed to take on part of the debt. New receivers were appointed and supply continued. Had this not happened it would have taken nine months to find another supplier, according to Rover, with all that would have meant to its own survival. Chrysler faced a similar

---

16   *The Economist*, 12 January 2008.

challenge in 2008 from a failing US auto parts supplier. Could this be repeated on the supply chain's global scale?

5. State Planning as Alternative to Global Firms

State planning and economic micromanagement at both a national and a global scale have not been invented in post-Maoist China. Immediately after the end of World War II, the French government set up an economic planning commission and for nearly three decades *le Plan* was the alter ego of government action, until first its appeal and then its impact faded.

China practices a more covert but, according to some accounts, just as rigorous state planning which initially seems to have performed rather well. More recently, however, it has been taken over by a spirit of gigantism, and it is beginning to falter. Critics say that Chinese planners:

- have missed the signals that an over-leveraged global economy was heading down the slope; and

- kept on expanding capacity instead of taking a break.

To appreciate the reasons for this failure, it should be recalled that since China's opening to the west, economic performance has been export driven. If it new employment opportunities were created for the internal market alone, China could only find employment for half the 22 to 25 million young people who join the labour force year after year. In turn, the miscalculation of export elasticity has led to an unstoppable increase in China's industrial capacity.

At end of 2007 industrial production grew by 17.3 per cent year-on-year. Export growth remained at elevated levels, though following a declining path throughout the year, but the trade surplus continued to widen. At the same time, however, inflation grew, with food prices largely driving its rise.

As an example of unwarranted growth without limits, in early 2008 China had the fastest-growing stainless steel industry in the world, tripling output in just three years. China already generates 23 per cent of the world's stainless output, at 7 million tons, up from 5 per cent in 2001. A Merrill Lynch study estimated that:

- there are approximately 4 million tons of new stainless steel melting capacity to be developed in China between 2007 and 2010; and

- this will account for more than 60 per cent of the global increase in stainless steel capacity over the same period.[17]

It does not seem that the Chinese government's planners have considered the risk of growing stainless steel production from less than 1 million tons in 2001 to nearly 11 million tons in 2010, while world consumption more or less tapers off. Some experts wonder about the curious fact that between 2005 and 2008 western stainless steel producers have allowed their production capacity to dwindle; others are of the opinion that:

- poorly planned empty giant steel factories will shock the Chinese economy; and

- governments usually spend other people's money, while no private enterprise could afford such a mistake in capital expenditure.

By contrast, the Chinese planners have correctly seen the need for energy resources able to sustain the economy's expansion beyond the short to medium terms. China has projected becoming the world's largest oil importer soon after 2010. Therefore, it is seeking ever greater supplies from all over the world, Africa included, to keep the engines of its economic boom running.

In recent years, Chinese state-owned companies have made inroads into the large oilfields off West Africa, one of the world's hottest exploration zones. In its most expensive acquisition, China National Offshore Oil Corporation (CNOOC) has finalized a payment of $2.7 billion for a share of a lucrative oil block off Nigeria, Africa's biggest crude exporter, due to start pumping this year. In Angola, Africa's next biggest producer, China Petrochemical Corporation (Sinopec) has gained a 50 per cent stake in the BP-operated Greater Plutonio project.[18]

In the west, such deals have fuelled concerns that China's government is gobbling up vast reserves at the expense of developed countries. Already in 2005 (latest statistics available) Chinese national oil companies produced about 267,000 barrels of oil equivalent a day in Africa, about one third of the amount

---

17 Merrill Lynch, *Commodity Strategist*, 12 February 2008.
18 *Financial Times*, 24 January 2008.

produced by ExxonMobil, the largest foreign producer on the continent; and the Chinese firms' share is growing.

Closer to home, there is a Chinese line of claims to potential oil resources claims in the South China Sea, from Hainan Island to Brunei and Malaysia. As in other disputes concerning oil and gas, at issue are reserves believed to lie under waters not far from the Vietnamese coast. Vietnam says that a Chinese came close to its coast more than ten years ago when, on 7 March 1997, an oil rig, the Kan Tan III, entered its exclusive economic zone and started operating just over 64 nautical miles from its shore.

- Vietnam accused China of violating international law, and called for talks urgently.

- The Chinese were unconcerned, as opposition by Vietnam and the Philippines was limited to a war of words.

The Chinese planners search for energy is far from having spent its steam. In a 2008 analysis, the International Energy Agency expected China's imports of oil to triple by 2030. China has also swallowed up 80 per cent of the increase in the world's copper supply since 2000, and it is getting ever hungrier for other industrial raw materials which it needs for an ever-expanding production capacity which has, so far, defied market dynamics.

6. The Great Leap Forward in Technology Recalls Mao's Time

An ominous precedence for Chinese planners is Mao's Great Leap Forward, which cost the country a couple of lost decades while also destroying some of its wealth. A twenty-first century example of a great leap forward is electronics. China has been gaining a great deal in technological advantage through an open door policy. In late March 2007 Intel unveiled plans to open a $2.5 billion factory in the Chinese city of Dalian by 2010.

At face value, this decision was favourable to China's ambitions to be a centre for high-tech industry while remaining a low-cost producer but, with an eye on potential opposition to the export of sensitive technology from American politicians, Intel said that the new plant would make chips other than microchips. This was bad news for China because its own semiconductor firms are struggling.

- Shares in chip foundry SMIC have dropped by over 54 per cent since its 2004 initial public offering (IPO).

- Chinese CD makers need a large government bailout to keep from going under, as Korean and Taiwanese rivals power ahead.

- TCL and other Chinese handset makers have lost ground in their own country to Nokia, Samsung and Motorola.

- ZTE, the telecom manufacturer, saw its share plunge 40 per cent in 2006, a likely indicator of similar troubles at its competitor Huawei.

- Lenovo's stock price dropped 34 per cent in 2006, and in April 2007 said it would restructure, laying off 1,400 people.[19]

This is a far cry from Lenovo's (and the Chinese government's) original plans, whose acquisition of IBM's PC division in 2006 led to predictions that it would become a powerhouse capable of challenging Dell and Hewlett-Packard. Today, while Lenovo remains the leader in China, it is falling behind its competitors in the world's computer market, providing evidence that China's up and coming computer outfits are struggling overseas.

More serious is the loss of face in the global consumer market because of the decline in the quality of some products, with health hazards associated to quality issues. After warnings about contaminated pet food and toothpaste, which alerted authorities both in the US and in Europe, American safety regulators discovered a new problem demanding a recall of 450,000 defective tyres.[20]

In mid-August 2007, Nokia said that 100 reported incidents of overheating mobile phone batteries had prompted it to offer replacements to customers. Nokia identified a batch of 46 *million* batteries supplied by a Japanese firm, but made in China. (The factory at fault belonged to Japan's Matsushita, but this matters little because Nokia's image was on the line.) In 2006 Sony had to

---

19 *Business Week*, 14 May 2007.
20 It has been a deliberate choice not to include magnet defects and risk of paint poisoning on China-made Mattel toys, which made big news, because of the 21 September 2007 *coup de theatre* where a senior Mattel executive apologized to the Chinese people.

replace 9.6 million laptop batteries because of fears they could overheat.[21] At the origin are said to have been:

- sharp cost-cutting; and

- lack of appropriate quality control.

It goes without saying that Chinese companies must be very sensitive on quality assurance, because health hazards and exploding batteries or tyres can kill the goose that lays the golden egg. Indeed, as the US Congress scheduled a hearing on product safety, China stepped up its campaign to reassure consumers that goods made in the country are safe. Both China and the western outsourcing firms are to blame:

- China, because what is now being revealed proves that the country is miles behind in quality control policies, methods and tools; and

- Sony, Matsushita, Nokia, Mattel, and other outsourcers, because they have shown a great disrespect for their customers with these incidents, indicating that their own quality control systems may be in a shambles.

All outsources and, clearly, *all* importers must examine their supply chains very carefully, no matter who the insourcers might be. Not only is this 100 per cent their responsibility, but also they face legal risk as they can be sued by customers who have bought poisonous wares or exploding mobile telephones. There is also the suspicion that:

- what has come to the public eye is no more than the tip of the iceberg; and

- most likely, the future will bring other quality scandals to light, with a costly aftermath to all supply chain players.

The global western firms argue that, as far as goods produced in developing countries are concerned, monitoring contract manufacturers is not easy, because visits to factories are hard to arrange and when they do occur they are stage-managed. As an argument, this, too, is worse than half-baked because if the players in the international supply chain don't come forward with clearly

---

21 *The Economist*, 18 August 2007.

established quality standards, inspection rules and proofs of quality they should not be patronized – full stop.

The Chinese government itself must be greatly concerned about health hazards connected to the country's produce, because this new, 'great leap forward' could kill its export markets. Additionally, China's government often said that subcontractors making electronics, toys, tyres, batteries or other wares are not violators when it comes to safety and labour standards.

Somehow hidden in these pronouncements about responsibility for quality problems is the fact that such products were typically bought by big firms, large enough to carry out regular inspections. It is, however, a false assumption that the producer bears no accountability. Two wrongs don't make a right.

7. Pollution, Too, Got Out of Hand

One of key contributors to the so-called *China Price* (Chapter 4) is the lack of environmental standards, as well as expertise and budgets to deal with them. The no. 1 priority China put on industrial development without limits has led to wholesale pollution of rivers, lakes and land. It was recently that in one of the provinces west of Shanghai an estimated 70 per cent of water resources are polluted and the fish are either dead or inedible.

- The pollution of land, air and water resources is not just devastating the local fish industry, which is bad enough.

- It also impacts on the quality of China's food exports entering into the global food chain, as the lightweight negotiators of the Doha Round should have pointed out.

To say the least, pollution control has not been in the Chinese government's list of priorities. All departments and ministries are oriented towards beefing up the GDP. Theoretically, a couple of the central government's comprehensive economic departments should be looking after the environment; but practically all they do is to authorize projects. Local leaders do the same. The Environmental Protection Agency is pretty weak, commented Pan Yue, vice-minister of the State Environmental Protection Agency.[22]

---

22 *The Economist*, 9 September 2006.

This disregard for quality of life and pollution's after-effects also seems to prevail among Chinese enterprises abroad. In the small French town of Commentry, a chicken farm, Adisseo, formerly controlled by Rhône-Poulenc the French pharmaceutical company, was bought by Blue Star, a subsidiary of Chem China. In 2003 CGT, the French labour union, said that 10 workers of a single production unit were diagnosed with cancer of the kidneys because of using a molecule 'chloracetal C5'. By 2006 the number of workers with kidney cancer had grown to 26.[23]

Experts suggest that the true scale of China's land, air and water pollution problems has been kept away from public knowledge for some time, but now it is coming to the surface. According to an article in the *Financial Times*, China engineered the removal of nearly a third of a World Bank report on pollution because of concern that findings on premature deaths could provoke social unrest.[24]

The World Bank's report stated that it is critically important that existing health and environmental data be made publicly available. Other studies have reached the same conclusion. Post-mortem, however, Chinese authorities said that by some standards the quality of the air in Chinese cities has improved in recent years, evidently without mentioning that air pollution in Chinese cities is among the worst in the world. An estimated 750,000 people die prematurely in China each year mainly in large cities, with deaths attributed to poor air and water quality. This is not surprising because:

- millions of traditional bicycle drivers have morphed into millions of car drivers; and

- Beijing today has 3 million cars, as well as traffic jams and long stagnant car queues.

At the beginning of August 2007, in a glittering televised show in Tiananmen Square through which China's government celebrated the beginning of the one-year countdown to the Beijing Olympics, viewers could see a thick grey curtain of smog engulfing the city, its skyscrapers and its cars stuck on the turnpike. Reportedly, concerns were raised about the potential effects of the city's choking air pollution on athletes running for the gold.

23 *Le Canard Enchaîné*, 25 October 2006.
24 *Financial Times*, 3 March 2007. The aforementioned World Bank study was produced in cooperation with Chinese government ministries over several years.

According to reliable reports, some 45,000 km of turnpikes and auto-routes have been built or are under construction. Through subsidized cheap gas prices the government is supporting a domestic car industry which it sees as an engine of future economic growth, having probably read that in America one out of seven people work for industry sectors producing and servicing motor vehicles.

What the Chinese government probably has not read is that the growth of pollution and over-consumption of natural resources correlate, the moderator being technology used for control of emissions. This failure in getting informed is a pity, because 20 of the world's 30 most polluted cities are in China – and the rate at which the country uses up natural resources is not sustainable. Taking only one example:

- domestic crude oil production is rising only slowly,

- but oil imports are growing by more than 30 per cent a year.

China also works intensively in liquefying coal, in an effort to provide oil substitutes. Critics, however, point out that abundant use of coal means that by 2009 China will probably overtake the US as the world's largest producer of carbon emissions. Its current share is 17 per cent of the world's total, while America's share is 22 per cent. Neither is a good record.

In mid-April 2007, *The Economist* published an article with the headline 'Come in Number One, Your Time Is Up', whose target was galloping air pollution. This is a direct result of the fact that environmental protection targets are weak or nonexistent, while provincial and local party officials have been judged and promoted on their ability to drive economic growth.

- A policy change can be effective only when there is greater openness about environmental problems; and

- This is not easy because the Chinese government remains sensitive about exposing too many details for fear of backlash from its own population and from the west.

In recent years, an increasing number of local protests in China have been provoked by local environmental degradation, commonly against factories that have polluted surrounding farmland and water supplies. Some experts say that, in social terms, the situation may also be serious in Chinese cities because a huge proportion of the rural population has moved to urban centres. Estimates indicate that by 2020 around 60 per cent of China's population will be living in cities or towns, and some of them in slums, with urban children quite likely to die from respiratory and water-borne diseases.

These statistics and estimates on the level of pollution in the largest of the developing countries should be seen in conjunction to the half-baked decisions of western countries (particularly European) to cut *their* level of pollution to imaginary low numbers by 2040 and 2050. Particularly funny, for example, have been the announced 'commitments' at the July 2008 G8 summit in Hokkaido, Japan – a 'summit' whose only concrete environmental act was the planting of a dozen trees.

A Japanese diplomat put Hokkaido's record straight when he worried that the relationship between the G8 and India, China, Brazil, Mexico and South Africa over climate change may soon resemble classical management-and-labour stand-offs at their worst. And a Russian diplomat aptly pointed out how absurd it is for meeting goals four decades from now.

The lack of authority of the developed countries' top brass making grandiose commitments on CO_2 trading is also quite cynical. As an article in *The Economist* pointed out, Japan's Fukuda is weak domestically, Britain's Brown looks little better, America's Bush was a lame and unpopular duck and France's Sarkozy struggles to comprehend how and why his voters' enthusiasm has evaporated.[25]

Nor were the aforementioned prime ministers and presidents, or their peers, in full accord on what to do and when to start doing it. The European Union wanted CO_2 measurements based on tough pollution targets to begin from 1990 (which is silly at best). Japan, which unilaterally says it will aim for a 60 per cent or more cut in emissions, thought it was more realistic to start from 2005 or perhaps 2008. The G8 could not come up with common timetables or even outline tangible nearer-term goals to cut emissions. The only thing on which the leaders of states seemed to agree was on setting far-out distant targets, so distant that (quite probably), they themselves would all have turned to minerals.

---

25 *The Economist*, 12 July 2008.

8. Contrarian Opinions about China's Commercial Threat

Some economists downplay China's challenge to US and EU, their argument being that its surge in international GDP statistics is considerably tempered by looking at the large population across which GDP results are spread. According to this school of thought, even if China's GDP is growing by leaps and bounds, ultimately the country still lags far behind the main industrial nations. The same economists point out that in 2006 per-capita income was:

- just above 4 per cent of the comparable figure for the United States; and

- about 5 per cent of the relevant figure for Germany, leaving plenty of room for catching up.

Such arguments, however, can be misleading because the statistics they refer to could also be interpreted in the opposite way. The 20 to 25 per cent multiplier to reach American and German living standards is roughly the demodulator of labour costs – making Chinese products so much more attractive to westerners in price terms. Table 2.1 presents a bird's eye view of minimum hourly wages in three western and three Asian countries.

In terms of labour costs not only America but also Europe and Japan have a problem because the scales of industrial production are tilting in a way that has been neither expected nor experienced so far. And there is also a certain conflict of interest embedded in the China challenge: by outsourcing components and

Table 2.1   Minimum hourly wages in EU and US typical wages in South and East Asia*

Country	Wage in Euro
France	8.27
Britain	7.48
United States	4.00
India	0.31
China	0.10
Bangladesh	0.07

*   Statistics by *EuroNews*, December 8, 2006

hardware from China, as well as information technology services from India, US companies have sharply boosted their return on capital.

Experts also add that it would be a mistake to underestimate the influence big banks exercise on Western governments. Bankers and investors see China's economy not only as being many times bigger than that of other developing countries, but also more efficient, growing faster and characterized by political stability.

According to the US Conference Board, the fact that China capitalized on foreign know-how and technology has seen to it that productivity of private industry has grown an impressive *17 per cent* annually over five consecutive years. By contrast, with their profit margins squeezed in order to be able to meet their Chinese competitors' prices, American companies are no longer investing much in new capacity and greater productivity at home. The same is true of European companies, at a time when China is emerging as a conglomeration of very competitive manufacturing platforms.

Contrarians believe that the lack of independent labour unions and of the right to strike is a cause of unfair competitive advantages enjoyed by China in the global market. Theoretically, the government promotes labour union membership. Practically, workers' unions in China are controlled by the Communist Party (a misnomer) through an umbrella organization to which all unions must be affiliated: The All-China Federation of Trade Unions (ACFTU).

These arguments made by critics have a point, but at the same time they fail to account for some progress in recent years. A couple of decades ago, when China's economy was largely run by the state, almost all urban workers belonged to trades unions set up in the state-owned enterprises for which they were working.

- These unions had very little, if any, bargaining power; and

- Strikes as well as other forms of collective pressure were effectively banned.

Things have changed somewhat since then, with some independent labour unions popping up. Critics say that this does not promote a free labour movement. The party simply wants ACFTU labour unions to keep workers off the streets. Be that as it may, what happens with labour unions in China is definitely not the west's problem. Much more worrisome is the scale of environmental damageand of food imported from China.

Moreover, it should be the responsibility of the United Nations and not of the inefficient and ineffectual WTO (Chapter 4) to come up with universal health standards and controls regarding food production, transport and distribution. An example is provided by China's mid-September 2008 tainted milk powder scandal, which escalated dramatically as not one or two but 22 Chinese dairy companies were found to have produced infant formulae containing a chemical blamed for killing two infants and poisoning a score of others.[26]

The adulterated formula reportedly contains the chemical melamine, which is normally used in plastics, fertilizers and cleaning products.[27] Adding melamine to milk is a tactic used to mask its dilution with water, because it tends to increase the apparent protein content of diluted milk. This infant formula scare is the latest in a series of product safety scandals involving everything from lead in toys to contaminants in pet food:

- severely damaging China's image as an exporter; and

- posing critical questions regarding health hazard in global procurement of food.

Health hazards aside, what I find curious is that labour unions in the west did not care, or did not dare, to demonstrate their anger about the fact that free labour movements are not allowed in China. They reserve all their action for the west, which makes a tense employment situation worse and increases the risk that the slide in America's and Europe's industrial power will accelerate until it becomes a rolling disaster.

One of the opinions heard these days is that a quota system can be a *deus ex machina* in putting limits to the torrent of China's exports, while benefiting other less developed countries. A variation of this was the discussion in France about an extra value added tax of some 5 per cent, applied to Chinese origin products, never enacted because of the risk of violating World Trade Organization (WTO) agreements and rules.

---

26 The list of companies caught up by the tainted milk scandal included Yili, one of China's largest dairy groups and a sponsor of the Beijing Olympics.

27 On 23 February 2008 it was reported that infant formulae containing melamine had reached New Zealand.

Opponents to unilateral trade barriers point out that apart from the fact these approaches would violate the liberal rules of WTO, a major factor working against quotas for Chinese products is that it would not create unanimity among western countries and its policing would be ineffectual. Also, once a system of quotas took hold, it would expand to the produts of other countries through its own devices, eventually leading to trade wars.

The notions outlined in the preceding paragraphs are basic reasons why Dr Paul Samuelson, the economist and Professor Emeritus at MIT, as well as many other economists and trade experts, now look with awe at developing events. They say the huge price challenge from China, and some other developing countries, can overpower any gains that western countries, companies and consumers get from globalization.

There is evidence that an economy can be made worse off if trade lowers the price of products in which it has a significant global advantage, let alone lowers them by 30 per cent or more. The pain that several western economies feel from globalization has seen to it that what now happens is in direct contradiction to the previously prevailing concept that ultimately globalization benefits more than it hurts.

As Samuelson suggests, the evidence of the recent years is that comparative advantage cannot be counted on to create net gains greater than the net losses from trade. For the first time, highly-skilled US workers have been exposed to intensive international competition. It is not clear whether it will hurt their wages, says Jagdish Bhagwati, of Columbia University, but a growing number of experts think that this has already taken place.

3

Globalization and the European Union

1. Free Market, Competition, Globalization and the EU

Clearly, each country and each region has a different set of goals and of conditions when confronting the challenges of globalization, whose opportunities, problems and limits were the theme of Chapter 1 – with emphasis on the United States, China and India. The focal point of this chapter is the European Union (EU).

Globalization's questions and the responses to them are not the same for all countries of the EU. For different reasons, the reactions of Britain, Germany, Finland, Holland, Ireland, Sweden tend to be positive. By contrast, France, Italy, Spain and other EU members don't appreciate that globalization has attached to it a significant dose of *economic liberalism*.

The level of acceptable economic liberalism contrasts British public policy to that of several continental European countries. To appreciate the background reasons the reader should recall that the roots of modern liberalism date back to the seventeenth and eighteenth centuries, when politicians tried to limit the arbitrary power of English kings and the Church while in continental Europe sovereign power remained absolute. Eventually, the English reaction led to:

- a political movement;

- the advent of liberal democracy; and

- the growth of free international trade.

It goes without saying that economic liberalism is far from being the only regime with which society has experimented since the mid-nineteenth century's Industrial Revolution, which altered the societal paradigm. As most readers will remember, some from personal experience and others from having read or heard about them, other forms have been socialism, fascism, nazism, communism and populism.

- None proved to be a success;

- but some of them are still around, as a memory or as a regime.

Distilled from two centuries of Continental European politics the relics of different *'isms'* are found in the form of big government; economic and other sorts of nationalism and protectionism; high social costs associated to the *state supermarket*,[1] and more. Such references are vital in understanding the anti-liberal, anti-free trade reaction by both the people and the government in several countries characterized by:

- state interventionism; and

- a big amount of authoritarianism.

These attitudes are more or less alien to England which, since the mid-nineteenth century, has taken the opposite stance. After his electoral victory in the 1841, Robert Peel, a Conservative Party prime minister, championed free trade, which became his most important legacy. Adopting the motto 'Advance, not recede', he recognized the need to unleash individual initiative through a proactive government stance which has persisted since his time (with the exception of the post-WWII years when the Labour government created the huge National Health Service (NHS)).

It would be wrong to think that all right-wing regimes in the world are liberal, while all left-wing are protectionist and therefore conservative – while other people believe that exactly the opposite is true. *Liberalism* versus *protectionism* in the wider possible sense is a much more accurate description then the one between political right and left. Additionally, the contrast provided by liberalism versus protectionism and vice versa also:

---

1   Where the state is expected to provide all sorts of goods to individuals, after milking them dry through taxes.

- helps in defining the attitude of several EU nations towards globalization; and

- explains the measures that both governments and companies take to gain some of globalization's advantages.

The fortunes of the European Union's economies are diverging along the liberalism versus protectionism lines. Even if the euro is overvalued, the mood of some EU countries is upbeat. 'I love the strong euro,' said a German industrialist in a meeting. In other EU countries, however, business confidence is low and the public's response to different surveys is negative.

Italy provides both good and bad examples of company survival in a globalized market. One of the good is that of Luxottica, a world leader in sunglasses. 'Ten years ago, sunglasses were a functional device,' said Andrea Guerra, its chief executive.[2] But today a successful business strategy would capitalize on fashion and innovation.

Luxottica thinks it can persuade European, American, Asian and other consumers to spend more on sunglasses which come with coloured lenses, oddly-shaped frames and different adornments, including logos in silver and gold as well as special linings. This change in design has seen to it that prices and margins have risen in proportion to the perceived novelty of the products.

Another facet of Luxottica's strategic plan is to capitalize on globalization to gain cross-border alliances. In this remit, it has won lucrative contracts, including licences from Burberry, a British fashion house and Polo Ralph Lauren, an American one, as well as Tiffany, the jeweller.

The company has also grown through acquisitions in the markets which it is targeting. In 1995, it bought LensCrafters, the biggest optical retailer in the US, followed by the acquisition of Sunglass Hut, a global leading retailer of sunglasses and Cole National, another big outlet. In June 2007, it also announced the purchase of a portfolio of brands with the $2.1 billion takeover of Oakley, a California-based sunglasses firm.

As this and other similar cases document, in today's globalized economy with its growing number of competitive players, one cannot survive, let alone

---

2   *The Economist*, 18 August 2007.

thrive, without expanding, innovating and caring for customers' satisfaction in a proactive manner. To be ahead of the curve, a company needs:

- managers and employees loaded with talent and energy; and

- people who are not with the company because of its paternalism, but because there are excellent opportunities for career development.

When he was at the helm of General Electric, Jack Welch called such individuals 'people who are happy to stay but ready to leave'. These are the winners. The concept of employee loyalty for the sake of it, or as a corporate and societal virtue, went out the window with lifetime employment – which itself had to go when competition intensified. *Differentiation* is now the golden rule and along with it the ability to put oneself and the company back on the radar screen of intensified global competition.

2. Failed Tests of Globalization in the EU

According to estimates by the European Commission, over the past 50 years roughly 20 per cent of the rise in standards of living in EU countries has been due to the greater openness of the world economy.[3] This documents the thesis advanced by the foreign trade theory which says that, under competitive conditions, the international division of labour, which exploits comparative cost advantages:

- leads to efficiency gains; and

- helps in increasing the average per capita income.

Moreover, at enterprise level the dynamics of intensified competition oblige companies to keep in shape. But as has already noted, globalization increases the individual's economic need for adjustment and accelerates macro-economic structural changes, with the result of significantly affecting:

- certain sections of the population; and

- the country's economic activity as a whole.

---

3   Deutsche Bundesbank, Monthly Report, December 2006.

'... domestic policymakers have always faced the challenge of responding to external shocks but, in our globalized and market-driven world, these have become ever more significant', says the 2006 Annual Report of the Bank for International Settlements (BIS). The same document states that '... the actions of domestic policymakers increasingly have external effects on others. These interactions apply in good times, but perhaps become more important in bad ones: when the efforts of many national authorities need to be harnessed to manage international problems at the least cost'.[4]

What the BIS correctly castigates is the still far too strong tendency for national authorities to go it alone, no matter what the effect is on other national authorities. Also criticized is the fact that international dialogue goes no further than vague agreements on principles. Both points are well made and they fit the EU reality hand-in-glove, because the European Union:

- lacks a unique government structure; and

- its overblown membership of 27 nations guarantees that governments are never in accord on anything that matters.

The result is a paradox. While, in my judgement, globalization – or at least regionalization – has improved the standard of living of EU citizen, perceived job insecurity has increased and so has the number of people (and governments) who see globalization as a scapegoat. Even if many economists argue that rising inequality has far more to do with skills and technology, politicians say that its key reason is global trade.

Instead of paying attention to the fact that success in global trade requires that liberalization is protected by structural changes that allow local industry to become competitive again and financial systems to remain resilient in the face of both domestic and external shocks, several EU governments take inspiration from the increasing protectionism in America – and raise trade barriers of their own.

'If America becomes protectionist, why shouldn't we?', some Continental EU governments ask. Little attention is paid to the fact that, while in the 1990s the US was indeed the largest trading partner of Euroland by a wide margin, today Continental European nations buy more goods from China than they do from America. Their purchases from Russia, other East European countries,

---

4   Bank for International Settlements, 77th Annual Report, Basel, 2007.

Turkey and other Asian nations are close to double what they import from the US.[5]

Additionally, little attention is paid to the very recent phenomenon of *decoupling*: the growth paths of the US on one side and the EU and Asia on the other, are diverging. While the American economy slowed in 2008, other regions of the world are less likely than in the past to travel in tandem with the US market. 'We think that decoupling will be with us for an extended period of time', says Alex Patelis, Head of International Economics at Merrill Lynch.[6]

Even so, the economies of some of the European Union's member states exhibit striking similarities to the 'Asian Tigers' of the previous decade. As should not be forgotten, in the early-to mid-1990s East Asia boasted low inflation, balanced budgets and a remarkable record of almost 8 per cent average growth – hardly the stuff of a sudden downturn. It was only after the meltdown of 1997 that analysts found major Asian flaws:

- weak financial systems;

- hasty opening of economies to foreign capital;

- a policy of tying local currencies to the dollar, and more.

Weak financial systems can be found all over the EU. As recently as 2007 Portugal came at the bottom of the EU economic growth league and economists called it 'the sick man of Europe'. Since 2000, the Czech Republic, Malta and Slovenia have overtaken Portugal in terms of GDP per head. Indeed, Portuguese GDP per head fell from just over 80 per cent of the then EU's 25 nations average in 1999 to just over 70 per cent in 2007.

In Iberia, Portugal has suffered more than Spain from higher oil prices and its unit labour costs have risen sharply, whereas Germany's have fallen. As an article in *The Economist* had it, renewed political instability has also taken a toll: on average governments in Lisbon have lasted just two years since the return of democracy in 1974.[7]

---

5   Crédit Suisse, Global Research, 24 April 2007.
6   From a Merrill Lynch 2007 publication.
7   *The Economist*, 14 April 2007.

Spain is better off than Portugal because it reformed its public sector and disciplined its public finances before joining the euro. But Spain, too, has glaring weaknesses when it comes to free trade and the presence of government-led financial nationalism. One of the better known nationalist barriers raised by the Socialist Spanish government against a company of another EU state (and a blow to the much-vaunted 'European unity') has been the case of E.on, the German energy company which was squeezed out of its bid for Endesa, Spain's largest power group, through an unholy alliance between Spanish and Italian politicians.

Apart from the glaring denial of EU spirit, the Spanish government's move (in collusion with the Italian's) saw to it that for the nth time minority shareholders – including foreign investors, who generate more than half the business in the Spanish Borsa – have been denied takeover premiums. Loopholes in Spain's takeover code mean that control of listed companies has often changed hands while minority shareholders are left holding the bag.

All this is social*ism* and protection*ism* under the economic national*ism* banner. Just like the French government, the Spanish has adopted the doctrine of national champions in strategic sectors, which is present and full denial of globalization. 'This government is clearly interventionist', says Juan Carlos Martinez-Lazaro, an economics professor at the Instituto de Empresa in Madrid.[8]

Other knowledgeable people suggest that what singles out the Socialist government of José Luis Rodriguez Zapatero is its inexperience, particularly in business affairs. The Prime Minister never worked in the private sector, having left academia to become a Member of Parliament at the age of 28. As for Joan Clos, Minister for Industry, Tourism and Trade, he is a former mayor of Barcelona and an anaesthetist by profession. (Does the Spanish economy need an anaesthetist?)

3. Aftermath of Globalization on the European Economy

As the reader is aware, globalization is causing the biggest shift in relative prices of labour, capital, materials and other commodities. In turn, this is creating a significant worldwide redistribution of income whose consequences should escape the attention neither of governments nor of the public.

---

8   *Financial Times*, 2 March 2007.

In Western Europe, low-skilled workers have been losing out relative to skilled workers. And because even the low-skilled workers are overpaid when their wages are compared to those of new accession countries (let alone to those in China and India), the inescapable after-effect is that they are losing their jobs. In France, this has contributed to the now famous myth that 'the Polish plumber' is taking away the job of the French plumber. Polls have shown that voters want the government to:

- protect jobs; and

- ensure that trade is *fair* rather than *free*.

An impressive quotient of the 2006 French vote against the European Constitution was against Turkey's entry to the EU – not against the Constitution itself. It's a safe bet that this will continue to be a major political theme for the decade ahead; a theme which does not lack reasons.

The message Figure 3.1 conveys is a 20-year trend (1980–2000) in France's share in total added value by industrial firms among 15 OECD member nations. (In terms of government, these two decades were shared almost equally by French socialist and right-wing parties – but at no time did the curve bend upwards.) France performed worse than the other 14 EU members because it is burdened with much heavier social costs than the OECD average.

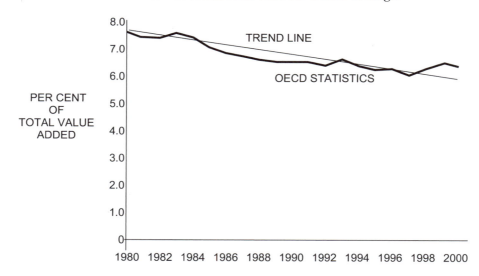

Figure 3.1   **The decline in France's share in total added value by industrial firms among 15 OECD member nations over two decades**

This process poses a challenge to the economies not only of the European Union but also of America, as entitlements are adding up to entitlements – the latest being Hillary Clinton's promise about universal health care. The more the social costs are, the more companies tend to dislocate and outsource as their way to survive. Entitlements, the so-called *aquis sociaux*, are demolishing whole economies.

France, Italy, Spain and Germany are examples of ballooning entitlements which kill economic competitiveness. When costs become too high, they diminish the ability of companies to compete globally. The share of health costs in a General Motors car is more than the cost of steel. In the end, countries where these firms are based pay a high price for having failed to introduce structural reforms in their labour market.

Many governments of EU member states are at a loss in adjusting their economy to the effects of global competition, which they themselves promoted. Restructuring is difficult even if, ironically, many politicians recognize that current labour laws are rigid and anachronistic. With money lavishly spend to fill every hole of the social net, little is left for:

- providing a competitive twenty-first century infrastructure; and

- revamping the expensive and inefficient public sector bureaucracy, which sucks up practically every penny available for renewal.

An evident answer is that of attaining higher productivity, but productivity and restructuring correlate. Many socialist regimes, and some centre-right governments such as Jacques Chirac's, fail to appreciate that an economy's growth and well-being depend on appropriate worker skills, higher productivity and the ability of companies to compete successfully in the global market. An example on the impact of renewal is the productivity boom that began in the US in the mid-1990s but then faded.

- Higher productivity pushed America's growth rate well above 3.5 per cent a year;

- *but* its momentum lasted only as long as it was accompanied by structural changes, including shifts in employment.

The necessary economic response in facing globalization's challenges is painful in the short term. It is also opposed by powerful interests, including those of labour unions. Yet, without radical labour reforms, unemployment will not be cut in any significant way; and without deep labour restructuring the labour unions' own membership will be destabilized – as has happened in America and Britain.

Persistent on-and-off two-digit or high one-digit unemployment – like that in Spain, France and Germany – could spark a social explosion, as angry workers fight changes with strikes; or, vote for extremist political parties. Many economists now say that this situation cannot last forever. Reformists point to the fact that a government worth its salt should take the lead in informing the citizen that there are really two options:

1.   we shape the future;

2.   or we all suffer from it.

Politicians should explain that suffering from social ossification can go on for a long time. Resistance to change is self-defeating, because the world is no longer what it used to be. In most of the EU's member countries, the current social system was established shortly after the Great Depression. Since World War II more and more entitlements have been added to it. The other side of the coin is that:

- *if* they are not careful with final product costs;

- nobody buys the products, even in the country where they are made.

Today *China price* has become the measure of all things in manufactured wares (Chapter 4). It is not at all a strange statistic that the world's 40 biggest multinationals:

- employ, on average, 55 per cent of their workforce in foreign countries; and

- earn nearly 60 per cent of their revenues abroad, in markets more vibrant than their home country.

Another interesting aftereffect of globalization is that, in America and Western Europe, while company profits surge, workers' real incomes have been flat or even falling. This is evidence that the old relationship between corporate and national prosperity has broken down. Globalization shifted the balance of power in the labour market in favour of companies, whether or not the different socialist regimes in the EU admit it.

At the same time, however, it would be wrong to conclude that globalization has broken European Union economies, because not every piece of news is bleak. While the global marketplace gave firms access to cheap labour abroad, it also helped to keep a lid on wages at home and by extension on inflation. As a result, working people:

- improve their living standard by buying low cost goods made abroad; and

- capitalize on low cost air transport coupled with low costs at destination, by taking vacations in North Africa, Thailand or Brazil.

Both points describe integral parts of the globalized economy. Even if many people don't see it that way, the fact is that the citizen of the European Union lives in an economy without borders. Therefore, they and their services are part of the international landscape of producers and consumers. The same is true of American citizens. Still, according to public opinion polls the word 'globalization' conveys negative images for nearly half of the respondents to EU surveys, while only for one third is it positive.

4. Italy's Decline as Industrial Power: An Example

Implicit in the preceding section has been the notion that prosperity of a nation depends both on good governance and on the way in which its citizens exercise their talents and their occupations without seeking *rent* (social and other subsidies). Work must be paid well, but at a cost affordable by both national and global markets. Other things being equal, the prosperity of pwople and families is directly proportional to the:

- freedom of each member of society in exercising his or her skills; and

- desire of each individual to contribute to common good, rather than making a living at public expense.

A 2005 study by the Deutsche Bundesbank focused on the lead or lag in *growth* of a dozen EU countries, as compared to that of the German economy. Way ahead, with 40 percentage points over Germany, came Ireland, followed by Luxembourg and Greece. Since then the German economy has accelerated while that of several EU members – including Italy and Portugal – has fallen way behind.

Not only has Italy been a laggard in growth and a big spender in a *current account* sense,[9] but also in mid-June 2005 it became the first European Union country to face disciplinary action under the revamped (read: watered down) Euroland Stability Pact[10] (see Chapter 9). Other EU member states thought that lack of sanctions regarding Italy's ballooning budget deficit would become an example for more countries to do the same, thought there is scant hope that a country which pays penalties would do what it takes to redress its financial condition while:

- caring for an aging population;

- continuing with the *dolce vita*;

- coping with paralyzing strikes;

- doing something to reverse the worrying loss of exports; and

- being chronologically mismanaged, independently of whether a right or left-wing government holds the reigns.

Italy's case also exemplifies the fact that, as far as budgetary and current account deficits are concerned, the descent into the abyss can happen very fast. In 2000, the Italian budget was in the red only 0.6 per cent of GDP, but a year later this 0.6 became over 3 per cent – surpassing the EU Stability Pact ceiling. After that, instead of being brought under control it kept on growing, reaching 4.3 per cent of GDP in 2005.

---

9   A country's *current account* is classically defined as the difference between gross national savings and gross fixed capital formation. It is, however, correct to add imported goods and exported tourism in the liabilities side of the balance sheet.

10 *Financial Times*, 11/12 June 2005.

By mid-2006 the torrent of red ink obliged the Italian government to institute austerity measures. Critics said that spending cuts and tax rises tended to fall more heavily on the poor, whom the new centre-left government had pledged to defend. This argument conveniently forgot that the whole population must contribute in redressing the budget, particularly so as the whole economy was in tatters.

There was a time, in the post-WWII years, when the Italian economy prospered. Not only were the ruins created by World War II repaired very fast by the hard-working Italian North, but also from Torino to Bergamo industries provided plenty of jobs for people from the impoverished South. Had Lombardy been an independent state, it would have been richer than Switzerland.

But the *Italian miracle* of the 1950s and early 1960s did not last long. The killer was not just political instability and inability, but also bloody strikes orchestrated by labour unions who asked for more than the Italian economy could afford. Additionally, Italy did not have the mass market to sustain first class technology companies like Olivetti, which died out:

- partly because of poor management; and

- partly because it was too small an entity on the global scale.

Under steady pressure from labour unions, which could not swallow the fact that Italian industry made profits, there was a steady and unreasonable increase in the cost of labour that the Italian economy could not sustain. For their part, Italian governments were too divided and too weak to strike a good balance between industrial competitiveness and social issues.

On 22 February 2007, the then Italian government, the so-called 'rainbow coalition' because of the nine centre-left parties supporting it, issued a list of 12 non-negotiable points which included respect for Italy's international commitments and undertaking to press ahead with two plans:

- a high-speed rail link with France; and

- a programme of some sort of market liberalization.

Neither had the power (or even was intended) to redress Italy's deteriorating industrial, financial- and demographic condition, but both were controversial, the first because of environmental damage; the second because of many deputies and senators who are die-hard corporatists, given that they get most of their votes from the south where a swarm of households depend on:

- welfare (hence rent); or

- public-sector employment.

As if all this was not enough, the 'rainbow coalition' retreated from a pension reform introduced by the centre-right administration which preceded it. This was supposed to respond to Italy's escalating welfare bill and to a central problem of the Italian economy, rhat too few younger people must now pay through taxation the fairly comfortable pension of the elderly, which is a pan-European problem.

To try to bring some sense of order, Tommaso Padoa-Schioppa, the coalition's finance minister (and former board member of the European Central Bank), crafted an austerity package that relied on tax increases to put the budget of the Republic on the right footing. Shortly thereafter, in late December 2006, polls taken for *La Repubblica*, Rome's major newspaper, suggested that support for the government had collapsed from a high point of 64 per cent in July to 38 per cent at 2006 year end.

5. Competitiveness Should Never Be Taken for Granted

Italians who care about their country's future suggest that its competitiveness is an even more worrying long-term concern than the state of its public finances. The reason can be found in a World Economic Forum report issued in December 2006, which flatly stated that Italy had fallen below all other European Union members save Poland.[11] In spite of its promise to redress Italian:

- industry; and

- the economy at large.

The 'rainbow' government had only scratched the surface with a few minor measures. These mainly focused on freeing up a couple of professions and such small businesses as taxi driving. Half-baked measures are a formula for

---

11   *The Economist*, 23 December 2006.

muddle. Yet such low profile ineffective formula has also been the preferred solution of other EU governments.

Apart from inertia, pressure groups, and corporatist institutions, there exist as well other similarities among European Union member states. One of the more obvious is their propensity to raise taxes rather than cut expenditures. With a debt level of 108 per cent of gross domestic product, Italy had no option but become more effective in its use of money and the same is true of Greece.

Additionally, neither Italy nor any other EU country can afford a patchwork of economic repairs, an intellectually flawed macro-economic strategy and a heart-stopping fear of cutting loose embedded interests. As the 'rainbow' coalition retreated from promised reforms, the liberalization of taxi drivers, pharmacists and notaries has not been followed by that of major professions, but by petrol stations. Worst of all, it left Italy's perversely overblown public sector unscathed. This is the twisted side of political economy:

- the more effectively an interest group is organized;

- the less vulnerable it is to a challenge to its vested interests.

Italy still has some excellent industries which have maintained their global export share. But these need to grow in their home market and this requires a government capable of formulating and implementing strategic principles, outlining clearly prioritized reforms and reigning in strikes promoting an industrial renaissance.

Deprived of far-sighted government leadership, many Italian companies (including some of the biggest) have failed to establish global plans for their products. Statistics document the degree of damages the lack of resolve can create. By the early years of the twenty-first century, Italy's high-tech exports made up only 12 per cent of total exports – half the European average.

Experts suggest that loss of technological position and of thrust in globalization are no chance event. Apart from the aforementioned general reasons, there also exist special reasons why Italy lost speed in world trade, with research and development (R&D) at top of the list:

- Italy spends only 1.1 per cent of its gross domestic product in R&D; and

- this compares poorly with the EU average of almost 2 per cent, which rises to 3 per cent in the US and 3.2 per cent in Japan.

To make matters worse, a good chunk of Italy's exports are and remain in industries such as textiles, ravaged by Chinese competition (more on this in the next section). Successive governments have been unable to come up with new ideas which promote the 'Made in Italy' label in new and more competitive domains. Nor have most Italian entrepreneurs been successful in:

- reinventing their industries; and

- channelling the country's productive skills in fields profiting from globalization.

Sure enough, some Italian industrialists have tried to create new companies focused on activities that can stand up to Chinese competition. A late 2006 example of such a firm which went public is specialty furniture maker *Poltrona Frau*. To warn equity investors, it issued a prospectus containing seven pages of risk factors which include:

- the highly competitive nature of its industry; and

- warnings about potential difficulties in enforcing intellectual property rights.

Analysts said that both points are code for China. 'Chinese competition and a weakening dollar have made the past four years terribly painful,' said Pasquale Natuzzi, whose firm is the largest in the Italian furniture-making cluster which sprang up in the 1960s around the southeastern town of Matera. Natuzzi's firm sells half its produce in America.[12]

But even go-ahead enterprises are not immune to natural selection. In 2000 the Matera cluster had some 400 furniture-making firms. Roughly one third of those businesses are gone. Like many furniture companies in other western countries, the Matera's sofa cluster did not foresee the threat to high quality leather furniture posed by low-wage economies in emerging countries. Experts also say that:

---

12 *The Economist*, 25 November 2006.

- the quality of Chinese furniture was just as good as Italian;[13] and

- the Chinese furniture outfits copied Italian designs quickly and accurately.

As if all this was not enough, the bad situation created by lack of new directions in global trade by the Italian government was worsened by continuing labour strikes and by the fact Italy's labour market liberalization was incomplete, its infrastructure deteriorating and social costs that push up labour costs among the largest in Europe. As shown in Table 3.1, they ranked just below the exuberant French social costs.

Taken together, all these reasons work against creating the right conditions to attract investment, while the lag in R&D does not encourage innovation. This contrasts dramatically with the fact that just four or five decades ago, at the time of the *Italian miracle,* the country was praised as a clock whose cogs meshed perfectl, and its production machine never seemed to break down. For more than a decade, Italy was not far from the *German model* which, also at that time, performed brilliantly because:

- the West German economy was upbeat;

- the country's industrial products were much in demand; and

Table 3.1   **Social cost contribution to social security as a percent of salary***

	By Companies	**By Workers**
France	57	19
Italy	38	8
Japan	16	14
Ireland	13	6
Britain	13	11
United States	10	10
Denmark	1	18

*   *La Republica,* May 18, 2005

13   Which led Italian furniture firms to set up their own manufacturing operation in China.

- the pace of economic change was relatively slow, while the social safety net was a fraction of what is today.

It is indeed a tragic part of Italy's and Germany's histories, as well as of France's, that social costs and entitlements continued to expand without anybody measuring the consequences. This happened while it was quite evident than in the global market low cost is king – and uncompetitively high wages, lavish retirement benefits and an unprecedented level of health care have become the enemies of workers.

As far as Italy is concerned, the good times ended with a spike, the new famous 1987 *sorpasso* when the Italian government officially and proudly announced that the country's GDP exceeded that of Britain. Then, as it happens also in the engineering and financial businesses, that spike was followed by a collapse, with growth over the past two decades the slowest in the European Union. The figures in Table 3.2 suggest that Italy is way behind the averages in the EU.

- Italian performance both in services and in industry has taken a dive.

- Costs have risen, while productivity remained flat or declined.

With this, the country's competitiveness has been deteriorating. While its share of world exports becomes lower and lower, foreign direct investments (FDI, see Chapter 1) have practically disappeared. Therefore, it comes as no surprise that Italy's economy is now only about 80 per cent the size of Britain's, and the gap widens.

Table 3.2   Italy vs the European Union

	Italy	European Union
1. Industrial Productivity	+0.7%	+2.1%
2. Added Value in Industry	+0.8%	+1.8%
3. Productivity in Services	-0.1%	+0.9%
4. Added Value in Services	+2.5%	+3.4%

*   *La Repubblica*, May 18, 2005

Italy's demographics make all that bad news even more bleak. Giovanni Antonio d'Amato, a former prime minister and more recently Interior Minister is rumoured to have said that Italy has no sons only *nepoti* (nephews). At an average of 1.3 children per woman, the country has one of the lowest birth rates in western Europe. Not only is the population rapidly shrinking, but Italians are also living longer; hence, society is rapidly aging with awful economic consequences.

6. Italian Textiles versus Chinese Textiles. A Case Study

It is no secret that China's clothing imports are piling up at the racks of hypermarkets, department stores and individual clothing shops throughout Europe and America. And because they are rather good quality but low price, they sell like hot cakes. The same happens with shoes made in China (and in Vietnam). 'You should not be scared', went the text of a cartoon on Chinese textiles in a French newspaper, 'in a short time saying Chinese textile will be redundant'.[14]

Because of its massive textile exports, since mid-2005 China has become the No. 1 exporter to France. Even before this happened, according to official statistics France had lost 250,000 jobs over the first five years in the twenty-first century, not only to China. French textile jobs that don't go to China delocalize to Tunis.

Another interesting hindsight is the speed with which all this has taken place. As far as industrial conquest is concerned, the reader should appreciate that China emerged as dominant force in textiles in no time, using the best equipment it could buy in the west. Only tariffs have kept some Chinese textile imports at bay, but these are waning and threats of trade wars are shortlived.

China's clothing exports have been growing most rapidly since the system of global quotas ended in January 2005. The US decision to re-introduce quotas exposed a clear split in US industry, with retailers launching legal action against sanctions that would limit their access to cheap Chinese clothing – which is an example of the other side of globalization. A similar split in public response has happened in Europe.

---

14 *Le Canard Enchaîné*, 25 August 2005.

At the beginning of 2005, following a surge in textile imports, the EU and China started negotiations to limit their growth with an agreement of sorts reached on 10 June. Peter Mandelson, the EU trade commissioner who had threatened to impose new quotas on two types of Chinese imports, rushed to state: 'This is a significant demonstration of China's entry into the global economy as a responsible and valued partner.'[15]

- Mandelson's remarks came after his talks with the Chinese on an ill-defined kind of restraint on textile exports to the EU; and

- as Mandelson's critics had predicted, this soon became another one of the 'agreements' made but never kept.

For some time, the new limit had already been reached. In early August 2005 stocks began piling up in storage at various entry points into the European Union. A new 'agreement' was concluded by the same parties in September which allowed these stocks to be released whilst maintaining limits on the *future rate* of growth of textile imports from China. This too has been an 'agreement' signed but not observed. Therefore, it comes as no surprise that:

- patterns of 2006 and subsequent years reveal a continuation of the downward trend in EU employment in textiles; and

- this trend was considerably accelerated by the phasing-out of import quotas by the mismanagers of the EU, the trade negotiator included.

The fact is that the different EU busybodies have been overtaken on the clothing front in every angle from which one looks at this issue. What Mandelson repeatedly 'negotiated' with the Chinese has been nothing more than superficial stop-gap measures, taking no notice of priorities in Italy, France, Britain and other EU countries which used to have a significant textile production.

This is surprising inasmuch as Mandelson knows very well that it is only a matter of time before China's low labour costs and growing production skills crush their competitors in western economies. Quite similarly, European governments who think that curbs will revive the old Continent's ailing textile industry are sadly mistaken. Italy is not the only to suffer. Textile manufacture in Manchester, once the citadel of Britain's textile industry, is now history.

---

15 *The Financial Times*, 11/12 June 2006.

Varese was a small-sized Manchester of Italy. With the Chinese clothing wave, the number of workers in textiles and clothing in that province almost halved to 27,300, in two decades between the censuses of 1981 and 2001. At the same time, the number of firms employing them dropped by more than 40 per cent from 4,900 to 2,900, with another 440 firms closed since 2001.

It is sad to drive through Varese and see the rows of abandoned textile factories with broken windows. This industrial decay will continue, unless an imaginative solution is found – like the Swiss Swatch – along with a radical restructuring of social costs. Western economies can only fight a losing battle by trying to stop textile imports. If it is Italy which suffers the most from Chinese competition, this is because Italy *was* a leader in textiles.

Apart from the jobs textiles, shoes and other mass market items produce at home, foreign currency earnings also matters a great deal. China's current account surplus has soared over time, and year after year it continues to increase. By contrast to China's sprint, the United States, France, Italy and other western countries have large current account deficits.

Many economists suggest that low wages in emerging countries, particularly those with an educated work force, are a double-edged sword for those European countries with companies which have been producing goods for markets targetted by the Chinese. In fact, to gain advantage from low wages, Italian clothing manufacturers were among the first to flock to the Chinese factories for their wares.

- In 1990 almost 90 per cent of Benetton's colourful clothes were produced by Italian workers.

- Today Italian manufacturers supply less than 30 per cent of the total and this is projected to fall to 10 per cent over the next few years.

Dislocation and outsourcing intensified Italy's slide to oblivion. For generations after the country's independence, its economy relied on dense networks of firms, most of them small family entities with high quality textile products. Many of these family outfits, which could particularly be found in northern Italy, clustered together creating wealth by manufacturing clothing and shoes. Several supplied both:

- high-end fashion labels and designers; and

- the middle level with a wider market, thereby contributing greatly to Italy's GDP and current account.

Textiles has been chosen by the Chinese government as a market to conquer because it is universal and its size is huge. Italy is left with some first-class entrepreneurs of global standing who work in niches – like Carpigiani, the market of ice-cream machines and Luxottica (see section 1). Carpigiani is a private Italian firm which sellsthe Italian art of making ice-cream in more than 100 countries, but its survival is by no means assured.

The ice-cream machines company stagnated for much of the decade after the death of its leader in 1982; complacency set in, quality fell, complaints rose and Carpigiani's share of world sales slipped very dangerously. 'We had to relearn the importance of customer-service, of quality and of being ahead of competitors with new products,' says its new chief.[16] To prove that he meant business, he:

- cut costs;

- simplified the company's structure;

- introduced tough quality control;

- resorted to outsourcing in spite of having four factories; and

- redimensioned its 1,000-strong workforce to half its former size.

Other niche markets, too, are being revived – but unlike textiles they are too small to make a difference. Long ago, violin-making in Cremona flourished under such masters as Antonio Stradivari; by the 1950s it had died out. Recently it has been reborn in workshops overlooking the city's cobbled streets where over 100 craftspeople work on string instruments, more than in any other European city.

Cremona's instrument makers hope that their emphasis on quality, tradition and craftsmanship will keep cheaper foreign rivals at bay. But they are also concerned that differences in wages and social benefits are so great that they might consign the hand crafting industry to oblivion, taking away even a niche market.

---

16 *The Economist*, 18 August 2007.

7. The Italian Economy Needs Both Fiscal Discipline and Discipline at Large

The condition in which Italy finds itself in Euroland includes both good and bad news. The good news is the benefit of lower interest rates and a relative constraint of fiscal and exchange rate discipline imposed by the euro – at least theoretically. The bad news is the Italian governments' inability to control runaway expenses, the impact loose social policies have had on wages and pensions, and the burden of taxation on private firms.

How long can this imbalance last? At best, successive governments have paid lip service to fiscal discipline. Different acts of unwillingness or inability to live within the Italian economy's limits have made it impossible for the country to:

- redress the balances; and

- provide relief for overtaxed and overburdened industries.

Without leadership, people ask for more entitlements rather than for the changes the Italian economy badly needs. As for the common currency, many knowledgeable Italians now say that altogether the euro has had a negative effect; and they suggest two variants of a scenario that may lead Italy to fall out of the common currency:

1. Italy's public finances are deteriorating to the point that its debt loses investment grade.[17]

Italy is not alone on this path. All over the EU, France and Germany included, failure to revamp labour laws, restructure the economy and apply fiscal discipline makes the underlying situation worse than it would otherwise have been. In spite of his electoral promises to curb wild deficits, Romano Prodi has been ready to trim his planned budget cuts – not his budget – and this evidently caused serious concern about pruning Italy's balance sheet.

The OECD said it was 'disappointed'. Lorenzo Bini Smaghi, executive board member of the European Central Bank, noted that revenue increases were a 'temporary factor which may not be repeated'. Joaquin Almunia, the European Union's Economics Commissioner, stressed that for a country whose

---

17 See also in Chapter 10 the problems faced by Euroland.

debts exceed annual output 'tidying up public finances is not merely a case of bringing the budget deficit down.'[18]

Neither did it help in terms of public confidence that a satirical programme on Italian television was able to trap 50 Members of Parliament through a test which provided evidence of drug use. Twelve cases of cannabis use and four of cocaine use were documented, which meant that 16 out of a sample of 50 Italian parliamentarians had been breaking the law. Critics of Prodi's government were quick to add that his Cabinet, too, broke the law because its budget treated cash as revenue, not as a debt that had to be repaid.

2.   Government after government falls victim to complacency, and finds it difficult to wake up to reality.

Contributing to the country's deteriorating financial condition is continuing support for nationalized industries which have been solidly in the red for several decades. Alitalia, the country's flagship airline, which has been steadily losing attitude, is an example of a mismanaged company operating under the thumb of labour unions, losing 1 million euro every day, surviving only through huge state subsidies taken out of the taxpayer's pocket.

'The situation is totally out of control and I don't see any parachutes,' Romano Prodi told the trades unions at end of October 2006.[19] His transport minister was also against further subsidies, but neither the boss nor the minister had the courage to ground Alitalia – so good money continued to be thrown after bad money.

Prodi thought he had found a white knight for the national airline in AirFrance-KLM, thanks to the support of his friend Jacques Chirac. In late November 2006, Chirac called on Air France to take over Alitalia. Behind this friendly *geste* was no extraordinary goodwill among euroland bureaucrats, but the fact that Chirac owed Prodi some kind of gift to compensate for the French government's refusal to let Italy's ENEL buy Suez, the French energy holding.

AirFrance-KLM, however, is a well-run private company and Alitalia's wild strikers, as well as its flood of red ink, frightened its CEO. As a condition, he demanded that Alitalia's labour unions subscribe to and underwrite his company's offer, which after prolonged negotiations they refused to do.

---

18   *The Economist,* 16 September 2006.
19   *The Economist,* 21 October 2006.

Sorting out the problems at Alitalia, where more than 10 trades unions defend long-established privileges and flex their muscles by striking, is an Herculean task.

Nor is Alitalia the only 'national treasure' whose fortunes have been darkened because of too much interference by bureaucrats and politicians. Telecom Italia (TI) provides another example. The government made it known that it has no intention of letting foreigners control TI's fixed network.

In early 2007, AT&T and America Mobil (a Mexican company) were the frontrunners to buy some or all of Telecom Italia's equity and assets, but that did not sit well with politicians. After a meeting between Prodi and Spain's Zapatero, another leftist and economic nationalist, Telefonica set up a holding company through a consortium involving Italian banks to buy a 16.3 per cent stake in Telecom Italia, and 23.6 per cent of voting rights. As Telefonica took a a share in TI, Italy's ENEL bought a stake in Spain's Endesa, the energy company, keeping Germany's E.on out. That's the EU.

From creative accounting at government level in connection to the huge budget deficit, to behind the door manipulations for economic nationalism reason, these are not the sort of thing one would have expected from a former president of the EU Commission. It also shows how far Romano Prodi had to bend to placate demands by left-wing parties within his coalition where every single vote counts. In a normal world politicians would give priority to the important issues; not to trivia. But are we in a normal world?

4

World Trade, China Price and the Doha Round

1. The Management of Change in a Service Economy

As far as the western nations are concerned, high wages, entitlements and other unaffordable social benefits, as well as the skyrocketing price of energy and raw materials (because of the shrinking dollar), are not the only challenges they face in order to remain industrial powers. Cost pressures from budget deficits and 'cheat your neighbour' policies will continue growing in the coming years while globalization and stricter emission regulations lead to increasingly stringent conditions for their industries.

Taking just one example, emission regulations are very asymmetrical as regards Western companies and whole industry sectors. This is a self-inflicted wound perpetrated by third-class politicians. In connection to pollution control at large, and most particularly with regard to reining in CO_2 emissions (see Chapter 2), the problem is that industries will only meet the challenges through:

- international cooperation; and

- optimized technology solutions.

International cooperation is simply not happening, because to show they are 'good boys and girls', western politicians and trade negotiators have taken it upon themselves to solve the emission problems single handedly. This attitude simply forgets that competition in markets such as the car industry has reached a global level. Therefore, it is silly to put all costs of emission control (which is the most investment-intensive part) on to the western auto firms alone. This is preposterous when one knows that in the coming years by far the largest increase in auto population will be in China and in India (more on unilateral environmental control the next section).

Politicians coming out of the blue, and ill-prepared for their career, are being elected because they are photogenic. Bureaucrats assigned to important negotiations don't have the experience and flair of successful business owners like Henry Ford, Andrew Carnegie and Sam Walton or of far-sighted professional business managers like Alfred Sloan, to:

- recognize the stimulus and threats of competition; and

- put their intellectual and emotional strength in the balance.

By being forceful, incisive and controversial in their actions, great business leaders set the tone for industry. As a result, their companies became highly productive and established standards for the next generation who followed them at the helm. That's now past as lesser people have been unable to overcome the barriers in their way and have run the companies down. A similar statement is valid about second raters in country leadership being unable to master globalization's challenges.

Let us again take the auto industry as an example of optimized technology solutions. The reader should appreciate that it is not enough to make hypotheses about the development of engines and transmissions able to reduce fuel consumption and emissions. Meeting goals is a challenge; but goals which have been hastily put together in the Kyoto and other Protocols to impress the public are a disaster. The top priority in fulfilling objectives is the *management of change*.

- From the current highly polluting society;

- to the one we want to have, presumably at much lower pollution levels – which also means a lower standard of living, because the two correlate most strongly.

Change should be welcome. What is unwelcome is the sort of thinking that one can buy something for nothing. New technology has its risks. As a recent feature article had it: 'Whenever we publish an article describing a radical new technology of potential high value… we feel obliged to issue a "health warning" [which] normally suggests that as promising as the development may be, it will probably not progress any further in the mainstream... sector. At least, not for a very long time.'[1]

The short term holds many surprises about deliverables. In the longer run, success comes to those who not only love change but also are able to be in charge of it, and it leaves by the way side those who fall in love with the status quo and see change as their enemy. An example is *value adding* a process which is constantly working to enhance the current state of a product or process. Pollution control on a global scale is value adding within globalization's perspective.

Both the developed and the emerging countries (and not only the former) must acknowledge the impact the standard of living has on the environment, embracing an overall vision in which every party makes a contribution to sustained development without 'ifs', 'buts' and other excuses. This is written in full appreciation of the fact that one of the hardest moves a person, company, or nation can make is to change direction. That's precisely where leadership shows its impact, by:

- clarifying the issues involved;

- assisting in reshaping the principles guiding use of resources;

- assuring continuous support, as the direction of events alters its course and pace.

It is the duty of governments to explain, demonstrate and convince their citizens that they cannot have it both ways. This, however, becomes a hopeless task because the governments themselves are at the same time *for* and *against* globalization; while some of the governments use globalization only to further their aims, in plain disregard of the impact this has on other nations and on the Earth's pollution.

These are issues which, in the post-WW II years, the Organization for European Economic Cooperation and Development (OECD) and International Trade Organization (ITO) – which morphed into the General Agreement on Tariffs and Trade (GATT) and was succeeded by the World Trade Organization (WTO) – should have addressed. But the OECD had other aims, while GATT

---

1   *European Automotive Design*, March 2008.

and WTO have been hampered by inefficiencies and by internal political frictions.

The WTO may well answer that its charter is not pollution control and even less so the management of change. Such a response would be superficial at best, because intensified world trade contributes a great deal to pollution. Just count the thick lines of trucks on autoroutes, rapidly growing air traffic and CO_2 production by a horde of other transport media. Even purchases made on the Internet contribute to pollution, since goods bought have to be delivered to their new owners.

As for the management of change, *if* what the charter of the WTO states is to be fulfilled in an able manner *then* change is unavoidable, and change which is not managed leads to ineffectiveness as well as to an ugly sequence of events. Walking, talking and boasting are not for negotiators whose principal mission is to foresee the need for change, convert their prognostication into effective clauses and assure that these are implemented in an orderly, efficient manner so that globalization really works.

The evolution towards a global service economy has made the management of change mandatory. The international agreements themselves are in flux, as documented by the reference in Chapter 1 to the General Agreement on Trade in Services (GATS). There are plenty of challenges connected to the diversity of GATS *bilateral investment agreements* (BITs), of which the WTO is supposed to be in charge.

The January 2008 Staff Working Paper ERSD-1008-01 by the World Trade Organization notes that some 2,500 bilateral investment agreements have been signed. Of these, an estimated 1,900 are in operation, with about 640 existing between developing countries. Characteristically, these BITs cover all sectors of the economy including services in:

- insurance;

- banking; and

- other financial services.

Their negotiation and observance is a vast and complex project involving (and challenging) regional, linguistic, cultural and historical elements, as well as ties. Contrary to what may be true in a physical economy of import/export of raw materials and of many manufactured goods, linguistic, cultural and geographical elements are particularly important in the successful marketing of services. Distance also matters.

- As the distance between the importing and the exporting countries increases, trade in services declines faster than trade in goods.[2]

- By contrast, while a common border greatly enhances bilateral trade in goods, it does not seem to play a large role in trade in services.

Complexity is increased because of legal risk. The majority of BITs focus on the protection of foreign investors once established in a host country. Others provide for the automatic extension of domestic liberalization measures to new foreign entrants into host services. An example of associated challenges is provided by the fact that the coverage of services sectors in BITs often exceeds the number of sectors inscribed in the counterpart schedules of specific commitments by WTO members.

Additionally, a few BITs grandfather existing pre- and post-establishment limitations provide for new investment to be admitted in accordance with current laws and regulations whose conditions could be less favourable. Another issue concerns how the central GATS non-discrimination obligation, known as the most-favoured-nation (MFN) principle, applies to any preferential treatment that might be extended between the two parties to a BIT.

To further complicate matters, there are key elements of BITs that do not feature in the GATS provisions. These include guarantees against unlawful expropriation and related aspects, as well as investor-state dispute resolution. (The GATS provisions do not seem to capture the compensation requirement contained in investment treaties, such as seizure of property.) There are also other inconsistencies which must be addressed to provide a framework for trade in services, as GATS and BITs seem to be running ahead of WTO's ability to handle them. Still, the WTO's most important current duty is how to fence off one-sided exploitation of GATS clauses and how to be in charge of a steady process of change.

---

2   European Central Bank, Monthly Bulletin, July 2008.

2. Economic Integration and the Anticipation of 'Better Days'

Globalization is supposed to lead to *economic integration* as contrasted to the much simpler import/export of goods. So far it has not done so. Here is a practical example. Economic integration of an area like the European Union does not consist only of subsidies and a larger market; it also involves effective measures for promotion of living standards and absence of barriers raised by economic nationalism. By contrast,

- in Western Europe stagnant wages and price inflation see to it that the standard of living is static or falling; and

- economic nationalism is rampant among a number of EU member states, while the European Commission (impotent) EU Parliament and the WTO look the other way.

In a similar manner, *international trade* does not consist only of selling goods to foreigners; but also of being subject to *their* competition. But in spite of GATT, GATS and WTO there exist plenty of barriers to global trading services, and the same is true for a free market for currency exchange. Many currencies are still stage-managed by governments, China and Japan being examples.

Moreover, global trade should not be subject to various kinds of restrictive policies. Under protective tariffs, many goods produced abroad are still hit by manipulations to exclude them from 'this' or 'that' jurisdiction. Some are remnants of generalized practices after the first Great Depression, when a large number of nations adopted protective tariffs and other restrictive devices like import quotas. Others, like environmental taxation, are new-found devices which have become totally asymmetric at the expense of western industry (see also section 1).

When the issue of climate change reached its first climax, Western politicians, who wanted to be seen on TV in the evening news, brimming with selfless idealism, agreed to make deep cuts in carbon emissions by a fifth from 1990 levels, even if developing countries did not follow. The message was:

- Europe will start saving the planet now, even if the selfish Americans, Chinese, Indians and plenty of others were neither ready nor willing to follow;

- by 2008, however, some really slipped in, as politicians from countries with heavy industry called for explicit measures to protect European firms in case talks on a global climate-change deal failed and left the Europeans in a cleft stick;

- Austria, the Czech Republic, France, Germany and Italy asked the EU to plan for the after-effect of such a failure, with defensive measures agreed before climate change talks in Copenhagen at the end of 2009.

Car makers have been pressing the EU to shape upcoming legislation on future CO_2 emissions in a way that causes the least pain to the industry. They are asking that legislation is framed realistically and constructively around the industry's manufacturing cycle, without exorbitant and disproportionate penalties.

Awakening to the pollution created by biofuels, environmentalists want the gears of Bush's Energy Independence and Security Act to be reversed. This business has caused a fierce debate over the amount of water required to produce ethanol – a gallon of ethanol from corn uses 5 to 7 gallons of water – as well as the fact that to produce fuel from staple crops is morally unethical, when they should be used as food at a time of skyrocketing agricultural prices.[3]

To improve on a situation of unfavourable commitments made in the past by their incapable negotiators, some European Union countries like France, Germany, Italy and Japan back a carve-up for the most energy-guzzling factories, giving them continued access to free carbon credits from the EU's emissions trading scheme (ETS) after 2012.[4] By contrast, Britain, Denmark, the Netherlands, Sweden and the European Commission took the opposite stance. The latter group will supposedly 'analyze' and address carbon leakage in a Directive on the next generation of the ETS expected to come out in early 2009.

- But details remain vague; and

- the whole issue lacks the proverbial long hard look.

---

3   There is also a fierce argument about the deforestation taking place to free up land for fuel crops.
4   Basically, ETS is a joke; this, however, is not the present book's theme.

Just as a hindsight on how politicians live hopelessly on Cloud 9, Sweden suggested that emission control investments may actually be more effective outside the EU; building a clean new plant in China to replace Mao-era polluters might reduce global emissions more than investing in technology at European factories. In other words:

- on one hand the EU complains that through massive sky-high pollution the Chinese are engaging in unfair competition; and

- on the other hand, the EU countries would pay to clean up the Chinese mess, enabling a competitor to take away more of their market globally.

It is just nonsense. By contrast, the French position that there must be a carbon tax on imports from countries that don't play the game on climate change, has some merit. The French have asked the European Commission to find a way to penalize companies from such countries, though the existence of firms that source components from a dozen markets and manufacture on every continent could make this task nearly impossible.

Optimized technology solutions are at a premium because whether we talk of pollution control or mastery of markets, rapid and focused new product development is the cornerstone to competitiveness. Success in an environment characterized by economic integration largely rests on innovation of products and services, proactive work schedules and paradigm shifts. Government and companies have to study, analyze and stimulate – hence, experiment with ways and means to be ahead of likely future events .

The spirit of steady innovation, including control over environmental pollution, involves constant research in discovering new products and processes by bringing together universities and industry just as happened in the US during the Cold War years. The immediate goal should be damage control based on scientific facts and not on wild dreams.

Part of the inability to effectively plan for the coming years is due to inertia and to the tendency to follow the beaten path. When we are in the middle of a known paradigm it is hard to imagine any other. The set of rules which we follow establish boundaries for behaviour, which confine us to viewing a problem from only a single angle.

This raises questions of competence. Few politicians appreciate that the ability to anticipate is the cornerstone for all successful undertaking, economic integration and the control of CO_2 emissions included. Whether in business or in politics, effective leaders have always led from the front, where the action is; these days there is a scarcity of effective leaders.

A valid system of anticipation requires a first-class strategic exploration. Rather than waiting for a trend to develop, we should constantly monitor change through early indicators which permit us to capitalize on plenty of lead time. Typically, new paradigms start out slowly, until the rules become better known. If successful, however, they move quickly, often overtaking people, companies and states that fail to deal with them.

3. China Price and the WTO

The first section of this chapter explained why the management of change matters; the second discussed why it is important to look after economic integration and anticipate sensitive issues in order to be prepared for them. This is not a matter of being reactionary. Every nation tries to boost its exports while protecting its home market; a case in point being *China price*. Plenty of people believe that in the last five years of the 1990s and the first five years of the twenty-first century these two words somehow became the most frightening in US industry. The phrase has two meanings:

1. *Qualitatively*, China price represents what the US and EU have to pay in terms of lost exports for accommodating China's part of global trade and at the same time what their consumers might gain in low prices of manufactured products.

2. *Quantitatively*, the two words convey the message that Chinese prices stood at 30 to 50 per cent less than the lowest price that US-based industry can possibly achieve; they represent an even greater discrepancy when contrasted to EU production prices.

Given the fact that hourly wages in China are so low compared (in money terms) to those prevailing in the west, while societal costs are minimal and those resulting from protection of the environment non-existent, 30 to 50 per cent price reductions are not surprising. What is surprising is the failure of trade negotiators to bring to the table pollution, environmental damage and working conditions.

There is also a fair amount of fatalism in all this, all the way to the level of business leadership. As an article in the *Executive Intelligence Review* (*EIR*) had it, in an interview with Raisat (the Italian national television), Carlo de Benedetti, a former boss of Olivetti, developed two points.

- First, Italy has no future as a manufacturing country.

- Second, the Italian public must get used to thinking as consumers, rather than continue thinking as producers.

During the same interview, de Benedetti recounted how he tried to convince Enrico Berlinguer, the late Italian Communist Party Secretary General, that 'the working class does not exist any more. Today, the worker is a consumer, a wage-earner, and a taxpayer. If you think to protect him only from the standpoint as a wage-earner, you cheat him on consumption and taxes'.[5] What de Benedetti forgot to explain is from where the money the consumers and taxpayers need to survive will come.

A consumer-only society is not going to be around for long, as Italy and other countries with huge national debt have found. It is far better to take notice of one of the premises of foreign trade theory which associates potential effects of social costs with the need for structural change in labour markets. As cannot be repeated too often, a net effect of structural imbalances is that unemployment rises in countries where wages (and the labour force as a whole) do not react flexibly enough to fence off the negative effects of globalization. In terms of *China price*:

- the good news is that China's prices have started to rise;

- the bad news is that, according to economists and central bankers, this may create inflation in the west.

Economists say that export data offer some confirmation that Chinese manufacturers have raised prices in 2006 and 2007. In June 2006, Mervyn King, Governor of the Bank of England, spoke of upward pressure on export prices, based on prices of Chinese goods imported into Hong Kong.

---

5   *EIR*, 1 June 2007.

Prices in China rose because of greater input costs, particularly energy and materials. Manufacturing wages also grew, but not at a level which is a relief for US and EU manufacturers. Still, rising costs leave Chinese exporters with a tough choice:

• accept lower margins; or

• raise prices, thereby losing some of the *China price* advantage.

A crucial query is what will be the effect on China's exports overall, on US, French, Italian and other trade deficits and on future developments in world trade. Some perspective can be gained through a historical reference.

In 1830, America's share of global GDP was a mere 3 per cent; about equal to China's share of global GDP in 1980. The US took 83 years to reach 19 per cent of global GDP; this happened a year prior to WWI. China is expected to do so in less than 30 years. In 2007 it achieved an estimated 14 per cent; more than six times higher than its share in 1980. The irony associated with these statistics is that:

• for many years the US was hammering on the door for better access to China's market;

• now it is the Chinese who find themselves on the free-trade offensive.

Looking at the huge current account deficit the US has with China, optimists say that America has survived important waves of massive imports from Japan, South Korea, and Mexico and has come up from under. Pragmatists answer that something very different is happening this time around. The model which worked for nearly six decades after WWII was that the US and other western countries kept their lead in knowledge-intensive industries, while developing nations focused on lower-skills sectors. That is no more the case.

• What is particular with China is that it is progressing simultaneously on two fronts.

• For the first time, there is a nation with a huge population that can compete both with very low wages and in high tech.

The pattern of challenges created by China is not too different when it comes to European Union statistics. Since 2003 China has been Germany's tenth-largest customer for metals and metal products, given the buoyant rates of its construction industry. But, as Figure 4.1 shows, in the decade from 1995 to 2004 German imports from China have increased more rapidly than exports (statistics by Deutsche Bundesbank). China is now Germany's sixth-largest foreign supplier.

Worried about what the future holds, certain market watchers say that China's 9 to 11.5 per cent annual growth is essentially based on a strategy of

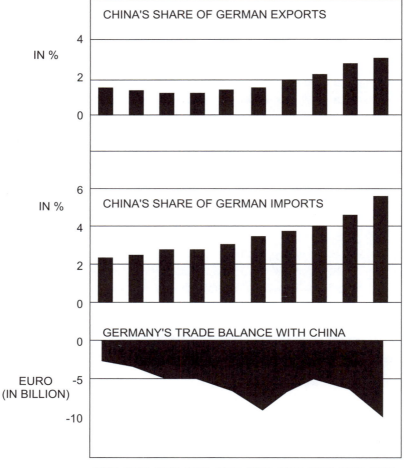

Figure 4.1   Germany and China: A 10-year trade balance

skimming the cream off the anaemic per capita GDP of other countries with which it trades, for instance, the 3 per cent in the US (prior to the subprimes debacle of 2007, and the rather depressed per capita increase in France, Italy, Germany and elsewhere, which stands at roughly a little over 2 per cent p.a.

The thinking underpinning this argument is that the real and pressing question is how to level the playing field while keeping globalization intact. Different ideas circulate, but none of them is a blockbuster. The most serious, and most controversial, is that of reopening World Trade Organization negotiations – a vast project, nearly equal to freeing the winds and spirits in Pandora's box.

The agreement that let China into the WTO was negotiated under very curious terms, since China was allowed to continue to protect certain strategic industries. This has been a two-speed WTO framework, under the rationale that China was a developing nation, which is no longer the case. These days, China is slowly lowering certain tariffs, but in some industries duties remain high by global standards. Foreign companies are still compelled to manufacture locally and to form joint ventures in cars, telecoms, construction and engineering. Additionally, Beijing has been able to:

- restrict the right of foreign companies to distribute within China on their own;

- resist opening up government contracts to foreign bidding; and

- keep the exchange rate of the yuan low, just as Japan has been doing over several decades with the yen.

Special cases in China abound. One of them is intellectual property, whose protection is complex and whose law enforcement leaves much to be wanted. Software is a product the US could be exporting in large volumes to China. However, US software exports to China are dismal and the WTO does nothing about it. The US Business Software Alliance estimates that 92 per cent of all software in Chinese computers is either unlicensed or pirated.

Additionally, there is the open wound of counterfeits: pharmaceuticals, fertilizers and other products which are joining the roster of pirated music CDs, books, movies and so on. While Beijing has brought some high-profile criminal cases to court, in general these represent small civil penalties that pirates shrug off. Based on these facts, critics say that the WTO is a paper tiger, unable to get a consensus on what to do on crucial global trade issues and even more incompetent in re-establishing order.

4. Is China Losing its Price Advantage?

The year of the Olympic Games in Beijing was supposed to bring China to the forefront of the international community. It did so in terms of the collection of gold medals, but it also brought on stage some very bad news. A June 2008 estimate suggested that import prices from China to the US would increase by 15 per cent in 2008 – that's the way to kill a market.

Not everyone has been surprised by this inflationary contagion. According to theory, global trade should cause prices in different countries to converge. Those of low-cost producers should gradually increase as wages rise, while the prices of high-cost producers should fall. Yes, but for the Chinese model this is not true in the case of managed prices; nor is short-term balancing of the books.

An important practical fact with managed prices is that, as long as they remain well below those in targeted export countries, their penetration of world markets will continue, albeit at slower pace than before. According to BCA Research, an economic analysis firm, the prices of Chinese exports of electric motors and generators doubled between 2003 and 2008,[6] but:

- they remained much cheaper than corresponding American products; and

- their share of the US market has more than doubled, forcing local producers to cut prices.

Nevertheless, inflation is working against the huge advantage China had in global markets and several companies are rethinking and revising their capital expenditures plans by hedging their bets. Canon is no longer building or expanding factories in China. Instead, it is doubling its work force to 8,000 at a factory outside Hanoi. Nissan, too, is expanding a vehicle engineering centre near the Vietnamese capital.

---

6   *The Economist*, 16 August 2008.

While even with these lost investments in 2008 China remained the most attractive destination for industrial sites worldwide, for Chinese leaders it's a bad omen that multinationals are worried about inflationary pressures, soaring costs and the fact of becoming overly dependent on factories in one country. The negatives include not only rapidly rising labour costs but also:

- shortages of skilled workers;

- a strengthening currency;

- shortages of energy supplies; and

- dwindling tax breaks for foreign investors.

With wages in China rising at close to 25 per cent a year in dollar terms in many industries, the *China price* for a growing list of goods, particularly low-technology products, is no longer much of a bargain. No wonder, therefore, that multinationals start thinking about other parts of the world and, as part of their strategy of keeping a balance, are encouraging suppliers to diversify out of China.

Those in favour say that there is no crisis and to a large extent the shifts taking place are part of a grand strategy on the part of the Chinese leadership. Factory investments going from China to elsewhere tend to be in low-skill, low-wage industries as the government focuses on industries like precision machining, computer components and auto manufacturing.[7] They add that even if costs in China are rising rapidly, after having made major strategic investments companies will not find it easy to move their manufacturing out of the country.

True enough, if the multinationals direct their new investments elsewhere they will be faced with fewer economies of scale. This, however, does not mean that a reduction in foreign direct investments (FDIs) and a loss of export markets are positive events. Even if China's manufacturing export industries do not seem to be in imminent danger, the government should not be insensitive to the fact that there is a shift in the global market which, over time, may have unexpected consequences.

---

7   Evidently these jobs are not moving to the United States or to Europe.

5. Doha Round: A Case Study in Globalization's Unexpected Consequences

A tournament of world trade negotiations may be enjoyable for its participants, since every session takes place in attractive surroundings and a selected city, with all expenses paid. But even in the Middle Ages tournaments did not go on forever. There must be an end sometime; and this is the case with the Doha Round.

Following in the footsteps of previous negotiations, like the Uruguay Round, which managed to come back to life from the Ades and reach some sort of conclusion, the Doha Round proved to be a slow vehicle for furthering world trade in agricultural goods, manufactured wares and financial services. It has also been a useless tournament, as it started with confused aims and without the least awareness of:

- where the real risks lie; and

- how big and open to destruction these might be – all the way from a major health hazard to a financial hecatomb.

It is not risk-taking per se that is to blame, but rather the lack of any serious effort to size up exposure, evaluate returns and keep big risks under lock and key. The reference to big risks is intended because there have always been risks in the process of trade liberalization, including periodic crises in negotiations because of too many conflicting aims and expectations resulting from compromises on sensitive issues such as:

- agriculture;

- manufacturing;

- banking; and

- special treatment for developing countries.

What Doha has shown specifically is that there is increased controversy over services liberalization as a whole, including issues such as water services, privatizations and the tearing apart of national frontiers for financial services, which has proved to be a highly sensitive issue to developing nations. Even more negative has been the contemplated destruction of Western agriculture.

Experts suggest that a great deal of complexity and controversy comes from national trade authorities which want to get out of WTO talks more than they contribute to it. The aftereffect is that agreements turn into disagreements and there are only losers. When it began in 2001, the Doha Round was billed as a big effort to boost growth in poorer countries, with the lowering of barriers to food trade being placed at its kernel. But:

- agriculture and its subsidies will not be gladly given up by the western world, and for good reason (see section 5);

- as disagreements persist, an American proposal for reducing its farm protection has been greeted by a much weaker response from the EU and none at all from Japan where the 'Sunday farmers' have political clout.

At the core of the unenthusiastic response to a reduction of agricultural subsidies by the EU lies the fact that Europe must remain an agricultural power even at the expense of world trade and of its own taxpayers. The no. 1 proponent of this thesis has been Jacques Chirac of France, and he has a point. In case of a major conflict or other catastrophe there is big difference between being short of manufactured goods one can postpone buying or even do without, and being short of food.

Three million Chinese grow apples for export. Some of these are exported whole, like Chinese apples to France, but the majority are made into apple juice and sold all over the world. There is no control for pesticides (rumour has it that many find their way into the apple juice) – and nobody from the WTO or any other organization is controlling the general sanitary conditions.

It simply does not make sense to have in place agencies like the Food and Drug Administration, who spend all their time and money on pharmaceutical health hazards, while the daily health hazards from imported food full of pesticides and antibiotics are left unattended. Because, Doha or not Doha, the Chinese and other East Asians do export huge quantities of food to the West – one of their best clients being the supermarkets.

Part, but only part, of the reason is failure to anticipate events to which reference was made earlier In August 2007 in France, the news that suddenly the country had a deficit of 100,000 milk cows was associated with the announcement of a forthcoming increase of the price of milk and milk products (butter, cheese, etc.). Henri Brichard, president of the National Federation of Milk Producers, explained in an interview to the *Canard Enchaîné* that this represented a deficit of 600,000 tons of milk.

This same phenomenon of underproduction of milk exists in practically all 27 EU countries and also characterizes two large milk exporters: Australia and New Zealand. Critics say that the reasons for the large and growing milk deficit in the EU can be traced to the ill-conceived Common Agricultural Policy (CAP). Since 1984, when the EU put the milk quotas in place, two out of three French milk producers have gone out of business: 'We are 100,000 today; in 2015 we will be 70,000,' says Brichard.[8]

Think of milk bureaucrats at the WTO repeating such blunders 100 times over. One of the silly decisions taken by the Brussels bureaucracy is that since 2003, when PAC was restructured, the financial aid provided to agriculture is no more linked to production and there is no prognostication attached to demand:

- farmers can reduce their milk delivery and increase their cereal production without any loss of financial support; and

- as it takes up to three years for a calf to become a milk cow, the situation in the next few years can only deteriorate.

Just as the EU's CAP has failed, the Doha Round has been handicapped not only because the management of a complex enterprise has been awfully weak, but also by a rush to a decision. The reason the self-imposed deadline for the Doha was set as the end of June 2007 is that negotiating the trade promotion authority granted by Congress to President Bush expired at that time. Yet, everyone knew the complexity of a negotiation involving:

- 148 countries; and

- a score of highly technical issues on which there was disagreement.

---

8   *Canard Enchaîné*, 15 August 2007. Typically considered to be a satirical paper, the *Canard Enchaîné* is a well-informed political and social independent weekly paper.

Both points meant that an agreement is not easy to reach – if it is reachable at all. Critics add that an accord along the Doha lines makes no sense, because practically everybody in it might be a loser, with the result that, for many countries, world trade becomes a foe rather than a friend. Another well-founded criticism is that Doha's promotion of a micromanaged world trade will eventually become over-regulated and therefore handicapped.

The often drummed-up argument of the pros – that the Doha Round should help the poorest countries and therefore the rich must be generous – is plain bad judgement. When it comes to trading, countries, companies and people should not depend on elimosinary handouts, but on their strengths – even if the way Doha has been conducted is mainly exploited by each party's weaknesses.

There exists, as well, the counter-argument that in the end the Doha Round would have given much better access to markets to companies of the biggest and richest nations, including their banks. Some representatives to WTO negotiations said in private discussions that the end result would be looting the poorer countries' resources through complex financial instruments sold to them, which they don't understand.[9] The crash of the subprimes in America which led to the huge July/August 2007 financial crisis proved those critics right.

6. Inflated Food Prices and Increased Health Hazard[10]

Not long ago, an article was published under the title 'Worker shortage takes toll on crops', discussing conditions in the agricultural labour market in the Pacific Northwest of the United States. This is a fairly complex topic with *for* and *against* arguments about illegal immigrants from Mexico. The article did little to convince its readers that food inflation is not a real issue because a shortage of farm workers means either:

- smaller harvests; or

- higher wages to lure workers.

---

9   D.N. Chorafas, *Alternative Investments and the Mismanagement of Risk*, Macmillan/Palgrave, London, 2003.

10 See also the discussion on health hazards in Chapter 2.

Both suggest that higher food prices are likely for all sorts of products from that region as, and not only from that region. In Côte d'Azur, in the South of France, which is on the other side of the world, the prices of agricultural products are also increasing, with specialists searching for and spelling out a number of reasons for this *agflation*:

- demographics;

- bad harvest in the global economy;

- heavy rains in some parts of the world;

- lack of water in other parts;

- the diversion of agricultural produce for ethanol and other vegetable fuels.

Prices for salads, soy beans, wheat, corn, cherries and apples may or may not be reliable economic indicators, but the fact remains that there is plenty of evidence from many parts of the globe that foretells bad news for consumers: with or without Doha, they will have to pay more for their food over the coming years, an additional reason why the attention paid to the quality of agricultural produce must be real, not merely skin deep.

Critics point out that while a great deal of time has been spent on 'national interests' and 'business interests' during this five-year long Doha Round, health hazards attracted very little attention. This has not been to the credit of the different negotiators. A similar statement is valid regarding the cost of production, transport, distribution and end effect on consumers – as well as pollution of the environment.

It is unavoidable that the growing demand for agricultural produce will translate into price inflation for agricultural goods. This is expected to last until 2015, if not longer. No wonder, therefore, that the European Union has been unwilling to relegate its food supply by opening its protected food markets and America has been slow to offer real cuts to its farm subsidies.

The European Commission would be greatly to blame if it lets the uncertainties of world trade in agricultural goods to devastate the old continent's farming. But while the EU has been daydreaming about Doha, American politicians faced a backlash. In 2007, the Democratic Party-controlled Congress expressed plenty of scepticism about globalization. Much of its reaction has been focused on China. But it is also wary of the offshoring of services to India and shows no willingness to give more concessions. Congress is also due to write a new farm bill.

All these references should be seen as evidence that the feeling that globalization may have reached its limits is becoming fairly widespread. Experts suggest this is the key reason why Europeans decided not to push America too hard on its farm subsidies and the Americans did not demand too much from a European Union notoriously reluctant to open its agricultural markets.

- Seen from a limited perspective, this looks like a newly found unity in protectionism.

- In reality, however, the new trend towards globalization's limits is pragmatism, which is now gaining ground.

For instance, the populous and increasingly prosperous emerging market represented by Brazil in the Doha talks has been of growing interest to western exporters and this gave the Brazilians a bargaining chip. But they overplayed their hand by greatly increasing their level of ambition. The Indians did likewise. Plenty of other emerging countries, too, misjudged their ability to force western nations to give major concessions.

After the liberalizing wave of the 1980s and 1990s, in which countries decided to open their economies without waiting for others to do likewise, there is now a new conservatism. Its after-effect is creating big differences in opinions between developed and emerging countries. Numbers are tricky. Brazil, Argentina and others have offered to lower their ceilings by over 40 per cent. But the WTO has calculated that this proposal would trim the tariffs Brazil and Argentina actually impose by less than a percentage point.[11]

No wonder that in the west the business world was never overwhelmed by enthusiasm about Doha. Moreover, the fact that the Doha Round focused on two sectors, farming and finance, in which sectional interests in both rich and poor nations are particularly entrenched, did not provide grounds for easy solutions.

- The industrialized countries feel that they have done a great deal with a matching effort; and

---

11   *The Economist*, 30 June 2007.

- not without reason, the less developed countries look with suspicion at the demand that they open up their financial market – the 2007/2009 banking crisis proved that they were right.

Additionally, it was a mistake to call these talks a *development round*, not only because it raised false expectations of how much most developing countries could gain in handouts, but also because the stagnation of the Doha talks gave the message there is nothing positive to be gained in pursuing them. The result has been a push towards bilateral trade deals that are generally better focused and more manageable than multilateral negotiations, but evidently have a more limited impact.

An article in the *Financial Times* also brought into perspective another ingredient of the failure of multinational negotiations: the changing corporate climate. One of the effects of the Sarbanes-Oxley legislation in the US, this article stated, has been to encourage boards to examine in detail the activities of their businesses.

- Executives have come under more pressure to justify policy debates; and

- supporting multilateral trade deals comes rather a long way down the list of their pressing policy concerns.[12]

There have been, as well, some theatrical acts. Quite unexpectedly, during the late January 2007 World Economic Forum in Davos, the Doha Round of trade talks came back to life, or at least they were temporarily resurrected. About 30 ministers instructed their officials to step up talks to reach a framework deal, especially on agriculture – the area most vulnerable to health problems and one developing countries tend to pay little attention with regard to the hazards to health and of pollution.

Cost, not health protection, has been the central point. A paper presented to a UN conference in 2004 has shown that at the time American rice cost $331 per ton to produce, compared with $70 for Thailand and $79 for Vietnam. Part of the difference in cost is due to the very accommodating health regulations in the two Asian countries.

---

12 *Financial Times*, 5 March 2007.

To the question of who is going to control the health hazard associated to Thailand-grown rice the answer is: 'Nobody!' – just as nobody today controls the overstuffing with antibiotics of Thailand-raised shrimps. (Thailand is taken as an example; it is not singled out as a 'bad case'. The same argument exists with China, Vietnam and plenty of other places raising food for western markets).

In conclusion, nobody can argue that health hazards associated to world trade in foodstuffs is not a major issue. Therefore, it would have been wise to involve the World Health Organization since Day 1 of the Doha Round talks (the same is true of the Uruguay Round). Contrary to the trade of coal, copper and other raw materials, foodstuffs should be handled with plenty of attention in regard to health hazards, and exporting countries must first and foremost raise their:

- health standards; and

- health inspection services.

The fact that this has not been a preoccupation of WTO and of the Doha negotiators is definitely wrong. It is a failure of professional obligations with dire consequences for all consumers, leading to the thought that, down to the bottom line, American and European consumers benefited greatly from Doha Round's failure – and so did Western farmers.

7. Conflicts of Interest in Global Trade Talks

One of the reasons for the criticism expressed in regard to ill-defined and poorly managed multilateral talks, finds its source in the fact that the Doha Round addressed the world trade in services. This is a relatively new concept; an uncharted territory whose scanty evidence is interpreted in different ways by different interests.

The pros say that the biggest economic gains from this round would have come from freer trade in financial services, medical services and accountancy. Critics respond that *services* is a huge but heterogeneous domain and it does not help to pile up diverse, ill-defined issues. Additionally, unlike other aspects of the talks, the *services deals* have been decentralized, with each country on the defensive. In this sense, there can be no consensus based on the sense of a meeting, on:

- what each country is prepared to liberalize;

- how it would like others to come forward; and

- what is the minimal contribution, to avoid the trap that each country will try to take out of the negotiation more than it brings to the table.

Some of the trade representatives, particularly those on the defensive, justified their concerns with the statement that, if one asks what other world trade negotiations have achieved, the precedent is not necessarily positive. As briefly stated earlier, the previous agricultural talks, known as the Uruguay Round, which were held in the early 1990s, went through considerable brinkmanship and delay before they were completed; and according to knowledgeable people their result is still disappointing in many ways.

Therefore, it comes as no surprise that the world's trade ministers who gathered in Geneva end of June 2006 for what was billed as a 'final attempt' to salvage Doha, ended nowhere in their negotiations. The way a news item had it, Kemal Nath, India's trade minister, turned up 90 minutes late for the first big meeting, because he had thought it more important to watch Germany beat Argentina in the World Cup.[13]

In retrospect, Kemal Nath became the hero of the financial rescue of India and all other developing countries from the world's financial abyss, which they would have fallen into if the 'final attempt' to salvage Doha had succeeded. In July/August 2007 the heavens broke loose with the subprimes crisis in the US, which soon morphed into a global banking crisis and credit crisis in one go.

- The banks of western countries suffered greatly.

- Those of developing countries largely avoided bankruptcies, thanks to Nath.

The doors to a hecatomb are not quite closed, however. Following some nice dinners, always associated with international events even if their results are

---

13 *The Economist*, 8 July 2006.

dismal, the negotiators promised to keep talking. So far, this has led nowhere and the general comment has been that the best way to characterize the Geneva gatherings is apathy coupled with second thoughts. Those who try to find the reasons for such a negative outcome come up with two hypotheses.

- America, the European Union and the large emerging economies have concluded that it does not matter if Doha fails; or

- they see no need to reach an agreement in a hurry, given the fact that other world trade talks have dragged on for years.

Referring to the ups and downs of Uruguay Round, some people have predicted that disappointments will probably increase with Doha, because these particular talks have had conflicting aims. For instance, India is reluctant to cut its own farm tariffs but has a big interest in liberalizing trade in services, wanting more freedom in everything:

- from insourcing;

- to health care and entertainment.

Given this background, at the end of the June 2006 Doha Round negotiations in Geneva, Susan Schwab, the US trade representative, made clear that she would offer no further cuts in subsidies. Instead, she dwelt on the inadequacy of others' proposals, particularly a black box full of loopholes, through which different countries could minimize the effect of reductions in tariffs.

During the Doha Round negotiations, Argentineans, Brazilians, Indians, Indonesians and others advanced the thesis that each developing country should set an individual level of ambition on tariffs based on its own 'average tariff level'. Western countries have scoffed at this idea, which they consider to be a king-sized loophole intended to work to their disfavour.

The fact is that everybody's proposals were weakened by a large number of exceptions, as most countries had an extra request for *special* products and services, for example, to protect subsistence farmers. This and similar requirements which were on the Doha table led to endless arguments with no or very minor agreements.

As another example of loopholes, emerging economies including China, India and Indonesia wanted the right to define 20 per cent of farm goods as *special*. They demanded that tariffs on these products should not be cut at all – a measure which could easily exempt more than 90 per cent of imported agricultural goods from tariff reductions.

For his part, Pascal Lamy, the WTO's boss, talked about a '20/20/20' deal: American should cut its subsidy ceiling to below $20 billion; the EU should agree to the G20s[14] proposal for farm tariff; and emerging economies should agree to cap their industrial tariffs at 20 per cent. But there have been no takers. Instead, there was a widening gap between the viewpoints of the different parties over what the Doha Round should achieve.

Positions changed during the negotiations. India, for example, became less flexible, determined that the round's professed aim of helping the poor means that poor 'countries should do nothing at all'.[15] This was most surprising because it came from a country which benefits hugely from the est's outsourcing. And it should also be remembered that, as an ancient Greek saying goes:

> *'God helps only those who help themselves.'*

On 16 July 2006, a couple of weeks past the end of June 2006 deadline, a sort of last-minute agreement struck at the G8 summit in St Petersburg set a new deadline in the middle of August, when the World Trade Organization usually closes for business. To settle the major outstanding issues of the world trade talks, the G8 heads of state (see Chapter 1) called on Pascal Lamy to report to the global trade body's members 'as soon as possible with the aim of facilitating agreement... within a month'.

Ironically this short deadline was set a day after Russia and the US failed to strike a separate deal on Russia's long-awaited entry to the WTO. 'This is not the forum for negotiating the Doha round,' said José Manuel Barroso, European Commission President. 'But if the G8 leaders cannot take the lead, who will do it?'[16] In one word, the answer is 'Nobody!' – a factual reply, since on 24 July 2006 the Doha Round talks were suspended.

---

14   China, India, Brazil and other large emerging economies are members of a group known as G20
15   *The Economist*, 8 July 2008.
16   *Financial Times*, 17 July 2006.

According to some opinions, whatever the results of the Doha Round, there will come a *post-Doha* in which fresh thought may be given to future strategies and methods for world trade, including liberalization of financial services. According to my opinion, the world trade negotiations are too anachronistic, deprived of cherished goals as well as pre-testing through worst case analysis and *a priori* experimentation which would permit educated guesses on 'pluses' and 'minuses' for a wide range of countries, their produce and their tariffs.

8. Dead Cat Walking: Doha in 2008

Years of negotiations at the World Trade Organization to shape an agreement on the Doha Round of trade talks collapsed for the fifth time in July 2008. Theoretically, the reason was that the United States, India and China failed to resolve differences over protection for agricultural goods in developing countries. Practically, the differences have been many and so widespread that reconciling them was an impossible task.

'There seems to be no chance of finishing the Round this year if at all,' one of the negotiators was heard to say. There is nothing surprising about that since nobody *truly* wanted such an agreement to 'succeed' at *their* expense. In fact, the only success story of this unstoppable resurrection of the Doha Round is to split the European Union into two camps.

Nine EU member states demanded better terms than the EU Trade commissioner, turned into mini-dictator, would permit. With the support of Italy, France organized a 'Club of the Volunteers' which also includes Cyprus, Greece, Hungary, Ireland, Lithuania, Poland and Portugal. All nine consider Peter Mandelson's position in giving way their prerogative to be unacceptable. Britain positioned itself on the other side of the fence.

To better appreciate the more profound reasons for this fifth failure we should briefly return to what happened in July 2007 a year after the Doha deadlines expired, for all practical purposes, and the negotiators files were put in the time closet. The subject of contention was not just agricultural. At that time, the chairmen of two formerly key Doha Round committees:

- one on agriculture; and

- the other on trade in non-farm goods;

put forward 'draft modalities', a kind of documents that, in the opinion of the promoters, should or could form the basis of some sort of further discussions. After a month or so for reflection, trade officials began meeting again in an attempt to close the many remaining gaps – but this too proved to be for no purpose.

All this happened when Hillary Clinton was riding high as US Democratic ticket presidential candidate and Doha addicts were saying that it was Bill Clinton who had skilfully steered through the previous agreement, the Uruguay Round. 'Maybe a second President Clinton will have to deal with Doha,' some diehards were saying, but the American people chose otherwise and Hilary's candidacy went down in flames.

Moreover, those who made this argument forgot that in 1994, with Uruguay, an agreement between the European Community (as it then was) and America was the main requirement for a Clinton-engineered deal. By contrast, with Doha the main stumbling block has been agreement between the industrialized and the developing parts of the globe where conflicts of interest exist in practically every chapter under discussion since the time of the post-WWII North–South confrontation.

Therefore, the only sure thing when, on 21 July 2008, trade ministers gathered once again at the World Trade Organization's headquarters beside Lake Geneva was a tourist bonanza. They had plenty of opportunities to visit nice places, eat excellent food and bring their spouses and partners; making a breakthrough in the interminable Doha Round of trade talks was not even the icing on the cake.

This is not necessarily a criticism, because those who went to Geneva in July 2008 at the WTO's invitation knew they had an impossible amount to sort out. Not the least were the still fresh aftershocks of the 2007–2009 credit and banking crisis, which had left the services side of the negotiations shattered. Most clear-eyed delegates also appreciated that 2007 and 2008 added something beyond the reasons which brought down the Doha round in 2006: *food security* at affordable prices. Both in richer and in poorer countries politicians seized on recent price spikes as proof that free farm trade:

- is a risky business; and

- that self-sufficiency is a worthy goal.

Striking a blow for reasonable self-sufficiency in foodstuffs carries a lot of political weight. Only intellectuals can believe that the concept of self-sufficiency was defeated by starving North Korea. Unilateral export restrictions, such as those recently imposed by Vietnam and India, have proved that sovereignty counts – and each government first and foremost looks after its own people.

The notion that trade in agricultural goods without bounds precludes food security should in no way be discarded. Not only food security but also food quality counts a great deal, and so do food prices.

- Theoretically, when countries cut their tariffs on farm goods, their consumers pay lower prices for food they eat.

- Practically, when farm subsidies are slashed world food prices rise because the subsidy part is removed but transport costs are added (though this has not been the reason for the 2008 spikes in food prices).

Another factor which must be added to the risk and return equation of the failed Doha Round is that, no matter what its proponents have said, it will not have liberated millions of people from poverty nor added hundreds of billions to global income. In most cases, it might have offered little more than locking in the status quo. Indeed,

- over the last few years, some large emerging markets have cut their tariffs unilaterally without waiting for WTO negotiations; and

- high food prices have also left the Doha Round looking anachronistic, if not obsolete; a mere excuse to justify bureaucrats' fat salaries.

Critics also point out that, had it become effective, Doha might (just might) have stopped its signatories from openly subsidising their farm exports, but it would have done nothing about the opposite, more pressing problem of governments banning food exports. Altogether, this would have been a meagre return for nearly seven years of expensive and protracted negotiations.

In conclusion, the July 2008 fifth collapse of Doha negotiations in Geneva did not come as a surprise. The negotiations began in Qatar in November

PART II

THE GLOBALIZATION OF FINANCE

5

Sovereign Wealth Funds

1. The Sovereign Wealth Fund Call[1]

Lenders never fail to pursue borrowers for paying back the loaned capital with interest. *State capitalism* is a way of doing so (see section 3), and in spite of the adulation of globalization, plenty of attention is now focused on *Sovereign Wealth Funds* (SWF). The oldest SWF is the Kuwait Investment Authority dating back to 1953 some five years after the first hedge fund was created.[2] More than three decades old are ADIA of the United Arab Emirates, Singapore's Temasek Holdings (which, along with other SWFs, has suffered severe losses) and the Permanent Fund Corporation of Alaska.

Currently there are an estimated 9,000 hedge funds handling $1.4 trillion;[3] but while there exists a much smaller number of SWFs, these have more money at their disposal than all hedge funds taken together. It has been estimated that as of late 2007 sovereign wealth funds controlled about $3 trillion, with 95 per cent of that sum under the wings of the top 20. In order of magnitude, the seven biggest were:

- Abu Dhabi's Investment Authority (ADIA) ($880 billion);

- Saudi Arabia's group of funds (amount undisclosed but believed to be over $500 billion);

---

1 An *option* contract gives the buyer the right, but not the obligation, to purchase or sell in the future a stated quantity and quality of the underlying commodity (or asset), at an agreed upon price (strike price). In the case of a *call* option (this section's theme) if the buyer (holder) exercises their rights, pays the strike price and receives delivery of the commodity. With a *put* option (next section's subject) he or she delivers the commodity and receives the price agreed to when the contract is first entered into.

2 Originally known as the Kuwait Investment Office, it ran into trouble in 1987 when it bought more than 20 per cent of British Petroleum, which had been privatized a short time earlier. Margaret Thatcher did not like it.

3 There used to be 11,000 hedge funds handling nearly £2 trillion but both their number and the amount have shrunk significantly.

- Norway's ($380 billion);

- Singapore's GIC[4] ($330 billion);

- Kuwait's ($250 billion);

- China Investment Corp ($200 billion);

- Singapore's Temasek ($160 billion);

- Russia ($160 billion).[5]

Smaller SWFs are Alaska's Permanent Fund, Australia's Future Fund, Qatar Investment Authority, Dubai Financial, Libya's Oil Reserve Fund, Algeria's Fond de Régulation des Recettes, Brunei's Investment Agency, a Canadian SWF and South Korea's Investment Corporation, as well as those of Trinidad and Tobago. According to different estimates, over 20 countries have sovereign funds and half a dozen more have expressed an interest in establishing one – including India and Japan.

Up to January 2008, the Sovereign Wealth Funds were the secretive high fliers of the investment community. However, following the severe banking crisis which started in July/August 2007 and the sharp drop in the price of oil, they have been facing strong headwinds. The losses they suffered with banking investments in 2007, 2008 and first couple of months of 2009 curtailed their appetite for the financial industry and they are now focusing on other western assets. Many people as well say that the SWFs' importance was exaggerated in the first place.

During the so-called 'good times' (i.e. from 2003 up to early- to mid-2008), as the current account surpluses of oil exporting Middle Eastern countries as well as trade returns of China and other Asian nations were recycled, western financial assets controlled by foreign governments soared. According to some estimates, these surpluses reached the equivalent to nearly 15 per cent of the value of all publicly traded shares and bonds worldwide with a quarter or more of this held by SWFs. For many countries with a current account surplus it made sense to establish a SWF.

---

4   Government Investment Corporation.
5   Notice that all these numbers are approximate. Another estimate is that by mid-2008 this
    amount grew to $4.8 trillion; then the curve bent.

- Good governance suggested the need to acquire reliable stores of value that can be sold easily if and when liquidity runs dry; and

- therefore, plenty of money was saved and shipped abroad, with America and Britain the favoured places because they had a good banking system as well as broad and liquid markets for securities.

The investment motives of Sovereign Wealth Funds have varied. Some of the Middle Eastern countries, like Abu Dhabi and Kuwait, want to save their oil endowment for future generations. Others, like Dubai, have been freewheeling, and some experts suggest that the entrepreneurial Dubai has done a much better job of gaining sustainable wealth. (The late 2008 real estate crisis in Dubai demolished this argument.)

There is also a hedging motive for the rise of Sovereign Wealth Funds – to form a buffer against volatile commodity prices. During the two oil shocks in the 1970s, major oil exporters profited hugely and adjusted their expenditures to their glut of oil revenues. But the crash of international oil prices after 1980 saw to it that they suddenly became debtor nations.

Therefore, it is not surprising that the better managed oil producers such as Russia have established *stabilization funds*. Another example of the need to hedge under a longer time horizon is provided by China, which amassed a huge amount of hard currency thanks to persistent large current account surpluses.

Singapore, too, whose economy depends on trade rather than a finite resource like oil, has locked up billions of dollars of its wealth in its two SWFs. So has Norway, whose economy depends on oil. These are the facts about countries which care to accumulate and manage wealth rather than overspend by ballooning their national debt and current account deficits (more on this later).

As the variety of these goals documents, the issue of Sovereign Wealth Funds is complex because it integrates so many other crucial subjects beyond petrodollars and trade surpluses. Financial assets have to be invested in terms satisfactory to their owners, and this raises several questions:

- Where are the investments being made?

- What exactly do they target?

- Do the new capitalists have the skills to be in charge?

- What's the impact of large SWF surpluses on the US dollar as global currency (see section 8).

In all likelihood tomorrow's challenges will centre around the *unintended consequence of SWF investments*. So far, Sovereign Wealth Funds have been conservative and have not raised many eyebrows in western countries, particularly in those states more liberal in allowing foreigners to buy their assets. But this is changing. As SWF managers gain experience,

- they become bolder and more active, with growing risk appetite;

- they also aim to diversify their risks, shifting away from the dollar given its inability to recover its past glory.

Theoretically, large SWF investments should be welcome in the US for the dollar's sake. Practically, Congress thinks that foreign capital should not be buying America's crucial assets, like Unocal and the Ports Authority. Experts, however, say that the shift of SWF investments away from the dollar could be even worse for the American economy, as sovereign funds seek alternatives in European equity markets that welcome them (and in emerging countries). One quarter of the Swedish stock market is owned by SWFs.

SWF investments aside, countries which in the globalized economy had pegged their currency to the dollar are also starting to look for alternatives. The Chinese have already allowed the yuan to appreciate, ironically under American pressure. There is also talk that the Saudis may unpeg their currency from the dollar because, among other negatives, the peg has proved to be inflationary – and other currencies are likely to follow suit, with wide-ranging consequences for:

- the United States; and

- the global economy at large.

While economists would not venture to predict the longer-term aftereffect of a major change in global currencies in case the dollar falls out of favour, there exist some short-term projections. One of them is that Saudi Arabia and other nations whose produce is pegged to the dollar, or who have inventoried hundreds of billions of dollars, are now confronted by two choices:

- revalue at a level of about 7 per cent, which is the Chinese solution; or

- abandon the dollar as reference currency and adopt a basket of currencies, like Kuwait did in 2007.

Seen as independent events, neither of these options carries an ominous message for the US currency; but the reasons behind them strongly correlate. Some experts now believe that it is not unlikely that the next major issue in financial globalization will be unpegging key commodities from being quoted in dollars; for instance, oil. This would have been simply unthinkable even five years ago, but with the American economy in the doldrums and the authorities letting the dollar roll to the abyss, it has become an alternative – one with rather ominous results, like those usually associated to a regime change.

2. The Sovereign Wealth Fund Put[6]

Though the label 'Sovereign Wealth Fund' is new, the practice of state capitalism is old. *If* nationalizations by governments during and after the Great Depression, as well as after World War II, are taken into account *then* in recent history sovereign funds have existed for nearly 80 years:

- this has been mainly inland state capitalism; and

- the difference is that today organizations managing assets held by governments are interesting in another country's wealth.[7]

From governments' perspective, having a sovereign fund is a better investment than spending lots of money on non-essentials. For instance, on 24 December 2007, Singapore's Temasek increased its financial control of Standard Chartered to 18 per cent and it invested $6.2 billion in Merrill Lynch, as the investment bank urgently needed cash to bring its finances up from under. The

---

6 A term derived from options trading. A *put* gjves the holder (buyer) the right to enter a long futures position, and obliges the seller (righter) to enter a long futures position at a specific price *if* he's assigned by the holder to do so.

7 At present, targeted currencies are typically dollars, euros and pounds.

hypothesis proved to be wrong and the latter investment (as well as the money poured into UBS) has been a disaster.

Year on year from the beginning of the 2007–2009 crisis to mid-2008, Sovereign Wealth Funds have pumped some $60 billion into western banks. This is about a sixth of the total bank capital raised since the subprime crisis erupted. By mid-2008, however, SWFs have been:

- distinctly less inclined to be exposed to financial stocks; and

- they have taken note of the fact that none of these investments has done well. (Private equity firms that have invested in financial banks are also facing serious paper losses.)

The severe economic crisis which started in September 2008 in America with the bankruptcy of Lehman Brothers, the virtual nationalization of AIG, Fannie Mae and Freddie Mac and, in October 2008, the $700 billion TARP fund, had evident aftereffects on SWFs' decisions. The mood became even bleaker when the British government practically nationalized the Royal Bank of Scotland and Lloyds TSB/HBOS.

As investors lick their wounds from losses in stock markets around the globe, SWFs have suffered a bleeding in their wealth of 'only' 27 per cent to 37 per cent[8] – the lower margin compares well with the loss of 25 per cent by Warren Buffett and is better than equity losses suffered by pension funds. Still, the mood is no longer one of rapid expansion, while the huge fall in the price of oil makes this red ink even more biting.

Current accounts of some big oil rich developing countries, too, have become negative. Russia, for example, has reportedly depleted its reserves to defend its currency from capital outflows and is tapping reserves of extra cash, which includes SWF funds. Other nations which still have a positive current account balance are in the process of asset reallocation.

The Abu Dhabi Investment Authority (ADIA) has significantly lowered the share of its equity investments (reportedly to 40 per cent from nearly 60 per cent), while increasing its liquid reserves. With over $500 billion of assets, the Saudi Arabian Monetary Authority, too, is being run much more conservatively

---

8   As of 23 February 2008.

than in previous years and (reportedly) it is significantly increasing its funds in gold and cash.

According to expert opinions, not only are net purchases of foreign assets by Gulf States likely to be close to zero in 2009 from a peak of over $300 billion annually, but they may also become net sellers if the price of oil hits the mid-$20s. The same parties who were pushing prices up would be selling foreign assets and that may hit western stock markets like a hammer, as has happened with hedge funds deleveraging.

Another scenario which is being discussed these days is that the US Treasuries may also be heading for turbulence if SWFs gradually move out of safe investments and into the stockmarket after the economic situation starts improving. This is particularly discussed in connection to Asian countries, like China and Japan, which account for about half of the world's foreign exchange reserves. At best (for the US Treasuries) the experts say, China's positive current account balance will stop growing rather than shrink.

Nevertheless, the 2008–2009 adversity should not divert thereader's attention from the fact that liquid financial assets are accumulating in what used to be called until quite recently the *Third World*, which was first renamed 'underdeveloped' then 'in the process of development' and eventually rebaptized 'emerging markets'. The large majority of SWFs, particularly the richer ones, are in Asia and in the Middle East.

- The former are fed through hard work;

- the latter, by a torrent of petrodollars.

At a time when derivative instruments are supreme, Asia has a put option on the West's economy: It delivers the commodity and expects to receive the prize. In his book *1492* Jacques Attali, the French writer and politician, uses as an allegory the resurgence of Europe in the late fifteenth century; but what he writes goes hand-in-glove with the resurgence of Asia in the early twenty-first century.

In ancient times, Attali's story goes, a giant made war, triumphed and dominated his world. One day, however, he got tired and retreated from the dominant position. Conquered and tortured, the giant was left for dead; then he was put in chains by different masters. But eventually the vigilance of his guards waned. Finding new energy through his beliefs and his reason, the former giant rattled his chains.

- at some distance, a shadowy figure menaced him;

- but the chained giant told that figure to get lost and, to his surprise, it obeyed.[9]

With his newly found confidence, the giant made a plan to recover his strength, break his chains and set out to conquer the world. In 1492 the awakening giant was Europe, but today it is Asia, whose wealthy institutions acquire western assets and loan to western banks, which have been silly to weaken themselves through their excesses and now face bankruptcy.

Asian and Middle Eastern SWFs have become the source of good money which greases the wheels of the global economy, as the formerly fabulous western financial resources run dry. One does not need to be an economist to appreciate that future results will largely depend on how these rapidly growing SWF assets are used.

Financial analysts have been the first to appreciate the sovereign wealth funds *put* for what it is: a potential shift out of safe into more risky instruments, and out of US into non-US assets, akin to the so-called 'Greenspan put'. Subsequently, however, the policy has changed but to more conservative investments, as the world's economy went into a tailspin.

In spite of these changes, western governments should be smart enough to know that Sovereign Wealth Funds are not going away. Their staying power is based on the current account surpluses of the state to which they belong, while with their steady current account deficits America and many European countries lack credibility when they say they are committed to reducing their imbalances and redressing their economic factors. Attali's wakening giant knows that they lie.

3. State Capitalism: A Way to Get Back Money Loaned to Rich Nations

Globalization was supposed to mean an efficient worldwide market economy, in which western companies and nations would have the upper hand because

---

9   Jacques Attali, *1492*, Fayard, Paris, 1991.

technologically, financially and militarily they dominated the planet. In reality, as Martin Wolf, the *Financial Times* columnist, points out, some of the most influential players are turning out to be newly-rich states, not private companies.

- States' treasuries play a dominant role in ownership and production of raw materials, other commodities and manufactured goods; and

- as the big banks of the West have entered a phase of self-destruction, the SWFs are emerging as their saviours.

In theory, Sovereign Wealth Funds exist because the country in which they are based has a surplus of savings over investments, which ends up in the governments' hands. In practice, the real reasons are that either the SWF's country owns a commodity wealth – such as oil – or, it features a large current account surplus from its export-oriented manufacturing economy and its services industry. China and Singapore are examples (see section 7).

Whether exporting commodities highly in demand by modern economies, or quality goods manufactured with cheap labour – and therefore having an unbeatable price tag – the nations whose current account balance is largely positive want to invest their money. After a rather brief learning period, they aim at achieving not only increasing returns and portfolio diversification but also strategic objectives, which include:

- a foothold in major western economies; and

- the development of domestic financial services expertise and skills.

Opinions on the after-effects of SWFs are divided, particularly on whether or not there are reasons for concern. The way one theory has it, *if* a government fund operates transparently and on established commercial lines, with a wide range of investments and with no more than 5 per cent ownership in a big company, *then* the counter-party knows what to expect. Norway's SWF is taken as an example of this policy.

Other Sovereign Wealth Funds don't limit their investments to such low percentages; still others are shifting their investment sights from banks to buildings, seeking stakes in big real estate assets in New York on the cheap. In the week of 19 May 2008, SWFs from Kuwait and Qatar emerged among a group of investors led by Boston Properties in talks to buy from a struggling New York property tycoon the GM building, a prized asset overlooking Central Park and four other Manhattan skyscrapers.[10]

The Abu Dhabi Investment Authority, as well as Meraas, a new real estate company of Sheikh Mohammed bin Rashid Al-Maktoum, the Dubai ruler, have also been among investors from the Middle East that looked at big American real estate. The attraction of New York property, and other US gateway cities such as Washington, Los Angeles, San Francisco and Boston, is:

- that the market is well known to Middle Eastern investors; and

- it is expected to recover earlier than other parts of the US when real estate turns around.

One of the reasons for this strategic change in SWF investments may well be the fact that in western minds questions are quickly raised *if* an SWF seeks a controlling interest in a strategic industry, in a big bank, or in some other American or European dominant company. Two issues arise:

1. whether the fund is fit to control that company; and

2. whether foreign ownership might threaten either public interest or national interest.

The latter point may or may not be linked to *economic nationalism*. The way to find the answer is through examples. Italy's Enel was a proper fit for the business of Suez; the French government's refusal of the merger was economic nationalism. The same is true of the projected (but not realized) acquisition of Spain's Endesa by Germany's E.on.

Moreover, neither E.on nor Enel got their financing from a Sovereign Wealth Fund. To the contrary, as many analysts point out there is accumulated evidence that some foreign funds do seek dominant positions or outright

---

10 The tycoon, Harry Macklowe has been caught short by the credit squeeze, and was desperately selling off buildings to pay his creditors. According to experts, the price of $2.8 billion, under negotiation for the GM building, was the highest ever to be paid for a single building in the US; and the trade one of the highest-profile foreign property acquisitions in the city.

ownership of strategically important firms. And these SWFs are loaded with money. Furthermore:

- *if* the fund belongs to a government deemed potentially hostile;

- *then* the concern becomes greater, taking on national security dimensions.

Even dedicated free traders have started thinking that it is reasonable to keep control of companies operating in defence or in high technology out of the ownership of funds belonging to any foreign government. This is an evident contradiction to the spirit of globalization and it finds its reason in the fact that during the last decade, globalization has brought into the acquisitions arena players who operate by different rules from those established in the western economy.

During the last few years, some of the governments of the country to which the targeted company belongs have taken countermeasures. In 2006 the US blocked the acquisition of five port terminals by Dubai World Ports, owned by the Gulf emirate; while before this a Chinese bid for Unocal, the US energy group, was scared off by Congressional opposition.

Along similar lines of thought about crucial industries, the German government is drafting legislation to block acquisitions by state-run funds in sectors related to national security and possibly energy. Led by France and Germany, the European Union is also preparing joint proposals on how to oversee such investments at the EU and at wider level, such as the Group of Seven leading industrial countries.

Is it too early or too late to do so? Part of the answer could be provided by a 2007 report by Claude Belot, a French senator. Belot suggested that three of the Kings of Oil – Saudi Arabia, Bahrain and United Arab Emirates – have so much cash that in less than two years they could buy all companies of CAC 40,[11] the French Stock Exchange Index.

But in July 2007, Lawrence Summers warned of the risks associated with ownership of commercial enterprises by government-controlled entities. Summers said that such risks could be greatly reduced if Sovereign Wealth Funds invested through intermediary asset managers accountable for producing

---

11 *Canard Enchainé*, 31 October 2007.

the best risk-adjusted returns, for instance, something similar to what they are supposed to do with endowments and pension funds. In Summers' words:

> 'The logic of the capitalist system depends on shareholders causing companies to act so as to maximize the value of their shares. It is far from obvious that this will over time be the only motivation of governments as shareholders. They may want to see their national companies compete effectively, or to extract technology or to achieve influence.'[12]

People who still believe in globalization demand that owners of Sovereign Wealth Funds understand that it is in their own best interest to play by established western rules, managing their money professionally and transparently and also to appreciate that visibility is the best way to minimize friction with host countries. This advice, however, contradicts the principle that

- the 'owner' is master of his or her funds and

- therefore, telling him or her what to do with his wealth is a contradiction to the principles of free enterprise.

4. Human Resources: One of the SWFs Main Challenges

A survey of 20 SWFs conducted in mid-2008 under the auspices of the IMF by the International Working Group of Sovereign Wealth Funds (IWG) found that a fifth of them were not accountable to a higher authority while three out of five reported to their legislatures through a board chair or minister of finance.[13] A different study, which focused on the SWFs needs for investments expertise and other skills, came to the conclusion that there is plenty of purpose for upgrading their current human resources. With the exception of some entities like Norway's and Singapore's SWFs, at least for the time being Sovereign Wealth Funds are considered to be averagely managed and several are poorly managed. Experts also worry that SWFs are particularly weak in risk control and in internal control procedures. Rogue traders are a serious issue for all investment entities and a major potential problem for sovereign funds.

The west is no stranger to rogue trader experiences, as documented by the fate of Allied Irish Bank's US subsidiary and myriad other cases. There are

---

12 *Financial Times*, 17 October 2007.
13 *Financial Times*, 15 September 2008.

plenty of instances in which, because of scant internal control, traders have taken very speculative positions and lost heavily. In several, though not in all, cases, these traders acted without senior management approval. Internal control and risk management share two prerequisites:

- full top management support;

- first-class human resources.

Today Sovereign Wealth Funds are struggling to attract top-level executives, investment professionals and risk managers to help deploy and control their assets. Headhunters are at work, but they don't seem to meet with unqualified success in hiring some of the most talented people from western private equity outfits and investment banks. Yet, state-backed funds in Asia and the Middle East urgently need:

- financial professionals with experience of western and Asian markets; and

- high profile executives and advisers to bolster their standing and political contacts.

For instance, a news item in the *Financial Times* carried the story that China Investment Corporation (CIC), planned to approach Alan Greenspan, former chairman of the US Federal Reserve Board, to join its international advisory board. CIC has also launched a recruitment website to help itself hire plenty of investment experts and boost its knowledge base.

Other Sovereign Wealth Funds, too, follow this policy. 'Nowadays, the only way to attract good people is by offering big salaries. Everyone uses headhunters – it is all based on price,' said one senior staffer at the Abu Dhabi Investment Authority.[14] For its part, in 2007, the Dubai fund has 75 professionals from more than 20 nationalities and is expected to increase this by 50 per cent by the end of 2008.

Since the brain drain of the mid-1960s from Europe to America, the discovery that brains are a highly-valued asset has stunned governments and industrial leaders, presenting them with complex questions. The realization

14 *Financial Times*, 3 January 2008.

that a modern economy's most important capital is not money, raw materials or equipments but *brains*, has been slow in coming – but it is here to stay.

Provided they can hire, retain and manage some of the best people in finance and investments, by all likelihood SWFs will become the ingredient of a major change in the global economy's weights. A rapidly growing body of opinion is that, should this happen, the big loser in the shift towards dominance by Asian economies will be the United States – a fact of geopolitical importance to which Washington does not seem to be sensitive enough. Nor are all American companies, particularly banks, fully aware of the fact that:

- money, the raw material of capital markets, is today more abundant in Asia and the Middle East;

- but being addicted to that source of easier funds can have dire consequences.

In flagrant violation of the ancient Greek principle on the wisdom of *not* making the same mistake twice, Citigroup lost its bearings (and its chief executive) for the second time in 16 years. In 1991 a private Saudi Arabian investor came to the rescue of Citicorp, which was strapped for cash as a result of an American property downturn and other leveraged trades which had turned sour.

Prince Waleed bin Talal largely owes his place on the world's top rich-list to that investment decision. Repeating the same mistakes of leveraged investments and poor risk management, Citigroup again went to the Middle East cap in hand and on 26 November 2007, the Abu Dhabi Investment Authority replaced Prince Waleed as Citigroup's biggest shareholder:

- paying $7.5 billion for a 4.9 per cent stake, at a hefty 11 per cent interest rate; and

- taking an option to convert its preferred shares into common stock in 2011, at a highly preferential rate.

These have been draconian conditions. The irony of such an investment is that, when it was made, ADIA's money could offset no more than about one third of the presumed writedowns on subprime-related Citigroup positions in the fourth quarter of 2007. Subsequently, the big bank's losses announced in January 2008 again obliged its management to seek capital infusion. Merrill Lynch, Morgan Stanley and other US banks, as well as Switzerland's UBS, have also gone to the SWFs for money they badly needed because their governance left much to be wanted.

While the full story of the descent into the abyss of the world's bigger global banks has still not been written, what is known documents that, in late 2007 and throughout 2008, SWFs' money was poured into financial carcasses. When it dried up, western governments and central banks replaced the SWFs in having throwing good money after bad.

By February 2009, the remaining shadow of the old prestigious Citigroup had received $45 billion of US taxpayers money, and the combined Bank of America/Merrill Lynch another $45 billion. In spite of these and all previous injections, on 20 February 2008 Citigroup's equity was trading at less than $2 (almost becoming a penny stock) and Bank of America's equity sank below $3. Twice, $45 billion of taxpayers money evaporated.

- Some analysts commented that the Troubled Assets Relief Program (TARP) was an American Sovereign Wealth Fund.

- Others said that SWF or not, the Troubled Asset Relief Program had all the characteristics of an enormously expensive failure.

On Wall Street the talk was that one-third or more of the amount invested via the TARP had been lost. People offering this view cited data from the Congressional Budget Office (CBO). More widespread is the view that, because it represents increased Treasury debt on the government's balance sheet, TARP has widely contributing to the US deficit. As unemployment in the US mounted, so did the fury over 'welfare for the banks, and the market' instead of 'for the rest of us'.

5. How to Destroy a Franchise

The developments discussed in Section 4 were not expected. As 2007 came to a close, analysts expressed the opinion that the $7.5 billion that Citigroup borrowed from Abu Dhabi would be a drop in the ocean compared with the amount of money the world's biggest bank needed to stay afloat. This educated guess was further reinforced by the fact that, most unwisely, Citigroup's board declared a dividend for 2007 – albeit one that was slashed by 41 per cent.

- Dividends are paid out of profits, not out of losses; and

- as Citigroup used borrowed money to pay the dividend, several economists wondered how the American supervisory authority allowed this to happen.

A 'dividend' paid out of red ink came as so much more of a surprise as the market knew that Citigroup was desperately looking for new large loans to redress its balance sheet. According to news from Wall Street, in the week of 7 January 2008, China Investment Corporation (CIC), the Sovereign Wealth Fund, had negotiated a major loan with Citigroup, but the deal met with opposition from the Chinese government and was dropped. Four reasons have been given for this negative reaction:

1. the issue was political, with the Chinese government worried about the American governments' reaction;

2. the stock market in Shanghai fell on the news of the projected Chinese SWF's investment;

3. in China itself there was a negative response to it, because the SWF's investment in Blackstone, Morgan Stanley and Barclays – as well as the one to Bear Stearns by Citic – were not profitable;

4. the Chinese government has been working on new strategic investment guidelines which called for diversification of exposure.

Critics said that the new strategic guidelines for investments in Europe, Africa and Latin America followed a pattern whereby the Chinese government could gain political leverage. The same sources also point out that, though not spoken about, there was also another reason why the Chinese government objected to its SWF's investment in Citigroup: Nobody really knows how the credit crunch crisis will unfold and how damaged the big bank's balance sheet will prove to be.

Contrary to China's adverse reaction, other Sovereign Wealth Funds came forward with enough money to satisfy not just one but two American banks who needed it badly. After $8.4 billion in mortgage-related 2007 writedowns, Merrill Lynch said it would issue $6.6 billion in preferred stock to a group that included three longtime investors:

1.   Korean Investment Corporation;

2.   Kuwait Investment Authority; and

3.   Mizuho Financial Group (MFG), Japan's second biggest bank.

Other investors in this latest round of preferred stock include TPG-Axon Capital, the New Jersey Division of Investment, Olayan Group and T. Rowe Price Group (TROW), which has acted on behalf of various clients. The price of the preferred stock was $52.40 a share (equal to three-day average closing price) paying a 9 per cent dividend – better terms than those Citigroup obtained from ADIA in December 2007.[15]

Experts said that so much red ink and so many loans made under draconian conditions destabilized the market position of many big banks. On 1 April 2008, it was announced that UBS, which had lost a cool $18.5 billion in 2007, had again been hit by a loss of another $19 billion from writedowns on credit risks – a torrent of red ink which compounded the pressure on Marcel Ospel, the bank's chairman and former CEO, to get out.

At stake has been nothing less than the big banks franchise and the willingness of foreign capitalists to make investments or lend money. The Dubai sovereign- wealth fund has seen the value of its stake in Och-Ziff, a hedge fund, tumble since the shares were floated in November 2007 and SWFs who invested in Barclays at the maximum price of £7.20 during its failed ABN AMRO bid of 2007,have regretted their move.

According to a contrarian opinion, however, in several cases, the gap in profits and losses was closed by intangible benefits. For instance, China Development Bank viewed its investment in Barclays as a valuable source of commodities expertise, while investments in private equity firms helped the SWFs to screen themselves from scrutiny. Ping An, China's largest insurer, said

---

15 Aimed at covering the investment bank's biggest loss in 93 years, this $6.6 billion infusion of capital, mainly by Asian and Middle Eastern interests, was over and above the $6.2 billion Merrill Lynch borrowed from Singapore's Temasek on 24 December 2007.

   Merrill Lynch, however, continued bleeding and more billions of dollars in writedowns were announced for first quarter of 2008.

that taking a 4.2 per cent stake in Fortis, Belgium's largest bank, provided it with the necessary expertise in bank assurance.

Still, some analysts pose the question: who will finance the big banks if the SWFs lose their appetite, given that the current credit crisis is not going to be over rapidly? A paper presented to the 2008 annual meeting of the American Economic Association (AEA) by Kenneth Rogoff and Carmen Reinhart finds parallels between the subprime mess and 18 previous banking crises in the west. It also identifies factors assisting in prognostication, which should have been used by central bankers and regulators but were not:

- rising home and equity prices;

- acceleration in capital inflows by optimistic foreign investors;

- a rapid build-up of debt; and

- immediately before the storm, an inverted V-path for the economy.

As Rogoff and Reinhart point out, while the export of subprime exposure through securitization has helped in preserving some of the capital of US banks, it has devastated the balance sheet of several poorly managed European banks. Against this backdrop, it is questionable whether the cash infusion by Sovereign Wealth Funds is bad for the wounded banking industry, particularly if one considers the financial market's reactions.[16]

A worst-case scenario, some experts now say, will be that of a further out major negative impact on the American economy, because the loss of global financial leadership will end with the US finding difficult to finance both capital-hungry banking mammoths and its billions of annual current account red ink.[17] This will probably have a severe after-effect on the global economy as a whole, raising the likelihood that the American economy will fall out of control – if the government does not come up with something big to turn it around.

---

16 Some readers may object to putting together big bank financing and current account deficits as being confusing. It is not so. If the American capital markets had retained their past glory, it would have been child's play to finance the recapitalization of big banks. But huge current account deficits and the falling dollar deprived the US capital market of foreign money and opened the way to the SWFs.

17 *The Economist*, 12 January 2008.

6. New Investment Strategies by SWFs

Kenneth Galbraith, the presumed author of the *Iron Mountain Report*, claimed in this small but impressive book that the armaments industry is the flywheel of the economy. With the exceptions of China and Brazil, the large majority of countries with Sovereign Wealth Funds don't have a weapons manufacturing industry. This leads some economists to suggest that in any major downturn governments are likely to use their SWFs as automatic stabilizers, in an effort to reduce downside business cycle risks.

At present, there are no reasons to believe that this will be the case, since the Asian economies sail under favourable winds; but no high times last forever. Should it happen, the resulting repatriation of capital is likely to put the currencies of the SWF-resident countries under great upward pressure. It will also increase global capital mobility and, above all, it will again rebalance wealth worldwide.

The role SWFs might play in the future in terms of currency exchange is not lost on some of them today. In December 2007 it was announced that Brazil had worked to create a Sovereign Wealth Fund with the primary aim of intervening in foreign exchange markets to counter the appreciation of the country's currency. 'It will have the function of reducing the offer of dollars in the market and helping the real to appreciate less,' Guido Mantega, Brazil's Finance Minister, told the *Financial Times*.[18]

Mantega's statement added to the controversy surrounding the fund, which first came to the public eye in October 2007. Under that plan, the new SWF would have drawn on Brazil's foreign reserves, which in 2007 grew to $180 billion. But what sparked a behind-the-scenes dispute between the Finance Ministry and the central bank was its projected intervention in currency markets. Brazilian economists commented that:

- this has been unorthodox; and

- the fund's level of firepower would have no lasting impact on exchange rates.

The term 'unorthodox' has been used by economists because, by a large majority, the goal of Sovereign Wealth Funds is *investments* in the classical

18 *Financial Times*, 10 December 2007.

sense of the word, enhanced by a new strategy: to buy just under 5 per cent of otherwise healthy companies and financial institutions which search to restructure their balance sheet after the silly losses they have suffered by taking inordinate and unwise risks.

A 5 per cent ceiling is not too far from what the equities market considers to be acceptable, and several western analysts are bullish on the support for equity markets from such investors. Part of their calculation is the fact that central banks of Asian and Middle Eastern countries currently control over $5.6 trillion in reserves, which is increasingly transferred into SWFs and helps in recalibrating investment goals.

- Currently, SWFs invest largely in government bonds;

- but investment banks expect that they will restructure their asset allocation, favouring equities.

The fact that Sovereign Wealth Funds have been recently insisting to be paid in high interest rate preferred stock for the loans they make, supports this opinion. According to an estimate by Morgan Stanley which has been widely quoted, from April to December 2007 Sovereign Wealth Funds have poured some $37 billion into mostly western financial institutions, and more is still to come.

This targeted money flow is not making western governments happy. But an article by an economist from the International Monetary Fund (IMF) and a very similar one by the Peterson Institute for International Economics (a newcomer linked to a private equity fund) are of the opposite opinion:[19] that SWFs are nothing for Americans or Europeans to fear. *If* anyone should worry about Sovereign Wealth Funds, the authors say, then it should be the people whose governments are amassing the assets, because they tend 'to be terrible' at managing money that is best left in the hands of private citizens (probably meaning the common citizens of China, Dubai and the rest, who are supposed to be experts in foreign investments).

At the opposite side of such ultra-favourable opinions stands the argument that while there should be 'no fear', it is proper to have a considerable amount

---

19 Simon Johnson, Economic Counsellor and Directir of the IMF's Research Department, *The Rise of Sovereign Wealth Funds*; and Anders Aslund, Peterson Institute for International Economics, *The Truth About Sovereign Wealth Funds*.

of *concern*. Therefore, it is better to plan ahead using 'What If' scenarios rather than calling the fire brigade afterwards. In the last analysis, the wounds of the western economy are self-inflicted and if we learn nothing from the subprimes abyss we will repeat the same mistakes.

This is above all, a principle of sound governance. *If* market players have doubts about whether the debt will be serviced properly, owing to what they perceive to be an increasingly mismanaged economy, *then* they will require higher interest rates for new debt. At every level of society leveraging has the nasty habit of increasing most rapidly, and somebody has to finance it.

Markets can operate effectively only *if* all players, including governments, make credible arrangements for limiting their liabilities and avoiding superleveraging. Only then could financial markets exert disciplinary effect.

- This is not what happens today in the majority of western countries; and

- recent evidence indicates that even big global banks have adopted the policy of swimming in a sea of red ink.

Governments, companies and people – not just hedge funds and private equity funds – are using higher and higher gearing ratios. For instance, a ratio of 20 would mean they borrow 20 times their own capital for consumption or transactions. In some cases, leverage is much higher than that and on a global scale this poses a significant danger to the world's financial systems:

- Long Term Capital Management had a leverage ratio of 340, when it went bankrupt in 1998;[20]

- Bear Stearns, the investment bank, had a leverage of 30 when it hit the wall of huge losses and sold itself for peanuts to J.P. Morgan Chase in 2008.

If superleverage and a growing government debt are bad, disorderly and steady current account deficits are even worse for the countries that have them. There are a lot of secrets about how governments manage their foreign exchange deficits, but the leading thought is they are not particularly concerned about such liabilities. It is *as if* traditionally they have been expecting that somebody

---

20   Merrill Lynch, *Bear Stearns*, 11 January 2008.

else will pick up the bill. In some quarters, Sovereign Wealth Funds are seen as destined to fill that role – but the cost may be forbidding.

7. SWFs of China and Singapore: An Example

Of Singapore's two Sovereign Wealth Funds, GIC is bigger than Temasek, which was one of the early SWFs worldwide. Temasek is watched closely by its peers, particularly in regard to the impact of rising nationalism on sovereign wealth investments and how to manage it, because it:

- no longer seeks controlling interests in companies outside Singapore;

- uses local partners when it makes investments abroad; and

- is sensitive to sentiments that may be aroused by its acquisitions.

Strategically speaking, all three points make sense. Tactically, however, many investments have turned sour, hurting the treasury of the SWF. Admittedly, however, this has been a widespread phenomenon as in 2008 the fortunes of many Sovereign Wealth Funds have wilted.

In February 2009 it was revealed that Temasek Holdings had suffered a 37 per cent fall in the value of its portfolio from $134 billion at the end of March 2008 to $84 billion at end of November 2008. This figure was disclosed by a Singapore government minister in parliament. At the eye of the storm were Temasek high-profile investments in western financial groups, including Merrill Lynch and Barclays, whose share prices have fallen sharply since the investments were made.[21]

It needs no explanation that these were large and poorly timed equity investments. Adding to them the stakes bought in UBS and Citigroup by Singapore's other sovereign fund, GIC, the city-state has bet up to 13 per cent of its GDP on bailing out struggling western banks. Temasek management can

---

21 For instance, it invested $5.8 billion in Merrill Lynch between December 2007 and July 2008. Merrill's share price fell 79 per cent in 2008 before the stock was delisted and the investment bank was taken over by Bank of America. Temasek acquired a stake in Bank of America as share swap in the Merrill deal.

always say that the '37 per cent' drop in dollar terms over the short period of eight months has practically tracked the MSCI world share index.

The decision not to seek controlling interests in investments probably had in its background an Indonesian government ruling in December 2007 penalizing Temasek for monopolizing Indonesia's telecommunications market, even if it only had indirect minority holdings, used the Indonesian government as local partner and its stakes were bought after the Asian financial crises in the late 1990s, when foreign money was most welcome in Indonesia.

Experts suggest that if Temasek's appeal fails, likely penalties include fines and a forced sale of its interest in either Indosat or Telkomsel, both Indonesian telecoms and the country's prized assets. This would follow another embarrassing case of a Temasek investment in a Thai telecommunications company purchased from the family of Thaksin Shinawatra, then prime minister.

The message the reader should retain from these references is that the political risk connected to SWFs' investments in some Asian countries is on the rise. This has not yet happened in any big way in the west, but it is believed that such a reaction may be coming in the near future. As we saw in preceding sections, Asian and Middle East SWF money is still welcome in America to restructure the balance sheet of wounded banks, just a shade below 10 per cent of equity. As 2007 came to a close, these investments stood at:

- 9.9 per cent of equity by China Investment, at Morgan Stanley;

- 9.4 per cent by Singapore's Temasek, at Merrill Lynch;

- 9.0 per cent by Singapore's GIC, at UBS;

- 4.9 per cent by ADIA of Abu Dhabi, plus 4.0 per cent by Al Waleed; a total of 8.9 per cent in Citigroup;

- 3 per cent by China Development Bank and 2 per cent by Temasek; a total of 5 per cent at Barclays;

- 4.18 per cent by China's Pin An Insurance, at Fortis (which ran into trouble); and

- over 2 per cent by Dubai International Financial in Deutsche
  Bank.[22]

For its part, China's Sovereign Wealth Fund does not make only foreign investments. It also gives a hand to needy companies in the home market. As 2007 became 2008, it made a $20 billion capital injection into state-owned China Development Bank ahead of its probable public offering. Singapore's Temasek also makes at-home investments. Among others, it owns Singapore International Airlines.

With $1.4 trillion war chest in foreign-exchange reserves, and this pool reportedly growing by more than $1 billion every day, China casts a giant shadow over the global financial market, above its massive buying of American Treasury bonds. China Investment Corporation first flexed its muscle with the announcement on 21 May 2007 that it would invest $3 billion of its reserves in Blackstone, the American private equity firm. The Blackstone deal did not prove to be successful, but it did stir others who invested money away from prying eyes.

China and its institutions still have much to learn in terms of the riskiness of financial assets. At the end of August 2007, the Bank of China, one of the country's biggest lenders, revealed that it held a $9.6 billion exposure to securities backed by American subprime mortgages – a greatly exposed investment even if this securitized paper was highly rated for the wrong reasons. Subsequently, China's two other large publicly-listed institutions, ICBC and China Construction Bank, disclosed subprime holdings above $1 billion each (see also Chapter 8).

Properly researched and studied, losses can contribute to the learning process, *to help* investors avoiding repeating the same mistake. For the Bank of China, for example, this $9.6 billion was more or less equal to the proceeds from selling in Hong Kong 18 per cent of its shareholders' equity. The Chinese authorities played down the seriousness of the problem, but this did not change the facts. Experts suggested that the reason the Bank of China took such a gamble reflected some of the problems of lack of expertise in managing a big bank's balance sheet, making complex cross-border asset allocation decisions and controlling risk in a rigorous way, to avoid losing the bank.

By contrast, the capital injections made by Sovereign Wealth Funds which are run by managers with experience in the market's swinging doors of risk and

---

22 Statistics by *Il Sole – 24 Ore*, 11 January 2008. Dubai International also made an investment at HSBC in an unspecified amount.

return have strings attached to them. At the end of July 2008, Merrill Lynch said that it had taken steps to shore up its finances with a $8.5 billion share offering. Raising more capital, however, brought the total since December 2007 to over $30 billion, triggering a reset provision that required it to pay $2.5 billion to Temasek, the SWF of Singapore that had invested in an earlier Merrill equity offering (at a higher price) and was pouring another $3.4 billion into the late July 2008 offering.

8. Sovereign Wealth Funds and the Dollar

The supporters suggest that for resource-rich countries it is only normal that the government should establish an agency, such as SWF, that can help limit monetary expansion, inflationary pressures and appreciation of real exchange rate – in spite of large foreign exchange inflows. A currency's strong real appreciation, known as the *Dutch disease*, is frequently a problem as it impairs the domestic economy's international competitiveness outside the commodity sector.

Nor is it unusual, according to supporters, that given their high and increasing wealth as well as mission to promote and diversify the domestic economy, Sovereign Wealth Funds are major players in the international financial market. Hence, this school of thought holds that their activities should tend to have positive effect on markets, to the extent that their longer-term horizon dampens volatility.

Critics answer that it cannot be ruled out that motives underlying SWF investments in the west are political rather than economic, and existing regulations do not suffice to control unwanted financial investments in sensitive areas. According to critics, security-related domains are not the only example of industries where major shareholdings pose intriguing questions and they see a 'nationalization' of private Western industries through the back door as even more frightening.

Effective answers to these worries do not come easily, not only because the issues involved are complex but also (if not mainly) because a subject on which most supporters and critics agree is that the principle of global free movement of capital should not be called into question. Closely related to this is the fact that, without foreign capital inflows by entities reliant on investment opportunities in the US, the dollar would have been shrinking even faster than it is presently.

But while from the American viewpoint the dollar has benefited from inflows of foreign capital to the US, a very weak dollar posed and continues to pose serious questions to SWF management. In the first quarter of 2008, Sovereign Wealth Funds from Asia and the Middle East lost billions of dollars by recapitalizing western banks. Further losses because of the rapid fall in the US currency increase the risk that SWFs will lose their appetite for dollar assets.

From November 2007 to the end of March 2008 Abu Dhabi's implied capital loss on its investment in Citigroup was about $2.5 billion. The December 2007 investment in Merrill Lynch by Temasek of Singapore lost about $600 million, and even that looks a lot healthier than Singapore's GIC, with which an unnamed Saudi investor lost $5.5 billion on their investment in UBS.

Financial analysts also point out that even those SWFs that have not recently loaned billions to distressed banks are hurt because of the sheer volume of their accumulated dollar assets. No wonder, therefore, that there are signs that several foreign investors are losing patience. Some are suggesting they may sell US Treasuries and buy higher-yielding European government debt. Should a rejection of dollar assets become a policy, it will be dangerous for the American economy.

- A short-term risk is that US companies will be confronted by unwillingness of their trading partners to price in dollars and bear currency risk.

- A long-term risk is that the dollar will lose its status as reserve currency, being replaced by a basket of currencies, with the loss of that status resulting in a permanent loss of wealth for America.

It needs no explaining that financial stability is a desirable, indeed fundamental, characteristic that makes up a reserve currency held to protect against unpleasant shocks that may hit one's money and wealth. Stability was also the most important concept underpinning the now defunct Bretton Woods agreement (Chapter 7). If the Fed's aggressive rate cuts unleash sustained inflation or create doubts about the dollar's stability, the pre-eminence of the dollar will be at an end and no one will be more hurt by that than America.

6

Risks and Opportunities in Globalized Financial Markets

1. Financial Markets

Financial markets are *assets markets*, a term generally used to include the notions of *both* assets and liabilities. If the market characteristics of the 1980s, 1990s and first decade of the twenty-first century were to be condensed into just one sentence, this would be that nowadays financial markets deal more in liabilities, particularly securitized liabilities, than in assets.

Money is, of course, underlying both sides of the balance sheet. Once confirmed, transactions result in streams of payments, either immediate or spread out over time. The trading of debt in financial markets enables dealers, investors, intermediaries and other players to place their bets using borrowed money. *Leverage*, however, sees to it that there is really no limit to what one can lose and derivative instruments can build leverage upon leverage in increasingly complex ways.[1]

It would be a mistake to equate the sophistication of financial markets with wisdom, just as one should not confuse complexity with modernity, or agreements made through compromises with completeness. It is unavoidable that there are some serious shortcomings in fast developing financial markets and instruments; the more important revolve around three questions:

- What are the main inputs of economic progress provided by the financial industry?

- Which preconditions must exist so that assumed risk is commensurate with expected benefit?

---

1   D.N. Chorafas, *An Introduction to Derivative Financial Instruments*, McGraw-Hill, New York, 2008.

- What must the regulators require from the different players in terms of exposure control, capital adequacy and liquidity to safeguard the financial system?

The regulators of financial markets have been asking themselves for years if the rapid innovation in financial products and services, especially the securitization of just about every form of liability into a tradable asset, is a good way to spread risk efficiently. Alternatively, does this leave the financial system prone to infrequent but high-impact seismic events to be met with a fire-brigade approach.

Since the third and fourth quarters of 2007, central banks in the US and Europe have lent tens of billions of dollars to restore confidence to debt markets that once handed out cash to all-comers. Suddenly, as the crisis hit, credit became tight or closed down altogether, because banks and institutional lenders had failed to properly price risk and sustain enough liquidity. Underneath all financial innovation and the fancy derivative instruments featuring strange names and acronyms is a dilemma as old as the banking business:

- How to judge if the borrower or the trader is a sound person or entity?

- Is the counterparty creditworthy or is it trying to hide its weaknesses with smoke and mirrors?

Frequently, though not always, the difference between a 'strong' and 'weak' counterparty is made through, respectively, low and high leverage. Gearing is a key reason why mistakes in financial markets, when they happen, can have much larger consequences than when they take place in connection with an economy's physical goods. Losses may cascade across a series of leveraged positions and shake up lenders, many of whom may not even have realized that they were exposed to an inordinate amount of risk.

Added to this scenario is ignorance characterizing some of the financial players, because very few people really know about the many market twists and hidden pockets of exposure that characterize a globalized environment. Another bunch of hurdles facing people entrusted with corporate governance comes from lust, greed, fat bonuses and irrational expectations typically based on disrespect of lessons taught by:

- centuries of banking practice; and

- myriad bankruptcies engineered by assuming an inordinate and unaffordable exposure.

An example is provided by *subprime lending* – which means lending to counter-parties of doubtful creditworthiness. The July/August 2007 subprimes abyss revealed the depth to which lenders had lowered their credit standards. Banks lent too easily by bending the rules of sound credit risk practices, but with every party securitizing and selling credit risk to everyone else (after it had been carved up and repackaged) nobody was sure any longer where the big potential losses lay.

The globalization of financial trades saw to it that plenty of credit risks ended up with counter-parties who least understood what they were getting into. The same is true of market risks. Quite often, the sheer complexity of positions in derivative financial instruments outruns the ability of institutions to manage their exposure, let alone the knowledge of private investors. Sophisticated instruments also see to it that banks become predisposed to take on more risk than they should.

- Derivatives and leverage increase the likely gain and loss from an investment of a given value; and

- the bewildering array of complex instrument mechanics makes it practically impossible to analyze its real value.

In theory, but only in theory, credit ratings agencies and mathematical models help bankers and investors price the risk they are taking, even if they don't quite understand its exact limits, and even if the securities they are buying are scarcely traded. But models reflect the limitations of their makers and users, this statement being true:

- from assumptions and equations employed by model designers;

- to properly taking account of how fast and how far asset prices fall when everyone wants to sell at the same time.

'The people at Goldman Sachs lost a packet when something happened that their computers told them should occur only once every 100 millennia,' said an article in *The Economist*.[2] Under these conditions, it is impossible to estimate gains and losses engineered by events – such as the amount of capital flowing

---

2   *The Economist*, 18 August 2007.

into complex instruments, when the market sentiment may change, how long liquidity lasts, whether the central bank will be taken hostage, and so on.

Because the sustenance of market liquidity and of money flows is never sure, the aftermath of mismanaged exposure hits individual investors, institutions and the banking system as a whole hard. The International Monetary Fund (IMF) has identified 64 banking crises and 79 currency crises since 1970.

- Most were relatively small affairs, national rather than international;

- but over time the risk of international financial breakdown has been rising.

Generalizations about the origin of financial earthquakes are often meaningless because each major crisis has its own causes. The crisis of the subprimes and collateralized debt obligations (CDOs)[3] was promoted by rock-bottom interest rates, irresponsibly low credit standards, a wide securitization of mortgages and misqualification of financial paper in terms of the creditworthiness it represented. The accumulation of such happenings proved that from time to time:

- financial discipline disappears and must be reestablished;

- plenty of embedded interests built up and they should be overcome; and

- the financial system must not only be surprised but also pruned and fine-tuned.

'There's going to be an enormous amount of financial engineering required to redo the national and international financial systems that have grown out of control and are going to have to be put back together,' said Felix Rohatyn, the investment banker. He made this statement not in 2007 but in a 1985 interview he gave to *Time* magazine. 'There are going to have to be people involved in public policy who understand financial structures, and who understand the

---

3   CDOs are complex structured instruments based on pools of debt that have been managed, repackaged and sliced into new products. They can contain a high two-digit number of mortgages or other debt and are allocated fictitious AAA credit ratings based on erroneous guesstimates of default.

relationship between financial structures and the real world. There are lots of people who understand financial structures but who don't understand the real world, and vice versa.'[4]

2. Financial Centres

Financial markets need organized and reliable exchanges typically found in financial centerres. Wall Street and the City of London are well-known and bursting with activity. The same is true of Tokyo, as well as of Frankfurt, Paris, Zurich and other European centers. Globalization, however, is rebalancing securities trading towards Asia with:

- Hong Kong,

- Shanghai,

- Mumbai and

- Dubai

being the most dynamic newcomers.

To keep themselves in the global picture, some of the older financial centres have been recycled to capitalize on niches of the banking industry. These include Geneva in private banking and Zurich in insurance and reinsurance. Others choose to remain financial capitals of big national markets; for example ,Tokyo, Frankfurt, Paris and Sydney. Still others act as gateways to emerging regions, like Singapore, or focus on a few but highly popular trades, like Chicago has done with commodities and derivatives.

Of the traditional financial centres only two, New York and London, have done their best to become truly global on a palette of trades. New York is home to six of the world's 10 largest investment firms and, along with London, outdistances the challengers by a large margin. New York and London, however, have different strengths among the financial products they offer and trade.

- New York focuses on a volume of work which creates huge employment (one in seven New Yorkers works in finance).

---

4   William D. Cohan, *The Last Tycoons*, Doubleday, New York, 2007.

At $33.6 trillion in 2006, a peak year, the *value* of equities traded in New York dwarfs the business done in all other financial centres. In the same year, London traded $7.5 trillion, Tokyo $5.8 trillion and Frankfurt just $2.8 trillion. By contrast, when it comes to *volume* traded in global derivatives, Chicago is at the top with nearly $3 billion, followed by Frankfurt/Zurich and at a distance by New York and London.

●   London tries to be more innovative in finance, with its own brand of fairly light supervision (the result has been Northern Rock). The leaders of London's financial industry say that it surpasses New York in structured finance; handles an impressive 42 per cent of the EU's share of trading new stock listings and in the wholesale side it accounts for nearly a quarter of the world's exports of financial services, against about 40 per cent for all of America's exchanges.

These are the present-day facts, but statistics on both *value* and *volume* will change in the future. The recent past gives a hint. Over the last few years, as investors diversified across asset types and geographic regions, the number of transactions *between* financial centres surged and there have been dislocations. To serve their clients in an able manner global firms are looking for financial centres with:

●   skilled people;

●   ready access to capital;

●   good infrastructure;

●   a rather friendly regulatory environment; and

●   an attractive tax structure for themselves and their clients.

Global firms also demand continued hand-holding, a reason why mergers and acquisitions flourish among exchanges. Beyond this, in a way not dissimilar to the principles prevailing in real estate, the top three criteria for financial centre selection are: location, location and location, followed in fourth place by the fluent use of English, which is the language of global finance.

Additionally, a new and not yet fully appreciated aftermath of the proliferation of global financial centers – yet, one of rapidly growing importance – is that complex new products created in one of them involve assets in another and are sold to investors in a third. Apart of the need for effective any-to-any networking, this is a system:

- which has totally escaped regulatory control; and

- where risk management is incomplete, if not nearly impossible.

Two problems underpin the second point. One is that capital markets have been racing ahead of regulators, which remain concentrated on their national systems in spite of Basel II.[5] As if this was not enough, technology has made regulatory barriers less important to financial players, raising worries –indeed major worries – about the supervisory authorities' ability to know at any given moment the location and magnitude of systemic risk.

The second crucial problem of a systemic nature is the continuously expanding leverage provided by debt markets. 'There is no limit to the amount of money that can be created by the banking system,' said Dr Marriner Eccles, a former chairman of the Federal Reserve, 'but there are facilities and our labor supply, which can be only slowly increased …'[6] (this increase is reflected in the growth of gross domestic product (GDP)).

'More leverage' is no way to grow the GDP. In fact, there exist both philosophical and practical questions regarding high gearing. 'A business like an individual, could remain free only if it kept out of debt,' Eccles was taught by his father, who also instructed his son that '… the West could remain free only if it kept out of debt to the East.'[7] (Compare this to the huge current account deficit of the United States and try to guess possible aftermath of China's $1.4 trillion in foreign exchange.)

Moreover, due to mounting leverage the *virtual economy* and the *physical economy* have become unstuck. *If* the support that the physical economy provides lags way behind the virtual economy's commitments, *then* the virtual economy will turn into a bubble, as it did in July/August 2007. Three numbers tell the state of the international financial system in the 2000 to 2007 timeframe just prior to the superbubble:

1. the global gross domestic product increased by a weighted 5 per cent per year, on average;

5   D.N. Chorafas, *Economic Capital Allocation with Basle II. Cost and Benefit Analysis*, Butterworth-Heinemann, London and Boston, 2004.
6   William Greider, *The Secrets of the Temple*, Touchstone/Simon and Schuster, New York, 1987.
7   Greider, *The Secrets of the Temple*.

2.   to sustain the equity value of companies, financial markets expected a 15 per cent annual return, way above global GDP growth;

3.   the money supply measure M3 (see Chapter 7) increases by 15 per cent or more annually, against 4.5 per cent projected by the G10 central banks. The difference is leverage, inflation and inflation potential.

Essentially, the rapid rise in money supply is a way of trying to reconcile the difference in the statistics of the first two points. This sort of 'filling the gap' by means of the printing press can happen over the short run, but in the longer term the steady and growing increase in money supply leads to serious mismatches between:

*   liquid debt; and

*   liquid assets.

This has been seen in the sequel to the subprime crisis of 2007, when the European Central Bank and the Fed found themselves obliged to inject liquidity into the market to avert a credit market crisis turning into a global debacle. Also known as *emergency liquidity assistance* (ELA), such liquidity injection is achieved by allowing individual banks to borrow from the monetary institution against adequate collateral. (And as the banks run out of adequate collateral, the Fed and ECB allowed them to deposit any kind of garbage financial paper, to avoid a severe liquidity crisis.)

Even the practice of adequate collateral is relatively new, although the idea behind it is not. In *Lombard Street* (1872), Walter Bagehot urged the Bank of England to stave off a panic by lending quickly, freely and readily – to any bank that could offer good securities as collateral, but at a penalty rate of interest. At the time, this was criticized as the most mischievous doctrine ever broached in the monetary or banking world. Today (save for the penalty rate) Bagehot's theory has become conventional wisdom among central banks.

3. Market Liquidity

Liquidity refers to an entity's ability to meet its current financial obligations as they become due. Therefore, liquidity is a relative concept having to do with the size and frequency of liabilities and with current assets which should (presumably) provide the source of funds to confront assumed obligations in a timely manner. In contrast, *solvency* refers to a person's or entity's ability to meet interest cost, repayment schedules and other obligations in the longer term. The most important elements in judging a company's solvency are:

- debt capital; and

- equity capital.

Debt capital is a different name for liabilities, particularly those of the medium to longer term. Failure to meet debt capital requirements usually leads creditors to take legal action which may force the entity into bankruptcy. *Equity capital* is much less risky to the firm, because shareholders receive dividends only at the discretion of the board, and equity is always at the front line in fulfilling assumed financial obligations.

As this brief description demonstrates, liquidity and solvency are not the same thing except that, in crisis an illiquid entity may become insolvent. Additionally there exist different types of liquidity, while the term itself is often used loosely, making it difficult to disentangle the precise concept meant in each particular case. Macroeconomic theory offers at least two different notions.

1.   *Monetary liquidity* relates to the quantity of liquid assets in the economy, typically connected to the level of interest rates.

2.   *Market liquidity* is generally seen as a measure of the ability of market players to undertake securities transactions without triggering large changes in their prices.

These definitions go beyond the notion of liquidity connected to an entity and they are generally considered as distinct, although they do have a rather complex relationship. Therefore, it is important to gauge patterns under all definitions of liquidity, because all three have an aftermath for markets, market players and the economy as a whole.

Monetary liquidity can exist at country and global level. In open markets with free movement of capital, some of the excess monetary liquidity in one market moves across borders through different financial transactions, the *carry trade* being an example. International capital flows have increased substantially on account of both global liquidity and wider financial imbalances. Excess savings relative to investment in some emerging market and oil-exporting economies led to:

- the accumulation of very large reserves of foreign currency-denominated assets in these markets; and

- the development of part of these reserves to purchase substantial amounts of assets in financial markets of developed economies (see Chapter 5 on SWF).

But high monetary liquidity has also negatives, inflationary pressures being an example. For financial stability reasons, reserve banks want to rein in monetary liquidity (as briefly mentioned in section 1). An assessment of the durability of monetary liquidity, and by extension of market liquidity, requires a good understanding of its sources. One possible major source is money supply (Chapter 7); another is the banks and other financial institutions.

From 2003/2004 to 2007 western banks, particularly American, did their best to prove that Dr Marriner Eccles was right when he said in the 1930s that there were no limits to the amount of money the banking system could create (see section 2). Banks did so through a (nearly) perpetual motion machine known as the *Originate and Distribute* (O&D) business model whereby:

- they extend a large amount of poorly researched loans;

- distribute much of the underlying credit risk through credit risk transfer (CRT) instruments; and

- follow a strategy of issuing more loans, having been relieved of reserve requirements imposed by regulators for loans they securitized (a loophole).

This way, the market of credit derivatives became wide. During 2003 to 2008 the global amount outstanding of credit default swaps (CDS)[8] multiplied more than tenfold – to a present level of about $60 trillion. Geared and risky

---

8   Theoretically, a CDS is an insurance-like contract promising to cover losses on a security in the event of a default. It does so by separating credit risk from other risks, like interest rates. Practically, a CDS is toxic waste, particularly when defaults are rising; it is also a highly geared instrument which can go through 15 or 20 trades.

products were sold to a heterogeneous groups of investors with deep pockets and a large amount of tolerance to growing exposure.

One way of looking at credit risk transfer and non-regulated instruments such as credit default swaps is that, while they provide a common ground between monetary liquidity and market liquidity, they also have the potential to tear apart the financial fabric. Their market's depth greatly affects asset prices but not necessarily the compensation required for assuming risk.

From late 2003 to the beginning of 2007, in the go-ahead years of the financial industry, credit default swaps were credited for engineering low market liquidity risk premiums because they exhibited low credit spreads in an environment of low market volatility. By contrast, in 2009, because defaults are rapidly rising, credit default swaps have become a sword of Damocles over the head of the western financial system.

One of the signs often observed with liquid markets is their relatively mild reaction to different events for which low liquidity could have triggered broad price adjustments. Yet, vulnerabilities had existed, even if no attention was paid to them. For instance:

- slippages in risk assessment standards, particularly in credit risk; and

- a growing tendency by bankers and investors to take too much credit risk and market risk, without having studied *a priori* limits and consequences.

It is indeed surprising that highly paid people failed to appreciate that market liquidity can vanish abruptly while investor uncertainty and, therefore, risk aversion rises. This led to significant 'unexpected' portfolio losses which hit a long list of banks. A sudden and sharp reduction in market liquidity taps deeply into newly devised structures of finance and nobody can say the worst is definitely over, just as nobody really knows who will bear what losses from an eventual lack of liquidity. For instance:

- it is fairly well known that tighter lending standards will oblige borrowers to raise more capital, triggering more sales in stockmarkets;

- it is fairly unknown how messy the inevitable bankruptcies will turn out to be as change in the financial environment takes place.

Clearly, banks faced heightened counter-party risks as people, companies or other entities to whom they had extended credit were thrown into financial distress. But how likely was the collapse of one, two or three big players, or of a group of medium-sized ones that were particularly active in the protection-selling side of the credit risk transfer market? The answer is far from certain because as the 2007 and 2008 events demonstrated, the whole process of credit protection turned around and hit on the head the credit derivatives originators. There is no place to hide in a globalized market.

4. The Central Banks' Liquidity Control

The statement was made in the preceding section that while by definition liquidity and solvency are two different concepts, under conditions of market stress such as panics, a huge drop in stock market values or a credit risk-generated earthquake, they tend to merge. Gerard Corrigan pointed this out to Alan Greenspan when in October 1987 the New York stock market descended into the abyss (a 14.5 standard deviation event). Illiquidity could morph into insolvency, hence the decision by the New York Fed to lend to banks which faced immediate illiquidity problems.

Twenty years later, central banks of the US and Euroland followed Corrigan's advice. In three days – Thursday, Friday and Monday 9–13 August 2007 – the European Central Bank (ECB, the first to respond to the market liquidity crisis) injected 200 billion euros to avoid credit institutions being torn apart because of illiquidity.[9] The objective of liquidity injection was to assure that:

- the interbank market, which acts as the red blood cells of the financial system by moving cash to where it is most needed, continued to perform its functions.[10]

To get the banking system moving again from August 2007 until the end of April 2008, the ECB, Federal Reserve (and to lesser extent, the Bank of

---

9   The ECB has always proved to be proactive. For instance, at the time of the Y2K rollover when interbank liquidity was squeezed ahead of the new millennium, the ECB had injected funds equaling 15 per cent of the money supply.
10   Apart from credit, the interbank market defines the price that banks charge each other for short-term lending.

England) injected a guestimated $1 trillion. But the banking system still had not resumed its functions as intermediary because the transmission mechanism of the monetary system had been impaired. Therefore, central banks and governments did not manage to get that liquidity down to the consumer and ease the servicing of mortgages. In the United States and Britain:

- The central banks brought down interest rates.

- By contrast, mortgage rates went up.

At the same time, continuous injection of liquidity feeds the flames of inflation. The market responded negatively to an optimistic forecast by the Federal Reserve and the US government that inflation would subside. Inflation is going up and governments find it increasingly difficult to justify interest rate reductions since inflation has escaped their control.

In other terms, while something had to be done to relieve the stress of the severe credit crisis, a major liquidity injection is not a move without risks, particularly since from 2002 until mid-2007 most major central banks' monetary policies were considered to be accommodative. Decisions about injecting liquidity are never easy, because central banks must also to look after their other two main functions:

1.   assurance of financial stability; and

2.   promotion of price stability in their jurisdiction.

Experts said that when, in July/August 2007, the sky was falling, injecting liquidity had much to do with market psychology which had turned negative almost overnight. On 9 and 10 August 2007, the rates commercial banks charged each other for overnight borrowing spiked in both Europe and the US:

- in America the rate hit almost 6 per cent, well above the Fed's target of 5.25 per cent;

- in Euroland, money market rates peaked briefly at 4.7 per cent, also sharply above the benchmark of 4 per cent.

With this, central bankers and politicians found themselves in the middle of a debate about whether it was better to continue increasing the euro's interest rate to stop inflation or to lower the interest rate to please the overleveraged market.

To their credit, in Euroland (and up to a point in Britain) the central bankers stood firm, while politicians bent to the temptation to send the value of money into the abyss. According to several opinions, the reason the ECB was the first to inject liquidity, and to do so to the tune of euro 200 billion ($300 billion) is that some European financial institutions had a major exposure to the American subprimes, massively bought by their incapable managers.

Mid-September 2007, as the credit crisis was gaining momentum, Hank Paulson, the US Treasury Secretary, warned that reverberations from the turmoil in the credit markets caused by defaults in Amercia's subprime mortgage market would be felt for some months. He also reiterated there were no easy fixes to shore up confidence,[11] which is true of all crises. Several financial experts wondered what would happen with large hedge funds which are largely unregulated and geared up, but in the end hedge funds proved to be better managed than big banks.

On 11 July 2007 Anthony Ryan, Assistant Secretary for Financial Markets at US Treasury, stated that hedge funds play major part in perpetuating dangers embedded in leveraged debt. Addressing the Managed Funds Association's Forum 2007, in Chicago, he warned about concentrating risk in certain financial industries.[12] A short time later at a hearing of the House Financial Services Committee, chairman Barney Frank pressed Hank Paulson on whether Ryan's speech had meant that the Treasury was now waiting for a systemic shock to hit the financial markets.

For their part, central bankers were particularly worried about concentrated exposure to collateralized debt obligations, especially CDOs filled with asset-backed securities such as US subprime mortgages. Mid-2007 the total US mortgage market stood at $10 trillion, with subprimes $1.3 trillion and the so-called Alt-As[13] another $1 trillion or more.

---

11 *The Economist*, 15 September 2007.
12 Ryan cited the fact that hedge funds account for 30 to 60 per cent of all trading activity, depending on the asset class and instrument. He also pointed out that the surge in liquidity has brought down lending standards, which is a generally held opinion.
13 'Alternative As' is a misnomer. They represent not an A credit rating but blue sky credit evaluations based on what the borrower declares to have as assets. Research in October 2007 found that 66 per cent of these borrowers had lied in a big way.

(The reader should notice that the risk pattern is not the same in the US and in Europe. Europe's exposure is less about asset-backed securities (ABS), which are largely mortgages, but it involves a concentration of lending to corporates, the bulk through collateralized loan obligations (CLOs), as well as lending to small and medium-sized companies (SME). This, too, is a concentration and any concentration is a negative (see section 5).)

One of the important after-effects of mid-August 2007 events was that they made Basel II, the new capital adequacy framework by the Basel Committee on Banking Supervision, obsolete at the very moment it began to be implemented. The lesson from overexposure to risky instruments like subprimes and CDOs, CDSs and other derivatives is that capital adequacy and liquidity are put way down the list of priorities, even if they are most vital to a sound banking system.

Therefore, not only capital adequacy but also liquidity should steadily be reported to regulators by each institution; and liquidity must be watched as carefully as solvency. This is not just a one-off duty, but a steady one to be done intraday, because liquidity changes all the time. Moreover, board members and the CEO should carry responsibility both individually and collectively for assumed inordinate liquidity risks by the bank.

The goal must be to ensure that supervised entities always have sufficient liquidity to meet their liabilities when due, without compromising their ability to respond quickly to strategic opportunities and without bringing themselves to the edge of the abyss. This goal must be extended to concentrations of liquidity exposure whether these exist in national markets or in the global financial market – a tough call.

5. The Globalization of Concentration Risk

Concentration risk in the banking industry identifies the exposure arising from a skew distribution of money and exposure in deals with counter-parties – whether these are in loans, trading or other business relationships. It also identifies the exposure arising from a concentration in geographic regions, industry sectors or other selection criteria which could possibly generate losses large enough to negatively affect a bank's liquidity and solvency.

The establishment of *credit limits* is the most widespread method for restricting concentration on individual counter-parties, industry sectors and regions/countries. It should, however, be appreciated that credit and market exposure limits are established not only for the above purpose, but also to provide a quantitative expression of a bank's strategic plan; – two birds cannot be hit with one stone.

For the market as a whole, concentration risk can lead to systemic risk endangering financial stability through economic disruptions affecting big banks, countries, regions, or the global economy. Many of the concentration risk reasons found in a national market are encountered as well in the global financial market, but magnified. Some of the background reasons are:

- the banks' senior management tends to be remote from the day-to-day reality of the markets in which the institution operates, even if managers travel for business most of the time;

- fairly often reports received at headquarters from foreign operations are neither objective nor precise on developing industry, sector, and country (or regional) concentrations;

- the trend among major credit institutions to follow their clients abroad increases single-name risk (more on this later); and

- credit institutions' internal control is not up to standard, while auditing misses much of the fine print, particularly with accounts connected to international operations.

Many global banks think, or at least say, that these reasons are irrelevant to them because they are diversified. However, over the last three decades a significant number of banking crises have arisen from increased concentration risk, disproving the diversification hypothesis. The problem is that no generally accepted standards and methods for risk-sensitive treatment of concentrations exist, because there may be 100 reasons behind them, making fun of the fact:

- many banks proudly herald their diversification; and

- apply low risk correlation *as if* such diversification was indeed highly effective.

Multiple concentrations are not unheard of. For instance, an institution's portfolio may be characterized not only by a concentration of borrowers, but also by a concentration of counter-parties in trading, of exposures in a particular currency, to certain types of collateral such as equitie, and of exposure to collateral providers and guarantors. Taken together these events lead to magnified concentration risk.

Concentrations may happen in assets and liabilities, leveraged debt, new versions of financial instruments (like securitized subprimes), refinancing similar types of projects, and more. In the past, such concentrations were considered to belong to a bank's general liquidity risk; today, not only has their impact increased but also they extend all the way to solvency risk.

The control of concentration risk is complex inasmuch as some credit risk concentrations may be required as part of a bank's business strategy. Mortgage banks are examples of specialized institutions which deliberately undertake credit concentrations in regard to the mortgage market and certain types of clients. For their part, investment banks specialize in derivative instruments concentrations – or even on certain types of derivatives leading to market risk concentration.

There is also the case of dual credit-and-market risk concentrations. Take as an example risks arising from a concentration of exposure to companies connected with one another through ownership of bilateral business relations. Some of these companies use the borrowed money for trading purposes, including trading with the lender. In the event of default on the part of one of the borrowers, contagion effects may propagate through lending and trading channels:

- among the enterprises in the group; and

- between these enterprises and the lender.

No wonder, therefore, that concentrations are one of the regulators' worries. The Basel II capital adequacy framework brings attention to them in respect of individual collateral providers as well as certain kinds of collateral (as a further risk category). Because they have an impact in the event of default, Basel II promotes model-based approaches to measuring such risk.

Model-based experimentation can be helpful but, as explained in connection to other issues, the problem with most models is that they have not been tested under real life crisis conditions. In fact, in the vast domain of house mortgages the nearest thing to such test came in July/August 2007 with the aftermath of the subprime crisis and disappearance of market liquidity.

- The results have not been convincing about the models' power in revealing the level of assumed exposure; and

- quite often, the models' limitations are the result of deliberate decisions made to permit greater leverage.

Avoidance of model complexity also plays a role. For instance, the Asymptotic Single Risk Factor (ASRF) model (which also serves in Basel II's Internal Ratings-Based (IRB) approaches), does not take into account the firm-specific risk arising from a concentration of single-name exposure. Because of this, a portfolio's overall risk is usually underestimated.

(To correct this shortcoming some experts suggest using the so-called *granularity adjustment*, calculated as the difference between unexpected loss in the real life portfolio and in a theoretical infinitely granular portfolio with the same or similar risk characteristics. This approach, however, is based on subjective assumptions and it is not foolproof.)

Recently new and little-known financial products are also employed as means of managing concentration risk. An often-used example is portfolio diversification through the securitization of loans, mortgages and other receivables. The result has been the 2007–2009 hecatomb characterized by credit risk, banking risk, credit rating risk and liquidity risk in one go. What this approach forgets is that:

- *if* concentration risk is to be limited effectively;

- *then* it must first be measured adequately, and this is not always properly done, if it is done at all.

Credit portfolios often exhibit concentration to which inadequate attention is paid, such as certain industry sectors, emerging countries or regions. Commercial credit risk models tend to measure different types of sectoral concentrations, but there exist biases, particularly when credit concentration in industry sectors is a driver of corporate and business loans. Hence the inducement to underestimate concentration risk arising from:

- credit dependencies between firms; and

- common sector affiliations, often influenced by the prevailing economic environment in a given business domain.

Generalizations are not helpful. In the European Union, for instance, nearly every country has specific industry sectors with risk concentrations. In Germany and Belgium, this is commercial services and supplies; in Spain it is capital and consumer discretionary goods. Other industry sectors generally found in classifications are utilities, energy, telecommunications, information technology, health care, consumer staples, transportation, materials and capital goods.

(Multi-factor models are often employed to determine the total risk of a credit portfolio, taking into account single-name and industry sector concentration. But they typically consider only default risk, rather than the more complex factor of rating migrations. Also, each borrower is often assigned to one industry sector, which is in itself an approximation.)

The analysis of regional concentration is, moreover, blurred by the attraction of emerging markets, leading to underestimates of concentration exposure. Risks resulting from regional concentration are different from those arising from industry sector concentration, including contagion effects. The most important country risks lie in the:

- economic;

- social;

- legal; and

- political environment of a particular country.

Modelling regional and country concentration requires the mapping of complex interdependencies. Because of this, and of the fact that individual components of country risk are difficult to quantify, country risk is often condensed into a single factor of exposure by means of some magic. This practice weakens the power of the model by increasing the likelihood of model risk.

6. The Difficulty of Distinguishing Bankers from Speculators

By April 2008, the collapse of the housing bubble in the United States had mutated into a global phenomenon, with real estate prices down from the Irish countryside and Spanish coastal areas to the Baltic shore and even parts of India.[14] A global slowdown which started with the subprimes mess became a cataclysm swallowing homes and jobs. It is therefore most interesting to know who engineered all that – bankers, gamblers or speculators.

In his book *My Own Story*, Bernard M. Baruch quotes Sir Ernest Cassell, private banker to King Edward VI, who once said: 'When as a young and unknown man I started to be successful I was referred to as a gambler. My operations increased in scope and volume. Then I was known as a speculator. The sphere of my activities continued to expand and presently I was known as a banker. Actually I had been doing the same thing all the time.'[15]

Yes, but this is not the general case; or, putting it in a different way, some bankers are more controversial than others in what they do and the way they do it. An example is John Law, the Scottish banker widely credited (or debited) with having created, together with like-minded Duke of Orleans, Regent of France (while Louis XV was an infant), the Great Mississippi Bubble of 1719.[16]

It all started with Banque Royale and Law's use of paper money (originally a Chinese invention), which sent the French economy into a speculative mania leading to hyper-inflation. As the gold backing the legal tender became less and less in relation to the Banque Royale's massive printing of money, Law and the Regent spread the news that there were mountains of pure gold in the Louisiana Territory (which then belonged to France) and Mississippi River.

The bankers who sliced, diced, securitized and sold the subprimes really invented nothing new in terms of financing swindling. They just applied John Law's recipe. That's also what the King of England did with the South Sea Chartered Company.[17] This was a huge speculation on British government debt (a forerunner of privatization and securitization), ending in a bubble which grew and burst in the short span between April and October 1720.

- The formation of the South Sea Company to raise money to finance British debt was originally considered a brilliant solution.

---

14 *International Herald Tribune*, 14 April 2008.
15 Bernard M. Baruch, *Baruch. My Own Story*, Henry Holt, New York, 1957.
16 Preceded by the Dutch Tulip Bubble of early seventeenth century.
17 At the time three investments were listed at the London Stock Exchange: Bank of England, East India Company and South Sea Company.

- In 1711 the company, whose assets were imaginary, received a royal warrant and King George I himself became the South Sea Company's governor.

After the crash, it was said in the House of Commons that Parliament should declare the South Sea Company directors guilty of parricide and subject them to the old Roman punishment for that transgression: to be sewn into sacks, each with a monkey and a snake, and drowned.[18] Why twenty-first century swindlers should be given a break and a golden parachute is one of the mysteries of the most recent crisis.

(It is an interesting hindsight that the British monarchy was involved in the scheme, along with most of Parliament and thousands of investors, who were wiped out. Among others, Sir Isaac Newton, the physicist, lost a packet. At the time, Newton was Master of the Mint (equivalent to governor of the Bank of England).)

In the years between WWI and WWII the model for a banker and speculator was Sweden's Ivar Kreuger, the king of match monopolies (who ended by committing suicide), who for some time was considered to be his country's national treasure.[19] In a 15-year career, however, he was estimated to have burned through $400 million of his investors' money (a big sum in the 1930s). Robert Shaplen wrote a book about him: *Kreuger: Genius and Swindler* (1960).

The twenty-first century's financial swindlers have been those who engineered the banking industry's subprime bubble of 2007–2009. One of the ironies of the first decade of this century is that outside banking and finance, companies expanded with caution, leaving them lean. As a result of this cautious strategy, many businesses, particularly American firms,

- do not have excess production capacity, bloated payrolls, or heavy inventories;

- therefore they have been better able to weather the credit crunch which followed the subprimes crisis.

Conversely, banking industry players, and most specifically the big banks, have been badly hurt. The events of 2003–2007 prove for one more time that

---

18 Robert Beckman, *Crushes*, Grafton/Collins, London, 1988.
19 *The Economist*, 22 December 2007.

the expansion of credit and rise of speculation go hand-in-hand. There are also some disturbing similarities between previous events and the subprimes.

- the 1719 Mississippi Bubble was engineered by John Law, the French Royal Bank and the Regent's lust for money;

- the 1720s South Sea Bubble was a comet that crossed the financial skies as Britain's budget skyrocketed and Chancellor Lawson sought a way to avoid further taxation;

- the subprimes bubble and credit crunch of 2007–2009 was set in motion by easy money and absence of bank supervision by Greenspan's Fed and the 'king' of the United States,[20] with the active participation of most global big banks.

An article in *EIR* by Washington Irving questioned whether any resemblance between John Law and Alan Greenspan was purely incidental or whether the situations in France in 1719 and in the United States in 2007 resembled one another more closely. The basic curiously common element between the Mississippi Bubble and the Housing Bubble was *phantom profits*.

7. Who is Responsible: Capitalism or Human Nature?

Capitalism did not exist, indeed even its present-day concept was unknown, in the early seventeenth century when the Regent of France created the Mississippi Bubble and the King of England the South Sea Bubble. By contrast, capitalism's excesses and the mistaken notion that markets correct their own mistakes have been at the origin of the housing subprimes bubble of 2007 and of the banking, credit, liquidity and confidence crises it brought along.

Therefore, many have appreciated the headline news that, in its mid-April 2008 meeting in Washington, the Group of Seven (G7) vowed to 'soften capitalism'.[21] But the substance has been missing because this headline is empty words, not too different from the fake profit figures which shook investors' confidence in the wake of the 2007–2009 market upheaval. The swindle went

---

20 When Jeb Bush, governor of Florida and brother of the then US president visited Spain he was received by the Prime Minister whom he reportedly addressed as 'Mr President of Spain'. Rumour has it that at the end of an interview King Juan Carlos asked him to convey his best regards to 'his brother, King of the United States'.

21 A headline in the *International Herald Tribune*, 14 April 2008.

like that. During the housing boom credit institutions aggressively sold risky adjustable rate mortgages (ARMs). Under the terms of those loans:

- borrowers paid less than the total interest owed each month;

- but lenders reported the full amount of interest as income, by adding the shortfall to the borrower's outstanding balance.

By exploiting an accounting loophole, banks recorded earnings up-front from mortgage-backed securities (MBS) they created and sold to investors. The trick is known as *gain on sale*. A lender bundles together a group of mortgages valued at, say, $25 million. Over the life of the bond – which can be as long as 30 years – the bank will collect up to $50 million in cash flows from that security.

The difference comes from compound interest, servicing rights and other payments. In reality, however, that money is still pie in the sky even if the bank counts the $50 million as income once the security is sold. This is at the edge of legality and it is deprived of good sense because everyone knows that the bank will not really receive those payments for years to come; it is a controversial practice but not totally illegal.

Another trick popular among banks in the housing bubble years is a category of on-balance sheet mortgages called *loans held for investment*. Exploiting another loophole lenders largely put loans they made to homeowners or bought from other lenders and brokers under that special clause until investment banks purchased and securitized them. Under Basel II's marking to market, the value on those loans must reflect the current market conditions which are very poor, but 'held for investment' escapes that clause.

Subjective judgement continued exploiting this loophole even after the housing market crash, because banks don't necessarily have to mark down the value of those loans if they consider the losses temporary rather than permanent. That leaves plenty of room for cooking the books – a practice that would have made John Law, Ivar Kreuger and Bernard Madoff very proud.

Every speculative financial bubble in history has been promoted by excesses and loopholes, particularly in lending. Current examples are not only the housing bubble with its subprimes, 'no doc', and 'Alt-A' mortgages, but also a long list of other substandard lending practices including huge loans for buy-outs and rapid leveraging of personal credit – a policy based on the misguided notion that:

- leveraging is the way to riches;[22] and

- 'this' or 'that' asset value would indefinitely appreciate, which is definitely untrue.

Steady leveraging is the avenue leading to crises and inflation, not to greater wealth. In the words of Bernard Baruch: 'If the government is really bent on protecting the public's earnings, it should begin at home with the purchasing power of the dollar. During World War II millions of families were persuaded to invest in US savings bonds as the patriotic thing to do. These people have seen the value of their savings slashed by the lowered purchasing power of the dollar, while others who did not heed these patriotic appeals have profited. If any company listed on the Stock Exchange had engaged in equivalent financial practices, its directors would be facing prosecution by the SEC.'[23]

- In the most recent financial crisis, while the few profited at the expense of the many, the governments saw nothing, heard nothing and thought of nothing.

- In the background of the bankers' disregard for credit risk and the subprimes' folly has been a roster of mistaken bets combined with king-sized bonuses.

- In the foreground, there is a torrent of financial losses obliging commercial and investment banks to sell their equity to Sovereign Wealth Funds (Chapter 5) cheaply, to get urgently-needed capital.

These are the facts. Their interpretation, and most particularly the kind of measures that need to be taken to come out of the long depressing tunnel, invite a whole spectrum of opinions. While it is unavoidable that the reputation for competence of current rulers is sorely strained, the remedies proposed by these opinions vary widely.

---

22 When he was chairman of the Federal Reserve, Alan Greenspan used to say that business had nothing to fear from leveraging because the Fed had lots of money and would rush to its rescue. This is another statement which, to put it mildly, could be made by speculators but not by central bankers.

23 Bertrand M. Baruch, idem.

Many will see the coming second Great Depression as the condemnation of capitalism and of everything it stands for. The irony is that capitalism's most severe critics belong to two quite different populations: the far left and the extreme right. What the two have in common is that in the twentieth century – after enslaving huge numbers of human beings – their national experiments proved to be singularly inept.[24]

At the basic level, the case is one of democracy and its weaknesses versus dictatorship and its vices. In her book *The Roman Way*, Edith Hamilton put the transition from democracy to autocracy and its after-effects into perspective. It did not escape her keen vision that all law is an empty form unless the moral feeling of the people is behind it. To explain her thesis, Hamilton has underlined the contrast between two civilizations.

> *'Harmony said the (ancient) Athenian. Freedom, because the good life was in conformity with a man's innermost desires.*
>
> *Discipline, said the Roman. Careful regulation, because the good life must be imposed upon human nature that desired evil.'*[25]

But even in the Roman way there existed huge differences in behaviour and in politics. In the last decades of the Republic, at the time of Cicero, Caesar and Pompei, the citizen body could not cope with its own corruption and civil wars were devastating – even when compared to the 30-year Peloponnesian War which destroyed ancient Greece (like the second 30-year Peloponnesian-type Great War of 1914–1945, which destroyed Europe).

That frightful time in Roman history had to be brought to an end and its resolution brought in the dictatorship of the Roman empire, with all the responsibility and all power to regulate everything in the state put in the hands of Octavius (Augustus) and the emperors who succeeded him. This led to the most irresponsible despotism the ancient world had seen. And let's not forget either that the first banking crisis ever came under Tiberius – hand-picked by Augustus to follow him onto the imperial throne.

Is this what we would like to see repeated? I doubt it. But nor would we like to have people bent on looting and supervisors with muddled thinking in

---

24 This is true of all the *isms*: socialism, fascism, national socialism, communism and the rest of them.
25 Edith Hamilton, *The Roman Way*, W.W. Norton, New York, 1932.

7

Monetary Policy in a Global Economy

1. Responsibility for Monetary Policy: The Fed in August 2007

In every jurisdiction, the system of laws constitutes a structural frame of reference, as well as of human relations, which reflects not only order but also meaningful continuity while keeping open the possibility of adaptation and change. A similar statement can be made of monetary policy: while it is setting a line of conduct in money supply and market liquidity, it is also subject to continuous revisions as:

- the factors whose order is being targeted change; and

- novel economic and financial events appear, calling for a new, better adapted set of rules.

The way a study by the Deutsche Bundesbank has it: '…the significance of the globalization process for monetary policy has come increasingly under the spotlight. There are two issues at play here: the influence of global factors on price developments – and thus on the monetary policy target – as well as the implications of globalization for the transmission of monetary policy.'[1]

Within the time horizon of monetary policy, which is practically for the medium term, central bankers confront several questions: are risks to price stability on the increase? Are challenges relating to the domestic side or to global economic developments also increasing? Is monetary and credit growth getting out of hand? Is liquidity disappearing because of a crisis? What's the best timing of corrective measures?

---

1   Deutsche Bundesbank, Monthly Report, October 2007.

To answer these questions in a factual and documented manner, central bankers need to monitor all developments closely. This must be done in a way able to assure that the market is not deprived of liquidity, while at the same time over the medium term risks to price stability are kept under control. It is not easy to achieve such balance. The task requires:

- monitoring and measuring;

- using both experience and experimentation;

- looking several years ahead; and

- acting in a firm and timely manner.

Attention must also be paid to the link between monetary policy and fiscal policy, because inflation is primarily created both by government deficits and by excessive money supply. Hence facts and figures about domestic deficits and current account balances are most important to central bankers who labour to regulate the supply of money. This is done at two levels:

1.   increasing or decreasing the monetary base, the former being known as injecting liquidity to the market (next section); and

2.   changing the velocity of the circulation of money, through interest rates and reserve requirements for banks.

Sometimes, particularly when the central bank wants to fight inflation, interest rates are taken sky high. This happened in the early 1980s when Dr Paul Volcker, then chairman of the Federal Reserve, decided to purge a high rate of inflation out of the economic and financial system of the United States. Under Alan Greenspan and Ben Bernanke, however, inflation came back to the American economy through the main door opened by the Fed policy.

Like any other important act, the purging of inflation requires tough decisions – not just words. Nobody is fooling a free market. In the medium to longer run, countries with fast monetary growth have experienced higher inflation. What many politicians and governments don't appreciate is that:

- by paying little attention to well-balances monetary policies they penalize the poor;

- as cannot be said too often, inflation is the taxation of those who are less well off in economic terms.

Shortly after the subprimes bubble the Fed rode to the rescue of the financial market by injecting liquidity and cutting the discount rate through giant steps in basis points. Just like the European Central Bank, the Federal Reserve faced a moral dilemma 'Cut rates now or let investors take more pain...'. The ECB chose the latter course; the Fed swamped interest rates.

While these events took place, the market raced ahead of central banks by applying wider credit spreads which materially increased the cost of loans. The news wires were alive with stories of 'high risk' companies being charged as much as 10 to 12 per cent for short-term funding. The market has its own way of punishing financial institutions and other companies silly enough:

- to be without appropriate reserves' and

- to have a low level of liquidity.

The simultaneous injection of liquidity and cut in interest rates fed the inflation fires. Other things being equal, economic risks rise both when interest rates are in two digits and when they are purposely kept at rock bottom. The latter happens when the central bank or the government intend to stimulate the market after a severe shock, for instance, after the collapse of the internet and other technology equities, known as the bubble of year 2000 and again after the housing bubble in 2007–2009. The central bank must always be diligent in raising rates a short while after rate cuts, because:

- when kept below the level of inflation, interest rates severely penalize all savers; and

- allow some bankers and other players to take huge risks, as happened from 2003 to 2007 with both big banks and pension funds.

Knowledgeable monetary policy executives must *a priori* appreciate that wholesale rate cuts lead to new bubbles and require a great deal of work to arrest inflationary post mortem. When the July/August 2007 bubble blew, Chinese inflation stood at 5.6 per cent (rising in 2008 to more than 8 per cent) and Russian inflation at 8.5 per cent – both worryingly high. To avert this likelihood, the South African, Norwegian and Australian central banks raised interest rates.

In their watch over money supply and inflationary pressures, central bankers always need to lean against asset-price bubbles, whether these assets are equities, commodities, real estate or anything else. Lack of steady observation and of proactive measures leads to many unexpected consequences.

Here is an example. On 28 March 2006, central bankers and regulators from around the world met in New York to measure the financial industry's progress in improving the stability of the global system and what they found was not at all disquieting. That one-day meeting was designed to gauge headway made since a report of July 2005 by an influential group of bankers, which identified a number of areas that needed improvement. The central issues were:

- risk management; and

- complex financial products such as credit derivatives.

The majority of central banks and bank supervisors were complacent but the evidence provided in the period which elapsed from March 2006 to July/August 2007 has been that both risk and novel financial products were badly mismanaged. 'There is a fundamental difference between the way that risk managers and accountants look at the world and it doesn't make sense. We need to square that circle,' said Gerald Corrigan,[2] a former president of the New York Fed, who convened that March 2006 meeting. Corrigan is a very wise person, but his voice was not heard.

2. Monetary Base and Money Supply; M1 and M3

Globalization is making the central bankers' job harder and this increase in difficulty is expected to get worse. Until the end of the twentieth century, central bankers were able to treat globalization as being largely benign: the prices of many goods were driven down and therefore inflation targets became easier to meet – or at least, nobody publicly questioned globalization's benefits.

---

2   At the time of writing a managing director at Goldman Sachs, Corrigan led the mid-2005 300-page report 'Counterparty Risk Management Policy Group II', to underline its link with 'CRMPG I', the report that followed the implosion of Long-Term Capital Management, a hedge fund in 1998.

The challenged to this concept of benign globalization began in the first years of this century, particularly after the rapid rise in commodity prices. From oil to copper to agricultural products, the commodities inflation gave the message that reductions in the relative prices of certain goods may have been mistaken for a reduction in general price pressures. In turn, this caused the monetary policy followed by the main central banks to look imprudent.

The newer theory is that globalization can cut both ways. As long as it lasts, the effect of cheap labour in emerging countries is beneficial to the price of goods consumed in the west; but increases in the price of oil, copper, grains and other commodities have become a source of inflationary pressure around the world. As such, they may become particularly devastating in the developed countries whose:

- years of loose credit policies, hence cheap credit reduced discipline; and

- a more complex economy finds it difficult to adapt to the globalization's twists and derives.

The first section of this chapter has explained the dilemma confronting central banks in their monetary policy. While decisions are by necessity more subjective than objective because (no matter what some economists say), there is no way to define mathematically what the right level of money supply is. Additionally, there is not one but several metrics of money supply even if one of them is mainly targeted: M3 (more on this later).

To appreciate the money supply's role in the economy, we need to go back to the fundamentals. In any financial system the *money supply* (MS) is a multiple of the legal tender (paper money) and coins in circulation,[3] generally known as *monetary base* (MB).[4] The multiplier is the *velocity of circulation of money, v.* The equation relating these three measures looks simple:

$$MS = MB \times v$$

In reality, however, v is a complex function. In the short term the velocity of circulation of money can be affected by, among other factors, general monetary

---

3   Usually coins represent between 7 per cent and 8 per cent of MB.
4   English economists suggest that the use of MB, which they call M0 (M zero) is a more reliable measure than M1, M3, etc.

and credit developments (including banks' willingness to lend), current interest rates, shape of yield curve, level of volatility and other external factors which are usually subject to a significant amount of uncertainty. Usually,

- low short-to-medium-term interest rates influence *monetary dynamics*;

- they impact the economy by beefing up the overall strength of underlying rate of monetary and credit expansion.

The opposite is true with high interest rates. If one were to state in one short sentence v's behaviour, this would be that it is conditioned by the annual growth rate of loans companies, households and to government(s), particularly when growth of loans becomes broad-based and (in a way) unstoppable. Algorithmically, a first approximation to the money supply's expansion is expressed by adding to MB overnight deposits:

$$M1 = MB + \text{overnight deposits}$$

The measurement expressed by M1 is sensitive to increases in short-term rates; as they rise, economic expansion moderates. The next, larger metric is M2, obtained by adding to M1 other short-term bank deposits, such as deposits with an agreed maturity of up to three years and those redeemable at notice of up to three months. The equation of M2, which has fallen out of favour as a yardstick, is:

$$M2 = M1 + \text{other short term deposits}$$

Presently, the focal measure for central bankers and for the financial community at large is M3. It is computed by adding to M2 *marketable financial instruments* such as loans to enterprises, loans to households, general government borrowing or savings (a negative input), monetary capital formation (which may also be a negative entry) and other component parts representing longer-term financial liabilities (excluding capital and reserves). The equation is:

$$M3 = M2 + \text{marketable instruments}$$

Globalization and, most significantly, financial innovation have greatly expanded the nature, realm and value of marketable financial instruments – securitized subprimes being only one example. Therefore, it comes as no surprise that, while central banks think of themselves as guardians of M3, it is the investment banks, commercial banks and hedge funds, who:

- took hold of it; and

- gave it wings to fly.

The irony of this, and the mother of the 2008 inflation in the west, is that through novel financial instruments banks and non-banks greatly expanded M3, unchecked by regulators. Then, when the financial games unravelled and the central banks' fire brigade moved in, their injection of more liquidity further fed inflation's fires.

From 1999 to 2007, the target for M3 growth (or at least the reference value) by the European Central Bank was 4.5 per cent, a level considered to keep excess liquidity in check and ease inflationary pressures. But, as Figure 7.1 documents, the market decided otherwise. A volatile M3:

- was equal to about 6 per cent in 1999;

- was 4.5 per cent on average in 2000;

- grew to 8 per cent in 2001;

- hovered between 7 and 8 per cent in 2002;

- further increased in 2003;

- shrank to 5.5 per cent in 2004;

- returned to 8 per cent in 2005;

- headed upwards in 2006; and

- hit *over 11 pe rcent* in 2007, the year of credit boom and credit crunch.

The numbers of M3's high stakes were too different for the Fed. On 5 June 2007, a *Global Money Trends* newsletter estimated that both the Federal Reserve and ECB had allowed an M3 at a nearly 12 per cent annual rate; in the Fed's

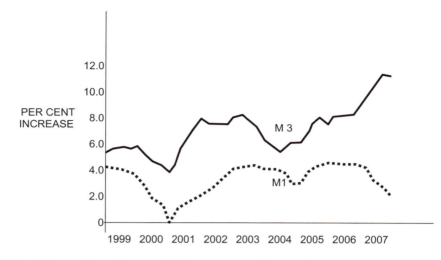

Figure 7.1   Growth rate of M3 versus M1 in Euroland, in 1999–2007

case this was the highest since 1995. At the same time (mid-2007), the Shadow Government Statistics firm in New York estimated that the Fed's money-printing was even at 14 per cent annual M3 growth rate – the highest since the 1987 stock market crash.

The fact that speculators have been doing as they please with money supply is an issue of greater concern. Milton Friedman had famously said that 'Inflation is always and everywhere a monetary phenomenon.'[5] Monetary aggregates are a guide to the economy, even if over longer periods other factors also add their weight. Many big mistakes in economic history are made when policymakers ignore monetary signals. Examples are the:

- Great Depression of 1929/1930;

- great inflation of the 1970s;

- Japanese financial bubble of late 1980s;

- East Asia meltdown of 1997;

- Russian bankruptcy of 1998;

- stockmarket bubble of 2000;

---

5   *The Economist*, 25 March 2006.

- sub-primes crisis of 2007;

- credit crunch of 2008;

- global economic crisis of 2009.

The first five have been warnings. But in June 2007, the *Monthly Bulletin* of the European Central Bank commented that: 'The monetary analysis confirms the prevailing upside risks to price stability at medium to longer horizons. The underlying rate of monetary expansion is reflected in the continued rapid growth of M3... as well as the still high level of credit growth.' A month later, all hell broke loose.

3. Who Establishes Global Monetary Supply?

The Bretton Woods agreement (see section 5) was succeeded by a liberalized vibrant foreign exchange market in which for nearly 30 years the Federal Reserve, as well as the British, German, French, Swiss and Japanese central banks, held the money supply strings. In the twenty-first century, however, global monetary policy rules changed without the benefit of a master plan.

The post-Bretton Woods decades led many economists, politicians, leaders of international institutions, investment bankers, commercial bankers and central bankers to the mistaken assumption that global monetary conditions are set by the central banks of rich economies. This was true in the 1970s, 1980s and early 1990s, but by now it has become history, because a rapidly advancing globalization radically altered not only the exchange system but also money supply factors. Highly paid people responsible for the fortunes of global economies should have been able to detect that since the late 1990s the larger of the so-called emerging countries started to flood the world with an unstoppable liquidity.

Countries thought to be key players in the global economy are also lousy managers of monetary policy. Russia, India, China, South Africa, Brazil and Saudi Arabia are example. This hides a number of unexpected consequences. Emulating the years of the Weimar Republic which led to hyperinflation, the aforementioned nations are working overtime with their printing presses, as Table 7.1 documents.

Table 7.1   M3 Money Supply Growth*, in percent, year on year, 2006-2008

Country	M3 annual growth (%)
Russia	48.3 to 51%
India	23.8 to 24%
China	18.5 to 22%
South Africa	about 22%
Brazil	about 20%
Saudi Arabia	18.4 to 20%
Euroland	9 to 12%
United States	just below 10%
Japan	1.3 to 1.8%

*   Basic on statistics and estimates by Bloomberg, Goldman Sachs, IMF, *The Economist*

- An uncontrollable and huge 60 per cent of the world's growth in broad money supply comes from 'emerging economies' and this flooding of the global market with newly printed money grows every year.

The message carried by the financial wires is that by now the Federal Reserve barely glances at money. Indeed, mid-2007 it announced that in August it will stop publishing M3 statistics, its broadest measure of money, claiming that M3 does not convey any extra information about the economy that is not already embodied in the narrower M2 measure This is:

- a reversal of the earlier policy which we saw in section 2; and

- a mistake because it takes no account of money supply growth due to novel financial instruments.

It is *as if* one does not want to hear the bad news. While it is true that M2 and M3 move in step for part of the time, there have also been large divergences. During the equity bubble of the late 1990s, M3 grew quite fast – not so M2; hence both must be watched. Additionally, there is good reason for developing not only US, British, Euroland and Japanese M2s and M3s, but also Russian, Indian, Chinese, Brazilian and others.

Additionally, a Merrill Lynch study suggests that policies of the central banks of Russia, China, India and Brazil might have a greater influence on performance of riskier assets than those of the Fed, European Central Bank, Bank of England or Bank of Japan.[6]

- Adjusted for inflation, the striking growth in money supply by the large developing countries is alarming; and

- the aftereffect is that in real terms the global money supply is growing at its fastest for decades, feeding inflation.

In 2006 and 2007, the BRIC (Brazil, Russia, India, China) put the printing presses of their central banks to work overtime, flooding the global market with money. By 2008, however, the central banks of western nations took it upon themselves to excel in that job and their zeal in money creation made them work overtime.

In the course of 2008, the last year of the Bush Administration, the Treasury made commitments way beyond appropriations by Congress – through leveraging. During the 10 February 2009 Bernanke hearings by the House Banking Committee, representative Carolyn Maloney, a Committee member, said that by some calculations the US government had guaranteed $7 trillion. Other estimates put the gearing higher, at over $8 trillion. This is by no means the end. Rather, it looks like being the beginning.

Britain is not very far behind, and the drama is that this is money largely poured down the drain. Take the Royal Bank of Scotland (RBS) as an example. Up to January 2009, the cost of its semi-nationalization has been (officially) £25 billion. On 10 February 2009 RBS had a market capitalization of £5 billion – or 20 per cent of what the Labour government had poured into its coffers. Even if every other asset of the bank was carried at zero value, the British taxpayer has been ripped off.

The governments of Euroland, too, are in a money-printing frenzy, forgetting about their obligations to price stability and low budget deficits[7] derived from

---

6   Merrill Lynch, *RIC – Monthly Investment Overview*, 8 January 2008.
7   Below 3 per cent.

the Stability and Growth Pact which they signed (Chapter 10). In February 2009, the European Union Executive mildly reprimanded France, Spain, Portugal and Greece for their deficit excesses – but it applied no penalties (as it should have done, using as an excuse 'the prevailing financial conditions').

As if all this has not been enough, practically from the start of the 2007–2009 crisis the Federal Reserve, Bank of England and European Central Bank have provided self-wounded big banks with ample liquidity, accepting as collateral useless financial paper. The garbage they collected includes not only securitized subprimes but as well asset-backed securities (ABS) freshly created for the purpose of getting liquidity from the central banks.[8] 'It could be burned eventually to heat the central banks' buildings,' said one of the experts.

Many economicts think that the more classical commodities like grains, copper and oil are no longer the only highly inflated assets. In a classical play of supply and demand, the value of money itself is going downhill. 'What makes the value of money?' Dr Karl Brunner, my professor of economics at UCLA used to ask his students; answering his own question with the statement: 'The fact that money is limited in supply.'

Several experts suggest that like the policies of the People's Bank of China (PBOC), Reserve Bank of India and Bank of Russia, these practices are having an increasingly negative impact on western economies. With globalization, capital controls have been greatly reduced and markets became not just more integrated but also more liberal and less prudent in their policies. Unfortunately, the same is true of central banks.

With these facts in mind, the answer to the query, 'Who establishes global monetary policy?' is 'nobody'! (The G20 which met on 15 November 2008 in Washington, DC and meet again in London on 2 April 2009 is just starting its work.) The huge money growth in developing economies comes over and above the rapid increase in MS among western countries.

Part of the reason lies in the fact that the monetary independence of developing countries central bankers – as well as Japan's – is constrained by their governments' desire to hold down exchange rates so that the country's produce sells well in the global market; particularly in America and in Europe.

---

8   D.N. Chorafas, *Financial Boom and Gloom*, Palgrave Macmillan, London, 2009.

This proves the strong link which exists between world trade and monetary policy and puts the blame squarely on the WTO (Chapter 4) for:

- not waking up in time to these facts;

- or, alternatively, looking the other way.

True enough, in the early 1990s, and even more so before that time, fast monetary growth in emerging economies was of little concern to the WTO, or to governments and central banks of the developed world. A monetary deluge in, say, Brazil simply caused hyperinflation there. Globalization, however, has seen to it that today the whole world economy suffers because:

- cross-border financial flows are large and intensifying; and

- the world economy is more integrated than ever before, passing the shocks from one country to the next.

By steadily keeping interest rates very low (the Greenspan mistake as Fed chairman), and by manipulating the exchange rate of their country (see the example with the Japanese yen in section 6), central banks of the large countries in the developing world *and* Japan distort the global financial system and lead it towards a systemic crisis. Their behaviour,

- forces several central banks to engage in heavy foreign-exchange intervention, which further inflates money supply; and

- sees to it that liquidity pumped out by central banks does not stay in their vaults, but flows somewhere else by travelling unimpeded through the global financial market.

An example is the huge purchase of US Treasury bonds by the Chinese, Japanese and other central banks whose countries have current account surpluses with the US. Economists say that such unprecedented hoards have reduced dollar bond yields and therefore spurred excessive borrowing in the United States. More opaque is the fact that under these conditions state capitalism has a ball, as Chapter 5 documents with the Sovereign Wealth Funds.

4. The Financial Industry's Money Supply Glut

In August 1977, a little over three decades ago, *The Economist* published an article by Dr Alan Greenspan who, writing as a private sector economist (not yet Fed chairman), listed five economic 'Don'ts'. One of these was: 'Don't allow money supply growth to spiral out of hand.' This is precisely what Alan 'Double Bubble'[9] Greenspan did in the early years of the twenty-first century.

It is unfortunate but true that as far as the money supply spiral is concerned, Greenspan found many imitators. The financial atomic bomb of the global economy is that governments and central banks of developing countries as well as the West's commercial and investment banks are now playing 'Greenspan Plus'.

- The bubble of the mismanaged credit markets has burst, but the bubble of the printing press continues expanding; and

- huge increases of asset prices have been encouraged by loose monetary policies and speculation in the global financial market.

Cognizant people suggest that part of the problem comes from the fact that the world over, both politicians and bankers have very short memories and even shorter-term horizons. Commercial and investment bankers use a myopic approach in pushing their favoured monetary policy decisions down the throats of central bankers and governments condone it while they should be bringing the errants to justice.

'Bringing to justice' is easier said than done because the governments themselves have poor policies. Not long ago, an IMF study ranked 163 central banks according to their political autonomy and discovered that, indeed, a few of the emerging countries' central banks have become more independent over the last couple of decades. Still, the IMF study said, they remain much less independent than the Bank of England or European Central Bank.

(Also under the thumb of the government is the Bank of Japan, with its irrational cheap money policy which has created, and continues creating, a flood of liquidity outside its borders. In large measure, this is done through the carry trade promoted by rock bottom interest rates – and for which, one day, the whole Japanese economy will pay dearly.)

---

9   Stockmarket bubble of 2000 and housing/subprimes bubble of 2007.

In the twenty-first century, however, even the central banks' printing presses pale when compared to the way big banks have found to inventory each other's garbage. When securitization was first practiced in connection to the construction boom of the mid-1920s, its size was manageable although some economists looked at it as a minor agent in the 1929 stock market crash. Today securitization has become:

- a huge liquidity engine;

- the booster of dubious credit risk trading; and

- a major agent of much lower lending standards, possibly leading to a new depression.

Banks no longer seem to care about credit quality, since they turn their substandard loans into products and sell them other banks, institutional investors and private individuals – feeding them with poorly-screened credit risk. 'Securitization,' says Aviniash Persaud of Intelligence Capital, a financial advisory firm, 'has meant that credit risks have moved from knowledgeable, long term hands to fast hands where the principal risk management strategy is to sell before prices fall more.'[10]

Critics say that this is a reckless policy which has the potential of tearing apart the global financial system. The original mistake was that the whole credit rating process was allowed to fall apart, as the independent rating agencies got involved in the promotion of securitized bad credits masquerading as 'AAAs':

- global investors no longer know the value of assets in their portfolio, or that of credit institutions; and

- the banks themselves find difficult to lend, because with credit standards broken down they no longer trust the creditworthiness ratings of their clients and of correspondent banks.

Confronted with such unexpected consequences, experts now regret that this transition of credit instruments from knowledgeable hands to fast hands did not ring alarm bells among regulatory authorities, when it was still time to stop it. They are also upset by the fact that it has been helped by the sugar

---

10 *The Economist*, 18 August 2007.

coating of securitized loans, where the upper tranche of junk has been turned into AAA by the magic of independent rating agencies.

On 29 June 2007, just prior to the subprimes crisis, BloombergNews reported that it had undertaken a broad review of mortgage-backed securities issues of debt on the American mortgage market and found that 65 per cent of them needed to be downgraded by rating agencies. Furthermore, three of 60 AAA-rated bonds failed credit criteria and the same was true of 22 of 60 AA-rated bonds, as well as of 50 A-rated bonds, also out of 60.[11]

Banks aside, people attracted by these supposedly safe investments that supposedly pay 'a high rate of return' have been high net worth individuals, managers of endowments and executives of pension funds – *as if* their goal was obliterating the savings of pensioners. In April 2006, the *Financial Times* reported on unprecedented amounts of UK pension funds flowing into speculative trades, while pension fund managers sought ways of increasing returns and diversifying risk.[12]

It is not only banks, insurance companies, pension funds and other institutional investors who have become careless in managing their assets and those of their clients: other companies too no longer give a fig about doing a neat job. Chaos marked the start of operations at Heathrow's Terminal 5, British Airways had to cancel hundreds of flights and problems in the baggage handling system were so severe that the airline had to send thousands of passengers' suitcases to a sorting facility in Italy (!).[13]

Mid-January 2008, American International Group (AIG), the world's largest insurer, had to bail out one of its off-balance sheet structured investment vehicles (SIVs) at the centre of the credit market turmoil. AIG Financial Products said it would repay all outstanding senior debt of Nightingale Finance, a $2.2 billion SIV. Big words. In September 2008 the US Treasury took over AIG to avoid the giant derivatives financial company, with insurance business on the side, going bankrupt. Experts say that if AIG had defaulted it would have pulled down with it several well-known banks.

Shortly after that decision, Moody's Investors Service downgraded Orion Finance, run by Eiger Capital Management, one of the oldest SIVs. Orion was

---

11   *EIR*, 6 July 2007.
12   *Financial Times*, 10 April 2006.
13   *The Economist*, 5 April 2008.

worth $2.3 billion in mid-2007, but its value had shrunk to about $800 million in January 2008, after it was forced to sell assets to repay maturing debt.

In the week of 11 February 2008, unexpected losses again at American International Group fuelled speculation that the financial industry was set for more of the same. AIG had to explain a discrepancy which forced it to write down CDO-related swaps by $4.9 billion – a figure five times higher than the number the insurer confidently offered in December 2007 – after its auditors identified a material weakness in how it values securities.

Financial analysts noted that AIG was also considered to be the world's largest seller of credit protection, with an estimated $63 billion of exposure to CDOs with subprime content. Other big financial firms were not far behind, nor were they any better in treating debt as assets. It is *as if* highly paid executives have difficulty in understanding that:

- if the assets of the system become an enormous liability;

- then a bubble built on leveraging of worthless assets will collapse in an *inverse leverage* chain reaction.

Every time a geared 'asset' goes to the wall, it increases the stress of an unstable financial system and carries to the abyss other geared 'assets', thereby accelerating the rate of the global financial system's disintegration. These debts securitized into assets are worthless if nobody buys them and they are also worthless if someone does.

Politicians who do appreciate what is happening, Lyndon LaRouche being an example, have proposed that sovereign governments should put the global economic and financial system through a bankruptcy reorganization, formulating a cooperative recovery programme. They also suggest that this should be based on the issuance of long-term sovereign credit, associated to the implementation of draconian austerity measures.

While such a plan has a point, it is unrealistic in democracies because politicians have neither the guts not the clout to elaborate its details and see it through. Instead, they are inclined to finance recovery by inflation – to the detriment of all stakeholders in economic life. It is therefore time to rethink what our economic and financial goals are, and how we can reach them without repeating crises which are instrumental in turning back the clock of economic and social life.

5. Economic Policy and Global Imbalances

Theoretically, risks to the global economic and financial outlook mainly emanate from sharp rises in commodity prices, growing protectionist pressures or tightness in 'this' or 'that' market, as well as continuing geopolitical tensions. Practically, many other factors come into play, the more important having to do with financial discipline and lack of it characterizing the global economic landscape. Examples are:

- runaway money supply;

- competitive devaluations;

- persistent current account deficits; and

- galloping inflation, in one or more of the main economic players.

Whether examined under a more limited or a broader view, persisting global imbalances, the risk of their disorderly unwinding and potential shifts in financial market sentiment affect the global market in a negative way. Take the diverging pattern of current account positions as an example. Two important issues have been raised in connection to its aftermath on the global economy.

While it can be expected that some countries may run deficits for considerable time, the fact that America (the world's largest economy) is recording wide deficits, which are absorbing about 75 per cent of world net savings, has a material effect on global trade and finance. When World War II ended, America's share of the *then* global economy was an impressive 60 per cent. Sixty-three years down the line, it has shrunk to 26 per cent. This is still a big number, but one which is steadily eroding while the US economy continues loading itself with debt which it will have to pay one day – a process which has already started and may have severe consequences.

Many economists are worried that the unstoppable accumulation of large deficits will eventually lead to creation of huge and probably unsustainable levels of net foreign liabilities. In turn, this will generate pressures to devalue the dollar in a way even more significant than the April 2008 rate of $1.6 to the euro. Contrary to expert opinions, by February 2009 the euro/dollar exchange rate had turned around, the dollar strengthened and it now hovers between 1.25 and 1.30.

Nevertheless, current account deficits have an impact. Experts suggest that, apart from other reasons of national nature, in the global market place the resolution of current account imbalances is complicated by the very nature of balance of payments and its metrics. The savings-and-investments aspect of current account management highlights the role of domestic factors, but downplays the role of foreign central banks which are increasingly important in the globalized economy. Added to this is the effect of more specific cross-border trading and investment issues.

Underpinning these two issues is the fact that modern economies are not parking lots of financial resources. Part of the challenge of evaluating *global imbalances*, and of doing something about them, is that different parties have different views about their meaning. The current sense of global imbalances is that of current account deficits; a broader developing notion, however, includes external positions of systemically important facts that:

- reflect distortions; and

- entail risks for the indebted economy, as well as the global financial landscape.

Persistent global imbalances convey the message that money flows are not a phenomenon related only to 'this' or 'that' standalone subject – like foreign direct investments and current account deficits. Instead, they have longer term impact on all sorts of assets and liabilities, both structural and cyclical.

Structural factors include longer-term trends which affect a system still characterized by incomplete financial globalization, with plenty of imperfections. Part of structural factors is the growing trade advance of emerging Asian countries, where saving rates tend to be structurally high leading to growth differentials across countries.

Other structural factors range from the effect of public savings and household savings to economic results of commodities prices, as well as of financial asset and house prices. Contrary to structural factors, *cyclical factors* may be reversed relatively quickly;[14] even so their existence impacts on the risk embedded to local economies and the global economy:

- a potentially disorderly unwinding of global imbalances could create a crisis for the global economy; and

- it will hit the stability of the international financial system in ways which are not necessarily predictable.

An example of exposure due to global imbalances in the twenty-first century is the current account deficit of the United States, which continues recording substantial increases: from less than 4 per cent of GDP in 2001 it rose to nearly 7 per cent in 2006. Economists say that this rise corresponds to a fall in net domestic savings from 4 per cent to almost zero – a statement which is at best optimistic, because it forgets that the debt of American households is also sky high.[15]

Conversely, like Japan in the post-WWII years, China has been running high current account surpluses and these continue to increase due to its very robust export trade along with a deceleration in imports. Part of these gains are related to Chinese price competitiveness, part to the undervalued yuan and part to the fact that the Chinese standard of living is way below the American and European – which has an impact on savings.

In other terms, foreign trade aside, the large increase in China's current account surplus is also associated with the rapid increase in domestic savings, which has risen from 2000 to 2007 (reliable statistics are missing). This comes in dramatic contrast to America's negative figure and the European Union's low one-digit number.

What the aforementioned examples demonstrate is that globalization as well as financial deregulation and innovation have given a negative slope to the surplus/deficit curve of Western nations, and made the rapid rise in the money supply harder to interpret, let alone control. In the background of these economic effects lie well-known issues of daily life, for instance, the fact that every day the US imports $2 billion worth of goods for local consumption, way above the level of US exports in spite of a shrinking dollar.

---

14   European Central Bank, Monthly Bulletin, August 2007.
15   Merrill Lynch, Investment Strategy Update, 14 August 2007.

6. Currencies and the Global Financial Market

Towards the end of World War II, lessons learned the hard way from the Great Depression of 1929–1933 were instrumental in leading American, British and Canadian political leaders to the 1944 Bretton Woods monetary agreement. At the time it was thought that this would do away with wild currency devaluation by contributing to currency stability through convertibility to US dollars and then to gold.

What the Bretton Woods signatories, including Roosevelt, Churchill, Keynes and White, forgot was that no international agreements last forever. The 1994 hypothesis was that with stable currencies, at least among western nations, financial stability would become the guiding light of global macroeconomic and monetary policy both:

- in the immediate post-World War II decades; and

- in the future at large with only periodic adjustments.

It did not happen that way. Even so, for two and a half decades the Bretton Woods agreement regulated international monetary arrangements. Its impact ended on 14 August 1971, when, in a televised address, President Nixon outlined his new economic policy. On the domestic side, he announced various measures to reduce both unemployment and inflation – such as investment credits, repeal of excise tax on cars and acceleration of income tax exemption, as well as:

- a $4.7 billion cut in government spending;

- postponement of government pay rises;

- a 90-day freeze on wages and prices;

- 10 per cent reduction in foreign economic assistance;

- 10 per cent surcharge on all imports; and

- suspension of the convertibility of the dollar into gold, or other reserve assets.

The suspension of dollar convertibility meant that the United States would no longer act as a guarantor of last resort of fixed exchange rates of key world currencies, a situation which had prevailed since the end of World War II. Each currency, including the US dollar, would have to stand on its own. With one dramatic gesture, Richard Nixon:

- broke the link between dollar and gold; and

- opened the way for effective devaluation of the US currency; the so-called 'shrinking Nixon dollar'.

Were the exchange rates decided at the Bretton Woods conference of 1944 *right* or *wrong*? No answer can be given to this question without considering two important elements: post-WWII economic realities and changes which took place over time in the economy of the most important industrial nations, as well as in those parts of the world in process of development.

The choice of exchange rates was based on economic realities of 1944, with only some thought about the foreseeable future. The rate of Japan's currency, for example, was set at 360 yen to the dollar during the immediate postwar period – and it remained at that level until 1971. Evidently this was wrong because from the mid-1940s to 1971 Japan's industrial competitiveness greatly increased.

For a quarter century Japan capitalized on an awfully undervalued yen which years later would reach a parity of about 85 to the dollar – a 423.5 per cent *revaluation* compared to Bretton Woods. Combined with hard work and engineering excellence, the dramatically undervalued yen gave Japan a tremendous advantage in conquering the world's markets. In a way quite similar to current Chinese policies (Chapters 1 and 2):

- it made Japanese goods very cheap in America; and

- it encouraged Japanese companies to aggressively export the world over.

Additionally, a weak yen versus a strong dollar led to mounting trade imbalances in Japan's favour, while in monetary terms US exports became uncompetitive. With the end of dollar's convertibility, all currencies were allowed to float free of the old fixed-rate limits, with the result that major currencies like yen and Deutschmark became more expensive against the dollar. (The mark had already been revalued by 5 pecent against the dollar in the early 1960s.)

The opinions of economists, as well as of business people, about floating currency exchange rates were divided. Many thought that a flexible exchange rate system was potentially superior to the fixed rate, because it could continually balance every nation's industrial competitiveness. Some experts, however:

- felt that a free market for money can lead to excesses; and

- foresaw the possibility of government interventions, which were anathema because of policies which had led to the Great Depression.

Economists who thought that the free market should be given a chance in setting currency exchange rates disagreed with this view, arguing that the world's growing economy would not allow government interventions for too long. Eventually they proved to be wrong, but at the time it looked as if that the money shipped around the world by globalization of financial markets would be the arbiter because it was enormous compared with the amount any single country could use to intervene. Hence the hypothesis that:

- *if* the amount of funds available to central banks for intervention in the market was insufficient to influence currency rates;

- *then* forex trading – spot, futures, forwards and options – would be in charge of the value of world currencies. This prophecy came unstuck, because many countries, like Japan and China, stage-manage their exchange rates.

Even *if* in the long run currency exchange markets are able to establish what some economists consider to be the 'right' rates – and this is a big IF – in the short term there may be government intervention as well as speculations, excesses, and anomalies in market action, exploited by sharp currency traders. In his book *Made in Japan*, published in 1987, Akio Morita, the animator and boss of Sony, regretted this growing impact of international currency exchange markets.

'The money traders,' Morita said, 'would begin to affect the value of world currencies. No mechanism had been set up to monitor the system and, figuratively speaking, to set the handicaps. Money speculators use only one criterion for buying one currency and selling another – profit. This resulted in a constant changing of rates that had nothing to do with industrial competitiveness.' Morita added:

- 'For those of us engaged in world-wide trade, it was as though some bully had come [in] everywhere.

- In this situation the price of our goods became a matter virtually beyond our control... Who could manufacture under such circumstances?'[16]

What Morita was essentially suggesting was that the futures and forwards forex markets are a dangerous thing to the manufacturing industry. Moreover, some people have found they can make more profits, more easily, by trading money rather than by manufacturing goods. And since manufacturers cannot forecast the return on potential investments:

- many have stopped investing in their own companies; and

- they are investing a lot of energy, time and money in financial alchemy.[17]

At about the time Morita published his book forex trading had hit $1 trillion per day. A few years earlier, as an aftereffect of the 1970s oil shocks, inflation leaped forward and in the early 1980s killing it ended in an overvalued dollar. All that economic turmoil had led to a period of negotiations, conflicts and confrontations regarding currency exchange rates – the most notable being the Athèné Palace agreement of the mid-1980s, which essentially devalued the dollar against European currencies. Since then, with minor exceptions, the US dollar has been falling in value.

---

16 Akio Morita, *Made in Japan*, Collins, London, 1987.
17 Recently, rumour has it that Porsche, which is a car manufacturer not a bank, makes more money from financial instruments than from selling automobiles.

7. Redressing a Falling Currency: A Case Study

Is the fall of the dollar good or bad news for the American economy and for the prestige of the United States in the world? Theoretically, a country's economy and its global prestige are more or less two different criteria separated and qualified by a horde of other factors. Practically, however, they correlate this being reflected through the country's currency which:

- reflects the strength of its economy; and

- significantly affects its prestige in the global market.

Currencies are like any other commodity; their value constantly fluctuates, but there is a big difference between volatility and a steady slide in value. The problem facing economists and monetary policymakers is that the current situation seems to be unprecedented. As the link between the value of the dollar and all sorts of balances has seemingly broken down, central bankers are at a loss about the monetary policy they should adopt.

- Should fighting inflation be given precedence? or

- Is it more important to keep interest rates low and money supply high, to stimulate the economy? and

- How far should they allow current account deficits to grow, given the message that the country is not in charge of its own house?

When an event like fear of a major currency's steady devaluation ripples through the market, investors regroup and fly back to safety in other currencies. They do so because they believe the shrinking currency is suffering much more than a temporary setback. The rout of any commodity, the value of currencies included, is a raw demonstration of market power.

- Can the dollar afford it?

- Or, is it better to find a way to pull itself out of trouble?

This has been a theme discussed in Chapter 5 in connection to Sovereign Wealth Funds. Here is another example from real life. As 1923 came to a close, five years after the end of World War I, the value of the French franc fell by

50 per cent and France found itself in full financial crisis. Frank Altschul, then leading partner of Lazard Frères New York, was invited by the French Minister of Finance to express his views on solving the crisis.

Altschul called for the French government to undertake what he called an *experiment*, aimed at stabilizing the plunging currency.[18] His approach was novel, as many experiments are. Using a $100 million dollar loan (big money at that time) from J.P. Morgan, the French government bid the franc from 124 to 61 to the dollar – and met the target in a few weeks. Speculators who had sold the franc short in expectation its value would continue falling were hit by huge losses and the franc stabilized.

All financial experiments involve risk, but when they are carried out under controlled conditions the insiders who are in charge know how far they can go; provided there are no leaks, the outsiders don't. The same applies to planning and testing our ability and preparation for dealing with issues confronting the dollar, or for that matter monetary policy in the global economy which this chapter is discussing. Notice, however, that experiments can be so much more successful if:

- we have established our goals;

- we design them properly; and

- there are clear responsibilities for carrying them out.

Post-mortems, too, are important – not in the heat of the moment but as playbacks. Some economists now contend that the 1929 crash on Wall Street need not have led to the Great Depression. It might have been an ordinary, albeit more severe, cyclical downturn which was turned into a cataclysm by bad politics.

According to this school of thinking, the New Deal made matters worse by prolonging the Depression, because of business bashing and big government programmes. US economic resurgence returned only with World War II but is now in the process of being lost because of a new bout of bad politics – which makes it so much more difficult to redress the dollar.

---

18 William D. Cohan, *The Last Tycoons*, Doubleday, New York, 2007.

8. The Chinese Sense of a Crisis

Since the 2000 stockmarket bubble and emergence of big developing economies, the floating currency exchange system which followed Bretton Woods (see section 5) has been in trouble. The pervasive housing-and-credit bubble of 2007 fed by the overleveraging of banks and households rang the first alarm bells about its ruin. *Crisis* is in the air, and there is a Chinese interpretation of this term as a word composed of two symbols,

- the first is 'danger';

- the second is 'opportunity'.

In the late 1990s, the exuberance of the massive stock-market bubble was a sign of danger that most investors either did not comprehend or paid no attention to. This danger did not dissipate with the 1 per cent interest rates for the dollar instituted by the Greenspan Fed. To the contrary, negative real interest rates presented new opportunities for overleveraging. What followed was the danger expressed in the subprimes and banking industry's bubble, which burst in July 2007.

Yet, cool minds had foreseen the coming danger. The 2006 Annual Report by the Bank for International Settlements offers an eye-opening commentary on risks embedded to the wild securitization of all forms of debt instruments: '... more skepticism might be expressed about some of the purported benefits of having new players, new instruments and new business models, in particular the "originate and distribute" approach which has become so widespread. These developments have clear benefits, but they may also have side effects, with associated costs.'[19]

Whether they are governments, companies or individual investors, the players in the global financial market should never forget that, like risk and return, the doors of opportunity and danger are adjacent and indistinguishable. Finance, and most particularly leveraged finance and derivative financial instruments, is a game of risk. The *virtual economy* has plenty of exposures:

- no policy, no regulator and no model can eliminate that element;

- the winner is the person who is in charge of exposure, sets rigorous limits and keeps steady watch.

---

19   Bank for International Settlements, 77th Annual Report, Basel, 2007.

A key notion underpinning the virtual economy, the system in which we presently live and work, is that the value derived from a process, instrument or product is no longer exclusively founded in the production of material goods. Increasingly, it depends on the utilization of services both within and outside the design, manufacturing, distribution and maintenance processes.

Because of this switch in value creation, the present key economic concepts are less and less those defined by the nineteenth-century Industrial Revolution and its notion of price equilibrium. Instead, they depend on dynamic estimates of risk and return as well as on the control of leverage, while:

- coping with a growing range of uncertainties; and

- facing vulnerabilities implicit in the financial system.

Managing risks and their underlying unknown, understanding new kinds of vulnerabilities and knowing how to stop before the precipice are examples of what lies behind the Chinese sense of a crisis. Appreciating today's economy for what it really is is most fundamental to longer-term success in business life because it permits the holding of the high ground as:

- the market is flush with liquidity;

- global competition intensifies; and

- the bastions of industrial economy lose their grip.

Some years ago, when the surge in world commodities prices became unstoppable, some economists warned that it signalled the near-term onset of inflation which might turn into hyperinflation. On an almost daily basis, copper, zinc, nickel, silver, gold, agricultural goods and other commodities hit a 10-year, 20-year, or all-time record high. What worried these economists most was:

- the *increase in the rate of increase* of commodities inflation; and

- the fact this acceleration defined a Weimar-type hyperinflationary environment.

While China usually has the finger pointed at it as being the reason for a rapid rise in commodity prices, several experts suggest that the leading force driving the shockwave by funnelling more and more funds into the commodities markets are hedge funds. Their speculations have created an alarming process that could easily lead to a commodities bubble over and above the US housing bubble. Some of these experts estimate that:

- the combined size of all investment in commodities could be one-quarter of a trillion dollars or more; and

- coupled with sizeable leverage, this amount could balloon into more than a trillion dollars.

Ironically, much of the seed money comes from people who could ill afford it. In the US, Greenwich Partners reported that 14 per cent of all US public pension plans are invested in hedge funds; and 49 per cent of pension fund managers expect to increase their hedge fund holdings during the next three years. As an example, the Pennsylvania State Employees' Retirement System (PSERS), with $27 billion in assets, has invested 23 per cent of its assets into hedge funds, the highest percentage by any state pension entity.

In 2006, in Britain, Sainsburys, the supermarket chain, announced that it would invest 5 per cent of its £5.5 billion pension fund into commodities. At the end of 2005 Hermes, manager of Britain's largest pension fund, launched a commodities fund into which it invested £1 billion ($2 billion) of its clients' money.

To appreciate why this can be disastrous when credit conditions are deteriorating, one must keep in mind that in western countries pension funds have put between 3 per cent and 5 per cent of their money into hedge funds – an amount which is now at high risk. The share of pension funds and endowments in hedge funds stands at about 30 per cent, and up to the July/August 2007 crisis an estimated 40 per cent of new flow of assets into hedge funds came from pensions.[20]

Some of the triggers of a possible global financial abyss are interlinked. The funds flooding the market from the yen carry trade, for example, have both fuelled the huge US housing bubble and fed speculation into such markets as Iceland, Australia and New Zealand. Not only are these markets more or less in

---

20 *EIR*, 6 July 2007.

crisis, but the same is also true of companies and households which have used the carry trade to finance their newly acquired assets. (British households have used the Swiss franc carry trade to get better terms for their mortgages.)

All in all, we are living in very interesting times. The reader should, however, notice that the Chinese saying 'May you live in interesting times' is not a way of well-wishing. It is a curse.

For some time there has been considerable speculation about when the next major financial crisis would happen and who would pay for it; but no one doubted that it would happen. In February 2009 we know the answer. A major economic crisis which started in 2007 spread around the globe. Speculating about when it may lift is like trying to catch a falling knife.

8

China's Banks and the Economy

1. Close Ties to the Government Breed Corruption

Financial panic hit Tokyo two years before the Wall Street crash in 1929. In a way quite similar to the Japanese banking crisis of 1990/91, the banking crisis of 1927 had everything to do with corruption and sweetheart deals, say Sterling and Peggy Seagrave.[1] In the 1920s and in the 1980s:

- large sums of money were lent by Japan's big banks to business run by their bosses, their relatives and friends;

- this created a false impression of prosperity, but the banks did not secure their loans and failed to audit their own accounts.

Sounds familiar? Add to the second point the voluntary total lack of risk control and you have what brought down the better-known names in American and European banking in 2007–2009. In most financial institutions risk control was just a label not a function. UBS employed 3,400 risk managers, yet up to and including the second quarter of 2008 it lost $37.5 billion (then Swiss francs 37.5 billion), the largest amount of all the big banks.

Losses continued to mount in the third and fourth quarters of 2008, with the result that in spite of fairly good profits made over the year, UBS posted an annual *net loss* of $18.2 billion (Swiss francs 19.7 billion in February 2009 when this red ink figure was announced). During 2008 the deeply wounded UBS had also benefited by the helping hand of the Swiss National Bank onto which it unloaded $52.2 billion (Swiss francs 60 billion) of toxic waste set up as a separate fund. One would have been allowed to believe that:

- these dismal figures translated into sanctioning and firing a very poorly performing management;

1   Sterling and Peggy Seagrave, *The Yamato Dynasty*, Corgi Books, London, 1999.

- instead, apart from the ousting of Marcel Ospel the CEO, everybody else continued warning his or her armchair.

Moreover, bonuses continued their course. According to the *Neue Zürcher Zeitung*, in 2008 the 17,200 investment bankers of UBS were paid in the average a yearly compensation of 284,000 Swiss francs – while investment banking booked the heaviest loss of all divisions. In other terms, the people who, during 2008, had nearly destroyed the once beautiful bank pocketed Swiss francs 2.2 billion ($1.9 billion) in bonuses for the year (and rumour had it that another $1.2 billion was hidden in the accounts to be distributed later). That tells a great deal of the story behind corporate patronage.[2]

If one adds to the first point lavish political patronage and associated corruption, *then* it would describe what was happening with China's banks before the regime's change in the 1990s. At that time, the Chinese government owned the country's banking industry, except for minority stakes in a few small and medium-sized institutions.

This wholesale equity of the banking sector has been at the origin of politically motivated reckless lending, with credit institutions finding nothing wrong in making bad loans. Patronage aside, because of domestic dangers of a slowing economy the Chinese government has erred for too long on the side of allowing banks to go on with their past practices without firm credit risk evaluation. As appendages of government:

- China's big banks were massive, bureaucratic and imbued with an intensely political culture;

- the big four alone had 1.4 million employees and 116,000 branches; and

- branch managers had closer ties to local party officials and businesspeople than to their own central authority.

Javed Hamid, head of East Asia for International Finance Corp. (IFC), the private-sector lending arm of World Bank, described the state of affairs at the bank of Shanghai, one of the better of the smaller city banks, when the IFC

---

2   Not to be left behind, the fired CEO of deeply wounded Merrill Lynch had hidden in the company's 2008 account $4 billion which he distributed as 'bonuses' to the unable, unwilling and unnecessary.

and HSBC took a stake in it in 2001: 'The minutes of board meetings would be written before the meeting. Decisions would be made on the basis of [the bank's lending] growth, not whether it would improve returns. Branch managers were like kings. They didn't know what a human-resources function was. People were rewarded not on the basis of market criteria, but on how loyal they were to the party.'[3] Altogether:

- by the end of 2003, outstanding loans had surged to 145 per cent of Chinese GDP, the highest such ratio in the world;

- bad debts to banks stood at 40 per cent of GDP and they were a threat to the country's future – not only to its fiscal stability.

Faced with these challenges, in late October 2004 China's central bank raised interest rates for the first time in nine years and it also lifted the ceiling on commercial loan rates, allowing banks to charge more to riskier borrowers. The counterweight to these early signs of a breeding clean house policy has been that, because China's capital markets were underdeveloped, a risk of market illiquidity since the domestic economy depended wholesale on bank loans.

- Bank assets comprised 77 per cent of all financial assets in China; and

- this was nearly three times higher than a corresponding 26 per cent in the US.

The Chinese government, however, seemed to have recognized the urgency of a change in banking policies – though it is less certain whether it also realized that a clean house policy would be most costly in implementing, given that almost all Chinese banks were state-controlled and broken. The quality of bank management also left much to be desired, with decisions characterized by:

- lack of attention to asset quality; and

- a breakneck build-up of non-performing loans.

Fraud, too, was rampant. According to available information, by the end of 2004 just one institution, the Bank of China, one of the big four, tried and penalized plenty of staff for fraud (more on this in section 4). Some China

---

3   *The Economist*, 20 March 2004.

observers commented that it was not easy to tell where plain fraud ended and political corruption started, because under political pressure to create jobs companies easily secured money for pet projects which led nowhere.

Some estimates point out that local governments had illegally underwritten $100 billion in loans to bankroll favoured investment projects while no one seems to have cared about repaying loans and the non-performing loan ratio (NPL) was a two-digit number. At the time, Standard & Poor's estimated that total non-performing loans in China's financial sector added up to anywhere from $384 billion at the low end to as much as $864 billion.

- A workout of the bad debt could have cost some $600 billion;

- this was roughly 40 per cent of China's (then) $1.4 trillion gross domestic product.

For large credit institutions recapitalization by the government led to a marked reduction in the bad loan burden, which was a step forward. The collapsing balance sheets of banking giants had to be shored up. The Bank of China, China Construction Bank (CCB) and Industrial and Commercial Bank of China (ICBC) received over $85 billion in government money between them, under the condition that they got their houses in order.

This was only part of the money invested to weed out all sorts of bad debts and unwarranted liabilities. After spending an estimated $160 billion to clean up the bad loans, the Chinese government again faced calls from banks for another loan bail out. Beijing was ill-prepared for that prospect, but the news continued to be poor.

According to estimates by Western rating agencies, borrowers altogether defaulted on nearly half of all bank loans in China. There was also news that Chinese banks continued to lend money to politically connected customers, making little effort to charge higher rates to riskier borrowers until the government got serious about the banks' solvency.

2. Solvency and Liquidity of Chinese Banks

With so much money being pumped into the market to promote the Chinese banking industry's solvency, by 2005 the economy was growing at 8 per cent a year, setting the pace for future years. However, in the opinion of many experts, the bail outs were no silver bullet. On their own they could do little if anything to reduce bad loans per se, because:

- the culture and attitude of China's bankers, too, had to change, which was not easy; and

- the new money was in the form of US dollar-denominated exchange reserves from the central bank, not in Chinese currency.

These reserves simply made the balance sheets appear stronger so the banks could write off more loans without shrinking their capital base. But tackling the bad loans policy required a new level of commitment from bank management. In the crisis of Chinese banking in the early years of this century, as in the crisis of American banking of 2007–2009, money was just one component of the overhaul.

As long as the country was an inward-looking giant, the chronic illness of Chinese banking was not only the virtual absence of credit-risk management but also shoddy bookkeeping practices. These were precisely the reasons that brought down the American and European big banks in 2007 and 2008. In both cases of financial mismanagement – Chinese bad loans and American/European subprimes exposure – losses were legion.

Poor management was responsible for the fact that at the end of 2002 (just before the events discussed in the first section of this chapter), Chinese banks had recovered just $8.1 billion on delinquent loans with a face value of $36 billion, a 77.5 per cent delinquency. To inject management skill into the chaos of the banks' bureaucratic culture, the Chinese government allowed foreign investors to take a stake of between 5 and 10 per cent.

- This share brought foreign banks into the picture;

- but limited their ability to steer too much the Chinese banks' management wheel.

Notice that the same 5 to 10 per cent bracket was what western governments were willing to accept when, in 2007–2009, American and European big banks found themselves obliged to go cap-in-hand to Sovereign Wealth Funds. It is indeed an irony that Citigroup – which a couple of years earlier had been lecturing Asian bankers on good governance and risk control – repeated the same mistakes and had to find cash urgently to avoid bankruptcy.

Another similarity lies in the fact that both with problem loans and collateralized loan obligations losses take time to surface. For this reason, it can take several years before the situation clears up. To hasten the process, the government instituted the China Banking Regulatory Commission (CBRC) which took oversight duties from People's Bank of China, thereby eliminating the conflict of interest in which the banking system's chief advocate was also its regulator (as happens in the US with the Fed).

CBRC raised capital requirements for banks under its jurisdiction, as well as risk weightings for some loans – particularly to state firms. The fact that China's banks would have to make larger and earlier provisions against bad debts was welcomed by the market. Critics, however, said that a capital-adequacy ratio of 8 per cent is too low for risky emerging countries and they wondered how sharp the CBRC's teeth will really be:

- those of a tiger;

- or of a paper tiger?

Westerners advised the Chinese government that in terms of better governance over the banking industry, CBRC would do well to adopt the chapter of Britain's Financial Services Authority (FSA). I don't agree with this because FSA failed in its duties with Northern Rock, Royal Bank of Scotland, HBOS, plenty of other smaller British banks and the subprimes in general. A better model is to emulate the recent restructuring by the Basel Committee on Banking Supervision which has reworked its organization and set up:

- the Policy Development Group (PDG); and

- the International Liaison Group (ILG);

in addition to the existing:

- Accord Implementation Group (AIG); and

- Accounting Task Force (ATF).

The working groups' work is related to, among other things, solvency risk, liquidity risk, regulatory capital, economic capital and fair value accounting (the *Guidelines to Computing Capital for Incremental Default Risk in the Trading Book* was published by Basel for consultation purposes).

Such an advice is valid not only for CBRC but for all national bank supervision authorities, as it allows a close coordination with, and representation in, the working groups of the Basel Committee. It is also a rational approach to organization and structure, as it represents important supervisory functions in a globalized economy.

Another policy decision which helps regulatory authorities to take charge of sprawling financial risk is that of being ready to learn a lesson from what well-managed commercial banks do in closing up channels of inordinate exposure. Sweden's Handelsbanken, the country's third largest commercial bank, provides an example.

An announcement on 31 March 2008 by Handelsbanken shows that even the conservative Swedish banks are being hit by the credit risk generated turmoil in the credit markets. Handelsbanken announced that it would close its New York proprietary trading operation and bear losses totalling SKr 1.4 billion ($236 million) after reducing its exposure to US asset-backed securities (ABS).[4]

As part of this shift, the Swedish bank sold its entire exposure to ABSs secured by credit card receivables worth SKr 11 billion at the end of 2007. 'We are conservative when it comes to risk,' said Mikael Hallaker, head of Investor Relations. 'In our view these types of assets don't have the same quality they used to have.'[5] Bank supervisors, as well as CEOs and board members, should engrave these words in golden letters and hang the engraving behind their desk.

Market and bank liquidity is another salient issue which CBRC (and all other supervisory authorities) should address. In 2008 China seemed to be suffering from a home-grown liquidity squeeze which, curiously enough, it is not so different from that afflicting America and western Europe. As inflation pushed higher, the Chinese government curbed lending by the banks, increasing the

---

4   In a meeting in London the president of an Australian bank said that his institution had greater derivative exposure at its New York branch than at its headquarters.
5   *Financial Times*, 1 April 2008.

reserve ratio for Chinese banks to 15.5 per cent in mid-March 2008. Classically, tighter credit tends to temper expansion.

In Hong Kong investment banks said they had huge pipelines of potential initial public offerings, but the liquidity was not there because investors had lost their risk appetite.[6] The global market had changed its attitude towards investments, which were overleveraged and/or have a significant exposure. China's once impregnable stockmarkets were off by over 30 per cent in first quarter 2008, while by comparison the US S&P 500 was down by 16 per cent. A falling stock market does not invite foreign investments.

3. China's Soft Underbelly is Financial Staying Power

It may sound ludicrous that a nation with a war chest of $1.4 trillion is weak in financials, but as the first section of this chapter brought to the reader's attention, China's banking system has feet of clay. The odds are that there are still some close ties to political cronies and government-run industries which lead to unpleasant surprises. Here is an example.

In mid-November 2006, eight months before the subprimes debacle, a Citigroup bidding consortium won control of the Guangdong credit institution, after a bruising auction that lasted more than a year. The Guangdong bank was a wreck, with non-performing loans representing up to 25 per cent of its credit assets (not unusual in China). Even if officials said this was exceptional, it has been the exception that proved the rule.

While rapid growth of the economy and huge reserves in foreign hard currencies look as if sent from heaven, they also engender consequences which translate into financial risks. Moreover, the complexity of the problem of bad credits exceeds the banking sector's confines. By keeping its tax threshold absurdly low, in recent years China has created wealth for a rapidly growing group of citizens who invested the money they earned, further expanding the economy. To do so, however, the highly stressed banking system had to issue more and more credit.

True enough, the government did its best to recapitalize the banks and to improve the their management by opening their capital to foreign investors.

---

6   *The Economist*, 22 March 2008.

Still, the Chinese banking industry is not in a position to follow the country's engagement in a growth course and rapid rise in GDP.

As if to confirm that China's financials may not be as good as they seem, a December 2007 study by the World Bank changed the calculations traditionally used to make international comparisons of the size of emerging economies. The underlying argument was that converting an emerging market's GDP into dollars at market exchange rates can understate the true size because a dollar buys much more in an emerging market, such as China, than it does in America. Hence, it had used purchasing power parities (PPPs) which take account of price differences between countries.

But, the World Bank adds, previous estimates of China's PPPs were largely guesswork, while a new basis has now been found. This reflects a survey of prices of more than 1,000 goods and services in 146 countries, with the result that GDP statistics changed significantly. The figures released by the World Bank indicated that:

- in 2005, China's GDP was $8.9 trillion with the old measures;

- in 2008, by using the new metrics, it had been reduced to just $5.3 trillion.

India's gross domestic product, too, was slashed with the newly discovered numbers;[7] but for both for China and India the annual GDP growth figures remain practically the same. As the reader will appreciate, there are plenty of things that can be done through statistical artifacts, but this does not change the fact that in economics the soft underbelly of every growth pattern is:

- unsustainable financing; and

- the rush to commercially conquer the world.

Japan has a great deal of experience on both points. Since 1991 it had tried to bring its economy out of the sick bed, but has not succeeded – even if successive governments have (unwisely) created mountains of national debt. Over a 17-year period (1991–2008), the Bank of Japan (BoJ) was alarmed enough to take any measure that might have stopped the economy's deflation,

---

7   By contrast, using the new World Bank metrics the GDP of the US, Euroland, Japan, Britain, Russia, Brazil, Mexico and Canada have increased.

including practically zero interest rates. But no matter how much cash it forced into the banking system, consumers and corporate borrowers cut back activity and repaid loans.

- The time of the go-ahead leveraged economy is past.

- For one and a half decades, no one wanted to lend or even borrow money any longer.

On several occasions, independent rating agencies downgraded the Japanese government's debt. As the standing of the country's banking sector deteriorated, in order to borrow money from other credit institutions Japanese banks had to pay the so-called *Japan premium*. Worse yet, after nearly every downgrading, Standard & Poor's and Moody's warned that they may soon cut their ratings on 12 major Japanese banks, including the country's largest and second-largest financial institutions

Leverage works up to a point. After that, all hell might break lose. The debacle of Japanese banks validated what Jean-Marie Eveillard, of Société Générale International Fund, once stated: 'We seldom get involved in bank stocks because it seems to me that bankers always find a way to hurt themselves.'[8] Governments, too, have this weakness.

We are not yet at that point with the Chinese economy and banking industry, but it is wise to learn a lesson from a neighbour's experience. In the 1990s, the collapse of Japan's strategy of 'growth without limits' led S&P to place on *credit watch*, with its negative implications, its topmost credit institutions: the Bank of Tokyo-Mitsubishi, Dai-Ichi Kangyo Bank, Fuji Bank, the Industrial Bank of Japan and others. The steady credit watch was necessary because credit rating agencies:

- saw high risk in the financial condition of Japanese banks' corporate borrowers; and

- thought this condition would continue to deteriorate for several years (it did), reflecting this opinion in credit ratings.

To make a bad situation worse, Japanese officials made several important policy errors at that time. For instance, to avoid further yen appreciation after

---

8   *Herald Tribune*, 14–15 November 1998.

the 1987 agreement at Plaza Athène which targeted the effective depreciation of the dollar against other hard currencies, they followed easy monetary and financial policies. These gave rise to:

- expansions in credit; and

- huge asset price bubbles.

Both set the stage for the subsequent downturn of the Japanese economy and deterioration of the country's finances. Easy monetary and financial policies in terms of stress (currently asked for by some of Euroland's governments) proved to be being implemented at the moment when Japanese consumers were enjoying increases in their wealth (like Euroland's citizen do today).

Since bad news never comes singly, the eggheads of Japanese bureaucracy also allowed problems in the banking system to fester rather than confronting them directly. These mistakes saw to it that Japan did much less than it could have done to prevent the serious problems which hit the Japanese economy on the head in 1990 and 1991 and left it in a coma.

In retrospect, many economists suggest that *if* the Japanese government had allowed the inevitable yen appreciation it might have saved the economy from overheating. It might also have skewed the prodigious rate of business expansion the world over towards a much more sustainable (and profitable) level. The Chinese government would be well advised to take note.

4. How to Prune the System of its Excesses

After the fall of Japan, Inc. in 1990/91 and of the Asian tigers in 1997, western economists advised that only abolition of archaic economic regulations could save these countries from a new downfall. Other advice provided by many Western economists has been that throwing money at the banks would not work unless they also started lending on the basis of credit analysis, rather than politics and nepotism – a reference most relevant to China's conditions.

Rather than betting the financial staying power of Chinese banks on political criteria and leveraging, the leaders of mainland China would have done better to take a leaf out of Hong Kong's financial book; the favourite economy of Milton Friedman. Why, Friedman asked, had Hong Kong thrived while Britain, which controlled it until 1997, was so static by comparison? He also wondered how much more might America have thrived had it kept its government as small, relative to its economy, as the little island off China had done.[9]

As the precarious situation of Chinese banking and financial sectors' weaknesses persisted in 2005, it led Richard d'Amato, a Congressman and chairman of the US-China Economic and Security Review Commission, to worry aloud about Chinese firms listing shares at NYSE. D'Amato was afraid that they will be siphoning American money into a *China bubble*.[10] These worries were probably promoted by the fact that a mid-2005 research conducted by international banks had shown that over the previous four years China's banking industry:

- was burdened by colossal bad loans;

- understood little about credit risk; and

- had a bureaucratic, antiquated culture which made risk management impossible.

As we saw at the beginning of this chapter, however, by 2006 this situation was slowly changing, under government prodding and a lavish recapitalization. Another positive sign in China's balance sheet was that finally Chinese banks were shedding jobs and modernizing their management. The Bank of China fired its personnel then rehired the best of 230,000 people in 11,000 branches – after having penalized at least 50,000 white-collar workers for fraud.

High-ranking heads also rolled. In March 2005 the chairman of China Construction Bank's (CCB) was fired for fraud. The removal of Zhang Enzhao as CCB chief executive, allegedly for taking bribes either in exchange for approving soft loans or for manipulating purchases of computer equipment, came at a bad time for China's state banks. CCB already faced four other embezzlement cases. More than 50 staff were accused of stealing equipment worth $85 million.[11]

There must have been a fraud pandemic in those years, because in 2003 Wang Xuebing, Zhang's predecessor, was also sentenced to 12 years in prison for misdeeds which took place years earlier when he was a junior official at

---

9   *The Economist*, 25 November 2006.
10   *The Economist*, 3 September 2005.
11   *The Economist*, 19 March 2005.

Bank of China. With such evidence in mind, Chinese banks have a long way to go in improving their:

- auditing;

- internal control; and

- risk management systems.

All three are 'musts' if a credit institution or investment bank wishes to become competitive at the global level. This is a comment which also applies to the American and European big banks, judging from the 2003 to 2007 subprimes fraud pandemic. The difference is that in China top banking executives and their underlings engaged in a policy of personal destruction through outright stealing, which is illegal, while in Western big banks senior executives exploited regulatory weaknesses and overall laxity in prudential supervision by:

- gratifying themselves with inordinate and out of place bonuses; and

- guaranteeing that by means of golden parachutes they would continue receiving self-awarded huge salaries even if they failed.

The negative reaction to such excesses is now reaching Wall Street, where money is the ultimate measure of success. The trigger has been that 50 hedge fund bosses earned $29 billion in 2007, practically a depression year; this made many people uneasy. 'There is nothing wrong with it – it's not illegal,' said Bill Gross, chief investment officer of Pimco. 'But it's ugly.'[12]

(In the last 100 years the United States witnessed only one other case of such unequal wealth distribution where the size of outsized winnings dwarfed common people's salaries. This was in 1928, a year before the stock market crash and Great Depression. Notice that 2007 and early 2008 have also seen scores of hedge funds which imploded because of overleverage, bad judgement in investments and client redemptions.)

'To some degree it's a very gigantic version of Las Vegas,' said Gary Burtless of Brookings Institution.[13] That's right. The difference is that the casinos in Las Vegas are supervised by a Commission, and there is also a sheriff. By contrast,

---

12 *New York Times*, 16 April 2008.
13 Idem.

nobody is supervising the hedge funds and no sheriff has brought anyone to justice. William Donaldson, the chairman of the Securities and Exchange Commission (SEC) and a former well-known investment banker, lost his job when he suggested that some form of hedge fund supervision was necessary.

In China, too, supervisory authorities will have to take action against illegal lending by fair-sized unlicensed banks. In 2005 a Shanghai-based opaque credit institution, which operated in a number of provinces, freely added cash to several business. In 2007 another illegal bank which was based across the border from Hong Kong in Shenzhen operated on a larger scale.

- It did business in every province; and

- its clients included both state-owned enterprises and foreign multinationals.

Either by omission or commission, these and similar unlicensed Chinese banks operated unnoticed by officials for up to eight years. In the Shenzhen area alone, the Hong Kong-based bank was reported to have done 4.3 billion yuan ($544 million) of unspecified transactions in the year and a half to May 2007.[14]

An interesting hindsight of this opaque and highly leveraged banking business is that most of the lending really went to companies making speculative investments in property and equity shares. This has added to Beijing's worries about the surge in the stock market and property prices, as well as about the fact that an estimated 3 to 4 per cent of the broad money supply is flowing underground unseen and uncontrollable by the authorities.

5. Economic Nationalism can Damage China's Economy

It is inescapable that, whenever reference is made to the global financial system, two of the world's most populous countries are centre stage. In principle, to judge whether an economy is overheating it is necessary to compare its expansion with what can be estimated as a *sustainable* rate of growth and India's sustainable pace is still much lower than China's. China's economy performs better than India's, because:

- it benefits from higher direct foreign investments;

---

14   *The Economist*, 11 August 2007.

- it has a more flexible labour market, without the skills shortages India has started to develop; and

- it features much lower wage increases than India.

On the other hand, the two Asian megastates' continuing rapid annual growth risk turning both of them into overleveraged economies, while there is no evidence that the people governing them will apply the brakes in time. Among other things, both lack the experience of how to control inflationary periods like those which hit France after WWII and the United States in the late 1970s/early 1980s.

In the West, bank supervisors worry because an overleveraged economy, with banks featuring plenty of toxic waste in their loaded derivatives books, is the best prescription for systemic risk. In the aftermath of the 2007–2009 subprimes hecatomb, some economists said that eventually Chinese banks would also face this challenge of unsupportable derivatives exposure, even if in the previous years the government had taken special care in recapitalizing the country's big banks with public money to tap their huge credit risk exposure. Additionally, in the opinion of the same economists, Chinese credit institutions were not the only ones which need recapitalizing. Hit by a dearth of flotations and bad management, the country's 130 odd securities companies had lost billions.

- For years Chinese brokers failed to make enough money to match the returns they guaranteed their customers; and

- according to reports, some had eaten into their capital, with the result that all but 10 or so brokers are technically insolvent.

Western economists suggests that the sorry state of Chinese investment banks is the prime reason why China's capital markets are still underdeveloped, thereby handicapping the creation of a healthy capital market. Critics of China's financial industry further say that a limping procedure of credit-based intermediation has made the whole economy dysfunctional. Evidently this is not in China's interest , but neither is it in the interest of the EU or the US. The great *ifs* of Asia today are what would happen:

- *if* China cannot sustain its growth; and

- *if* Japan cannot restart growth and cannot get its banking industry back on its feet.

Because of well-known twentieth century political and military history, there is no love affair between Japan and China, but this does not change the fact that post-WW II and for four decades Japan has been the motor of East Asia while China is the new one. If the two countries faltered, they would hurt economies throughout the Pacific Basin and, by extension, all over the globalized marketplace. That, economists say, is a shocking thought.

Both in China and in Japan, better management could help. In China's case much of it was thought to come from abroad. At least, that's what seemed to be the case some years ago. More recently, however, many people in the Chinese government's hierarchy have expressed misgivings about the impact of foreign investment and economic reform. This came to the fore in April 2006 when, during the annual session of the National People's Congress (China's parliament), the head of government's statistical service said that:

- *if* 'malicious' mergers and acquisitions by foreign companies in China continue unchecked;

- *then* China's brands and its innovative ability would disappear.[15]

This is, of course, nonsense, but it is also indicative of how people think. (A precedent is the licences Russia gave to oil companies in the 1990s, only to be revoked 14 years later with Kazakhstan following on Russia's heels.) China would do well to heed the advice not to close its doors to foreign skills and know-how, as Japan did in its heyday. *Brain gain* is the only commodity which has proved itself thrillingly effective in the gladiatorial arena of a globalized economy, on which China has (so far) capitalized so well.

Additionally, it should be noted that the National People's Congress is not the only institution to have second thoughts. Another organization with similar notions is the All China Federation of Industry and Commerce. This is a Party-backed lobby group which appealed to parliament for measures to protect the country's economic security by restricting takeovers in China by foreigners.

Some experts now suggest that it is quite likely that a new wave of economic nationalism is taking off in China, which might eventually emulate

---

15   *The Economist*, 1 April 2006.

the prevailing economic nationalism in some of European Union countries. If so, the different bureaucrats don't appreciate is that economic nationalism can cost their economy dearly, not only because of loss of foreign investments but also, if not mainly, because of loss of:

- technology transfer; and

- foreign management skills.

According to reports, China's debate over foreign acquisitions has recently intensified, with some papers publishing blunt criticism of the sale of stakes in Chinese state-owned banks to foreign banks. Critics say that these deals were priced too low, given the huge amount previously invested by the state in recapitalizing them because of bad debts – *as if* the Chinese banks' bad debts were the fault of foreign investors.

Chinese critics of privatizations and foreign acquisitions are also worried that the 25 per cent share allowed to be held by foreign companies in each Chinese bank would bring some of the country's vital financial levers close to foreign control. For their part, Chinese companies complain about tax privileges enjoyed by foreign investors, who have to pay income tax at only 15 per cent compared with a 33 per cent rate for domestic entities. (Compare this to the 55 per cent tax on profits paid by French firms.)

During recent parliamentary meetings, the current Chinese leadership were also at pains to ascertain that economic reforms remained on track. Rather than being deterred by the old guard's argument of China's takeover by foreign capital, which does not even make a bad joke, the current leadership should be careful on two theoretically distinct but practically interrelated issues:

- to protect the economy from overheating; and

- to avoid creative accounting in reporting financial results.

The risks that neighbouring Japan has faced over the last 20 years are a pointer to what China may be confronted with, *if* things go out of control. Both overheating and creative accounting are traps not only for banks, but also for industrial firms and the economy as a whole.

6. Mistakes Which Should Have Been Avoided

Plenty of economists have speculated on how long America can sustain the dual deficits of budget and current account. Today, 40 per cent of purchases in the US are of goods coming from abroad, leading some experts to suggest that globalization gives the central bank the option to let the US economy power ahead without much fear of fanning inflation. Recent data, however, disproves that hypothesis as:

- worldwide commodities prices have reached for the stars; and

- the prices of finished goods are also on the rise, no matter which might be their origin.

The negative side of 40 per cent of purchases in the US coming from abroad is that the American current account deficit will widen, while current account surpluses are accumulated by China, Japan and other Asia countries, by oil-exporting states and by some European nations including the German, Swiss and Scandinavian economies. By contrast, other EU countries like Italy and France post sizeable current account deficits. (The current account for the entire Euroland is more or less in balance.)

If the American economy were to collapse under heavy budget deficits and an unaffordable amount of red ink in its balance of payments, *then* the dollar would crash – with the European Union, Japan, South Korea, India and China paying the price associated to the loss of a huge market. This would cause a global crisis from which the world would not easily recover.

Because imbalances exist all over, in its 77th Annual Report the Bank for International Settlements (BIS) too a more global view, stating that in many countries both government deficits and debts were troublingly high. Countries with twin deficits, fiscal and 'external', should appreciate the urgency of taking steps towards fiscal consolidation. This could serve to:

- reduce exposures becoming unaffordable, as well as risk premia; and

- diminish the likelihood of disruptive capital flight in the event of future major economic setbacks.

Having made this statement, the Annual Report of BIS turns its attention to the Chinese yuan, advising that there should also be a greater willingness to let the currency rise, even if there exist major internal challenges to the Chinese authorities: 'While some in China seem to believe that the source of Japan's recent problems lay in allowing the yen to rise in the late 1980s, this is a misreading of history. The seeds of the Japanese bust were actually sown in the preceding, rampant monetary expansion designed to keep the yen down.'[16]

The likelihood of China taking Japan's road to oblivion is not at all to be discarded. As should be remembered, after rising from the ashes of World War II Japan tried once again to conquer the world, this time industrially and financially – just like von Neurath had advised Hitler to do, just prior to WWII. But once again:

- Japan overplayed its hand;

- ran short of resources; and

- in 1990/91 turned itself into Asia's sick man, a state from which it still has not recovered.

There are parallels between China and Japan. The BIS Annual Report points out that given the recent rates of credit expansion, asset price increases and massive investments in heavy industry, the Chinese economy seems to demonstrate some disquieting symptoms in spite of its current expansionist mood.

Financial experts suggest that there exist dangers in this expansion, because China's bankers have still not learned enough about risk management, particularly on how to be in charge of credit risk – as if European and American bankers knew how to be in charge of it. A September 2007 article gave a focused example: '…British banks have paid top prices for stakes in valueless Chinese banks whose bad lending makes Northern Rock[17] positively virtuous.'[18]

Nor are the Chinese bankers strong in controlling market risk. Bank of China reportedly lost $9.5 billion by buying securitized American subprime

---

16 BIS, 77th Annual Report, Basel.
17 The defunct British mortgage bank which experienced a full blown run not seen since the nineteenth century in Britain, and ended by being nationalized.
18 Article by Will Hutton, *The Observer*, 16 September 2007: <http://www.observer.co.uk>.

mortgages; that is about the amount it made (after a $20 billion recapitalization by the Chinese government) by selling a good chunk of its equity to foreign banks. For its part, China SWF placed $3 billion (at the time €2 billion) of its massive foreign exchange reserves with Blackstone, the American private equity group, just two months before all hell broke lose in the financial markets and the Blackstone stock lost altitude. The move suggested that:

- China started to switch investments from US Treasuries into riskier assets;

- but risk control has been wanting, therefore it put plenty of money in private equity just at the time this industrial sector was overheating.

This was not an investment decision made by wise men; and it is not the only one of its kind. A government-sponsored craze for milk production which went sour provides another example. 'Good cows, good grass and good feed produce good milk,' said a huge slogan inside a dairy farm built by villagers some years ago in Shaliuhe. 'Profit for the country, profit for the township, profit for the village and even more profit for the people.'[19]

Urban Chinese began to acquire a taste for milk and milk products around 2000. As nutrition improved and milk derivatives became a status symbol, the government-sponsored dairy industries looked like a sure way of making the peasants richer. In the aftermath:

- milk production skyrocketed from 8 to 210 million milk tons in 2005(!), or over 2,600 per cent in six years;

- but urban spending per person on milk products tapered off in 2002 while no bureaucrat took notice of it, leading to a 1,600 per cent overproduction of China milk.

Additionally, just as in the case of Japan in the 1970s and 1980s, China's inland investments are still in large part focused on export markets which would be badly affected should there be an economic shock or even greater protectionism in western nations. Just at the time the government is relying on export markets to maintain employment growth, this wide-open window of opportunity may be closing.

---

19 *The Economist*, 31 March 2007.

As if these mistakes were not enough, there is no evidence that the Chinese government used the buoyant economic and financial conditions of 2004 to early 2007 for structural reforms that would enhance a more stable pace of growth and put a lid on inflation.[20] Instead, since 2000 the curve of inflation has emulated that of China's economic growth – with a tendency to get out of hand.

In a way fairly similar to what has happened in other Asian countries, China's widening current-account surplus and its strong investment imply not only excess supply of material goods, but also excess money supply. As a result of a surge in foreign-exchange reserves and low interest rates, plenty of capital is flooding into shares. Households are withdrawing their savings from low-yielding bank accounts to bet on the stock market, and so on and so forth.

That's exactly how bubbles are created. The perpetual motion machine has not yet been invented, but governments (and central banks) are always timid in punching a nascent bubble. They chose to undertake damage control after the disaster, but the experience with the US subprimes demonstrates that such an attitude is the worst possible alternative for the economy.

7. Is China Ally or Antagonist of the United States?

For economists who are optimists about what surprises the future may hold, the rapid rise of China as an industrial power is one of the spectacular events in economic history. By contrast, economists who are by nature pessimists see mainly doom in China's rapid rise. The bottom line, however, is that both optimists and pessimists are wrong, because each looks at the challenge China poses from a limited perspective. The broader view is geopolitical.

China is, and save a major bust will continue to be, a challenger to industrial US and industrial EU. But a strong economic and industrial China can also be a much needed ally for the United States, as some of the EU countries are in free fall while radical Islamism is on the rise. Let me explain this statement by means of a provocative question: How can we establish a winning strategy,

---

20 China's inflation rate shot to 8.5 per cent in March 2008 (year-on-year). Included in this are food prices, but food is *core* inflation no matter what some economists say. The inflation caused Chinese share prices to wobble.

and who should be our allies in a likely (but not certain) head-on collision of unthinkable proportions between:

- the Judeo-Christian culture; and

- the evermore aggressive Radical Islam?

A couple of years before World War II ended, Marshall Cavallero, then Commander-in-Chief of Italian Armed Forces, confided to Dr Carlo Pesenti that for any practical purpose Germany, and with it Italy, had lost the war – and Japan would have the same end.[21] But this, the Marshall added, did not mean that America and Britain had won it.

Study the past, Confucius said, if you would define the future. Ugo Cavallero predicted that after the fall of Germany and of Japan two blocs would confront one another: the Soviet Empire and the Anglo Saxons. Reflecting on the size of this challenge, the Marshall added that:

- the outcome of the confrontation pitting the West against the Soviets was far from certain; and

- the bloc that would win was the one able to gain the support of defeated Germany and Japan.

We all know the events which followed Cavallero's 1943 prediction . Notice that his prognostication about two blocs which will confront one-another when the war against Hitler's Germany ended predated by several years Winston Churchill's lecture on the Iron Curtain. The reason why, at this point in time, the 1943 reference to Marshall Cavallero is important is that today the Western world is confronted by the greatest challenge since WWII against its:

- liberal culture;

- democratic values; and

- personal as well as civil freedoms

---

21 Recalled from a personal discussion in the mid-1970s with the late Dr Carlo Pesenti. Sometime before Cavallero's statement, General Udet, chief of the German Air Force, had come to the same conclusion about the outcome of WWII and he committed suicide.

There is no way of denying that there exists a real and present danger. In 2007, in the United States the National Intelligence Council published four widely differing scenarios of how the world might look in 2020 (just a dozen years down the line) and who might be holding the upper ground in the global arena. Briefly, these go as follows:

1. *Pax Americana*, where the US continues to shape the global order;

2. *Davos World*,[22] in which the present state of globalization continues, but with Asia playing a bigger role than today;

3. *New Caliphate*, with Islamic religious identity challenging the dominance of western culture;

4. *Cycle of Fear*, in which non-state forces create shocks characteristic of an Orwellian society.

These four scenarios are not written in order of decreasing likelihood. The study of the National Intelligence Council suggests that Davos World, the second option, is the more likely followed by Pax Americana and the New Caliphate (in that order). A sharp mind will easily perceive that behind these first three scenarios lies a *Chinese connection*.

China has a constructive role to play in Davos World. It can also be a valuable western ally in the New Caliphate – in an extension of the Cavallero Hypothesis – though it would have a contrarian position to Pax Americana (as the last few years have shown).

With all factors and likelihoods taken into account, it would be a bad deal to clash with China; with hostilities coming at the wrong time and for the wrong reasons. Theoretically, this may have already started. NATO's communications experts, and evidently its generals, are worried by the fact that in May 2007, Chinese spy software was discovered in computers in the office of Angela Merkel, the German chancellor, and some of the ministries. According to one source:

• this was a Trojan Horse program, attached to a seemingly innocuous electronic file; and

---

22 Named after the Swiss resort where the annual International World Economic Forum is held.

- it was siphoning off 160 gigabytes of information when it was stopped (the Germans suspected that China's People's Liberation Army was responsible).

A few weeks later, in June 2007, it became known that a similar Trojan Horse had penetrated computers in the office of Robert Gates, the US Secretary of Defense. Pentagon officials think the Chinese were behind this Trojan Horse. China of course is not alone in preparations for a cyber war. The US and Russia are also developing their own cyber offensive and defensive capabilities, integrating them with more traditional military weapons.

It is not easy to find out who is doing what to whom. According to an article in *The Economist*, US military planners worry that China is using cyberspace for reasons beyond simple espionage.[23] This is potentially troublesome because currently our society depends too much on computers and communications – therefore a first strike attack on networks could not only cripple military systems but also disrupt civilian life. The name of the game is *electromagnetic dominance*, which may be making the nuclear threat obsolete.

Critics of this thesis of perpetual confrontation point out that what is happening has nothing to do with denial of service (DOS). It has only proved that western defences look worryingly inadequate, as Estonia discovered to its dismay in April/May 2007 when the government's and banking system's websites came under fire from PCs located in several countries. (In that case it was thought the Russians were behind the cyber attacks.)

China is also accused of having fired a missile to kill one of its own obsolete space satellites. As an argument, this is one-sided because the United States did precisely the same thing. In fact, the most troublesome thing of all is the psychology surrounding these events. Some polls indicate that one out of three of Americans believe China will 'soon' dominate the world, even if China's current income per capita is only 4 per cent of the American counterpart (although the Chinese government has so far lifted 400 million people out of poverty).

The critics of the confrontational policy tell a different story. They suggest that all this is awfully exaggerated, and that what is happening in both sides is nothing more than hackers' business, with all that excitement simply targeting the evening news. Practically, the contrarians say, the US and China have a

---

23   *The Economist*, 8 September 2007.

good understanding of one another if not an alliance – and they need each other to keep in check North Korea's nuclear ambitions.

On 13 April 2008, on CNBC, the financial channel, the Mclaughlin group debated on whether George W. Bush should attend the opening ceremony of the 2008 Olympics in Beijing, given that Angela Merkel and Gordon Brown would abstain because of the Tibet story. Usually the group's five members disagree with one another, but in this case they were unanimous that the US president should attend even if other chiefs of state boycott the ceremony. Common interests between the US and China were, they said, an overriding reason for attending.

In conclusion, there is a growing body of opinion that while America will remain the most powerful country for the next dozen years, it will not be able to protect its citizens, let alone other western nations, by acting alone. Defeating Radical Islamist terror should have been, first and foremost, the responsibility of moderate Islam. Since this does not seem to be happening, being in charge requires international intelligence and police cooperation – not only classical military divisions deployed around the globe.

Let's not forget either that, according to the US National Intelligence Council, beyond the New Caliphate scenario lies the option of the Cycle of Fear. Nothing is cast in advance in terms of winners and losers in that huge approaching conflict with the many faces of the culture of terror. Having China and India on *our* side in the war against the enemies of personal freedom, and against fundamentalist conquest, may well make the difference between gaining or losing the high ground in World War III.

PART III

EUROLAND: CASE STUDY ON THE

LIMITS OF A REGIONAL GLOBALIZATION

9

Financial Integration in the European Union

1. Is the EU a Modern Integrated Economy?

This book has been supporting the thesis that globalization and greater openness of the world economy contribute to the increase of living standards *if*, and only *if*, people, companies and states meet its prerequisites. These revolve around innovation, lifelong learning, a focused effort to be ahead of the curve and the economic need for steady adjustments including the labour market and macro-economic structural changes.

Through case studies, the preceding eight chapters provided evidence that several sections of the population, and of economic sectors, may be affected quite differently by globalization because the necessary adjustments have not taken place. As the supply of goods and services confronts an intensification of competition, only those economies which have been restructured can profit from globalization.

The statements made in the preceding paragraphs are also valid for regional economic integration, such as the 27 countries of the European Union and most particularly the 15 countries of Euroland. Because the majority of member in the EU are industrialized, the trade in goods within a sector depends on:

- the existence of economies of scale; and

- the exploitation of comparative cost advantages.

There is no uniform research and development (R&D) policy in EU member countries, but even the higher share of GDP devoted to R&D is lower than that of the US or Japan. Economies of scale result from intensive use of capital for infrastructural and other capital investments, as well as investments in technical knowledge. Neither the EU nor the US spend enough money on infrastructure.

As for EU-wide marketing networks, the fact that economic nationalism in the European Union is rampant makes their financial integration questionable at best. As we saw in Chapter 3, the Spanish government did not allow E.on, the German energy company, to buy Endesa; and the French government did not permit ENEL, the Italian power company, to buy Suez.

The irony of a dysfunctional EU is that within Euroland foreign direct investments by Japanese and Chinese companies are more welcome than FDIs from major EU players, because they are not conceived of as threats. Just the same, products made by companies in developing countries find it easier to penetrate EU markets than competitive EU-made products – in this particular case because Asian-made products have a lower cost.

Statistics are eye-openers. Between 2001 and 2006, the import penetration in the euro area of goods originating in low-cost countries rose from 37 per cent to almost 50 per cent,[1] squeezing out intra-EU trade goods made in other European Union countries. Even price increases of goods made in China and other low-cost countries did not change the aforementioned trend, because prices of imports from other EU suppliers have followed the same escalator.

- Gone are the direct advantages of the intra-EU division of labour, which played an important role in the Treaty of Rome of 1957 (establishing the European Common Market).

- This lack of producer/consumer integration in the EU is not only present with manufactured goods but as well with financial and other services.

French banks merge with French banks. Italian banks with Italian banks; and while Italian banks acquire German banks, German banks are in principle not allowed to buy French banks or Dutch banks to acquire Italian banks – even if ABN Amro bought Antonvenetta after a long fight.[2] (More on the lack of financial integration in the EU in section 2.)

---

1   European Central Bank, *Monthly Bulletin*, June 2007.
2   After RBS, Fortis and Santander took over ABN Amro, Santander sold Antonveneta to Sienna-based Monte dei Paschi for 9 billion euro. With the equity crisis which hit financial firms, on

Such a highly defensive culture, which continues to characterize several EU governments is the antithesis of what is necessary for a modern integrated financial system in the European Union, or any other region. The criteria underpinning it can be derived from an MIT Sloan School of Management study of the late 1990s, which addressed globalization and internet commerce, but in really concentrated in four domains most valid from an EU perspective:

1. how businesses are investing in different assets to create economic value;

2. how financial markets evaluate the prospects of companies in the economy;

3. what is the best performance measurement and type of financial reporting of assets; and

4. what constitutes prudent risk management in today's rapidly changing business environment.

The first three of these points focus on the input and output of an economy, using the financial system as their pivot point. Translating their message into EU terms, the first point can be rephrased: How financial and industrial entities of member states are investing in different assets *and* in different EU countries. For reasons explained in the preceding paragraphs, under current conditions, the answer is deceptive – a statement also valid for the next two points.

MIT's fourth point concentrates on risk management. No EU member country is known to have a risk management system able to follow exposures associated not just to EU financial integration but to their banking industry as well, nor does the EU Executive,. Yet, as the credit and banking crisis of 2007–2009 has documented, a holistic risk management approach is important because financial integration has the potential to alter the:

*   nature;

*   frequency; and

*   impact of risks faced by the economic system.

---

20 February 2009 the capitalization of Monte dei Paschi including Antonveneta, stood at 5 billion euro.

This is particularly true for economies undergoing the painful steps of integration. A regional economy integrating different parochial financial systems structures, as is the case in Euroland, needs much more rigorous risk testing and control action than any one of the different economies individually. It requires at the same time:

- cultural and structural changes; and

- rigorous planning and control tools.

Additionally, not only the European Union as a whole but also Euroland's member countries have failed in establishing common rules for taxation and for red tape. In late 2006 PricewaterhouseCoopers, the international accounting and auditing firm, released the results of a global study which focused on two criteria:

1.   total tax rate as per cent of 2005 profits, for an emulated medium size retailer based on second year of trading; and

2.   time expressed in hours per day necessary to comply with rules, regulations and other issues demanded by a country's bureaucracy.

In calculating the total tax burden on firms, PricewaterhouseCoopers has taken into account not only corporate taxes but also other levies. These include social security contributions, which in some countries like Italy, Belgium, France and Spain, have run out of control. Attention has also been paid to overflowing *unproductive* labour used to satisfy the bureaucracy in countries like Spain, Italy, Japan and others. Table 9.1 provides very interesting statistics.

Optimists would respond to these remarks with the statement that there are good news in terms of accounting and financial reporting, because of the homogeneous basis provided by International Financial Reporting Standards (IFRS).[3] But they should not forget that some EU countries sought ways to escape IFRS rules and their aftermath on financial reporting. An example is France, which allegedly set up a Committee to study IFRS implementation and concluded that it would apply its own modified version.

---

3   D.N. Chorafas, *IFRS, Fair Value and Corporate Governance. Its Impact on Budgets, Balance Sheets and Management Accounts*, Butterworth-Heinemann, London and Boston, 2005.

Table 9.1   Tax burdens and red tape in the EU, US, Switzerland, New Zealand and Japan

1. Top Ten Levies on Business Profits

	Country	Percent
1	Italy	77%
2	Belgium	71%
3	France	69%
4	Greece	60%
5	Spain	59%
6	Germany	58%
7	Sweden	57%
8	Austria	56%
9	Japan	54%
10	Australia	53%
By comparison:		
United States		43%
Ireland		24%
Switzerland		23%[a]

2. Top Ten Bureaucracies in Daily Hours Needed for Compliance

	Country	Hours
1	Spain	602(!)[b]
2	Italy	360
3	Japan	350
4	Portugal	328
5	United States	325
6	Austria	272
7	Finalnd	264
8	Holland	250
9	Greece	204
10	Belgium	160
By comparison:		
Ireland		78
New Zealand		70
Switzerland		68

[a]   Bravo Switzerland!
[b]   Spain has found the best prescription for ruining companies.

2. The Low Road to Financial Integration

A *financial system* is comprised of six individual but closely related components, which must work in unison supporting each other and the economy as a whole in order to obtain commendable results. Member states belonging to a 'union' must aggregate these component parts to be able to claim that member country economies are characterized by financial integration.

The most fundamental of these six components is *financial infrastructure*, comprised of both privately and publicly-owned and operated institutions. Key activities include clearance, payment and settlement for financial transactions, as well as legal, accounting, regulatory, supervisory and surveillance agents. These are core functions and, with the possible exception of the payment system, they are far from being integrated in an EU-wide sense.

The second basic component is the *conduct of monetary policy* (Chapter 7). This includes not only decisions about monetary base and velocity of circulation of money, but also their maintenance within planned limits – established to swamp inflation and support price stability. In the EU, monetary policy was the first of the financial system's pillars which has been firmly established through a well-managed European Central Bank (ECB). Its decisions, however:

- concern mainly the 15 countries of Euroland (originally 12 plus Slovenia, Cyprus and Malta).

- The other 12 EU member states, including Britain, are out of ECB's reach in terms of monetary policy decisions.

Together with monetary policy, but also as an important self-standing issue, comes *fiscal policy*, which is the third major component of financial integration. In the EU, including the member states of Euroland, this is as diverse and heterogeneous as it could ever be. Indeed, fiscal policy would have been homogeneous *only if* there were political union, but by now this is just a pipe dream (Chapter 11).

The fourth essential component is free and vibrant *financial markets* which work in unison. Correctly, economists considered financial markets' integration as a very important step, because they match investors and entrepreneurs through the issuance and sale of equities and bonds. In the early 1990s the idea of aggregating the stock exchanges of the then 12 EU members into one system was discussed, but national rivalries saw to it that this fell by the wayside.

The fifth basic element of real integration is knowledgeable and capable *financial intermediaries* that pool funds and risks, allocating them to competing financial objectives.[4] Over the last three decades credit institutions have expanded the range of their services, well beyond taking deposits and making loans but, as noted above, economic nationalism sees to it that the EU features very few cross-border banks.

The sixth key component is the *financial system's players*. These are people and companies other than intermediaries; individuals, private firms and public entities (sometimes including the invisible hand of governmental authorities) who participate in financial markets and trade products to suit their purposes. Often known as *investors*, they:

- borrow in markets;

- aim for profits;

- hedge risks; and

- generally operate as buyers and sellers of assets and liabilities.

In spite of the fact that over 50 years have passed since the Treaty of Rome, the players in the EU's financial system have become European-minded only up to a relatively low point. To a large extent, they are still British, German, French, Italian, Dutch and other national investors – better players in the international market than in the EU market. The more EU-minded are American investors, and most particularly pension funds and hedge funds.

This lack of a holistic approach to the notion an integrated financial system which characterizes the EU is a serious handicap to the aggregation of its 27 different economies. Critics say that incentives for *financial integration* in the EU are not fully present, and since Day 1 hefty subsidies paid to the different member governments out of the common purse have delayed the day of economic aggregation. For instance, with a better than medium-sized EU economy, Spain continues to be treated with subsidies typically given to an underdeveloped country, with the result that it:

- gets vast sums of EU money, which it does not deserve;

- serves as gateway for illegal immigrants into other EU countries; and

- does whatever it can to feed the fire of economic nationalism in the EU.

In a way most similar to the bad policy of paying *rent*[5] to citizens who belong to different pressure groups within a country, the EU directs *rent money* towards its arm-twisting member states. This is evidently the wrong policy because the renters have every reason for blocking financial reform and integration. Some states act *as if* they want a situation of friction and discrimination between EU member states, industrial entities, and other economic agents in their access to capital.

Quite contrary to this sort of rotten culture is the definition that the European Central Bank applies to financial integration. True integration, the ECB says, is characterized by a situation of *no* friction and *no* discrimination in terms of access to capital and of capital investment.[6] The problem is that:

- *if* in a wider market area like the EU incentives for member states are not properly aligned;

- *then* market forces are not able to drive the member states' financial integration forward.

Some sort of collective action is therefore necessary to achieve integrative results, keeping in mind that among the benefits provided (and sustained) by a larger integrated financial market, like the United States, are more vibrant capital transactions, greater depth and liquidity, reduced transaction costs and broader business opportunities.

---

5   *Rent* is an American term meaning in one short word: to give away money, such as inordinate
     unemployment benefits, aid, economic support, monetized special savers – anything that
     members of special groups might get from the state or any other authority.
6   ECB Monthly Bulletin, October 2003.

3. Lisbon Agenda, The European Commission's Action and Inaction Plans

In November 2005, Charlie McCreevy, a former Irish Finance Minister and subsequently the EU's Internal Market Ccommissioner, said that the common man must see the benefit of what he calls *Europe*. 'The only way you get the message across to the public of Europe is to keep it simple,' contended a member of his staff. 'We need a single pan-European market.'[7]

Well said. But immediately two questions come to mind: What has been done so far to bring this concept to fruition, and how successful was the eventual initiative? To answer such queries we must look at the deliverables of European Commission's Financial Services Action Plan (FSAP)[8] which is already nine years old, having been elaborated in May 1999 and subsequently adopted by the EU member states. Containing a multitude of ambitious but vague measures, FSAP has been (at least so far) an ill-fated initiative for:

- integrating capital markets; and

- achieving a single market for financial services in the EU (somewhat along the lines already discussed).

Launched in March 2000 in Lisbon by the European Commission, this Financial Services Action Plan has been officially characterized as a core programme aimed at making Europe the world's most competitive economy by 2010. Big words. At the start (but not thereafter), the FSAP initiative found considerable support in the main European financial markets. But by 2007, just three years before its self-imposed deadline, it had become something of an orphan. The same is true of its key measures aimed at developing and implementing *EU-wide*:

- banking supervision;

- insurance and occupational pension supervision;

- supervision of securities and investment funds;

---

7 *The Economist*, 26 November 2005.
8 Not to be confused with the IMF's Financial System Assessment Program, which is now used by many central banks in the EU. The IMF's test is also called FSAP.

- cross-sector financial supervision;

- payments, clearing and settlement;

- accounting rules;

- company law;

- market integrity; and

- fairly uniform taxation.

This is admittedly a vast programme, difficult to implement in one country, very difficult to implement in six (the original Common Market), and practically impossible to push through with the current 27 EU member states. Obscure directives written by bureaucrats in Brussels did not help and the fact GDP growth differentials are observed among EU members makes their governments nervous and the whole FASP concept Cloud Cuckoo Land.

Looking back and trying to find out what did and did not happen in the lost years, one can see that the mood towards FSAP changed for several reasons. One of them is lack of clear cut *intermediate goals* and definition of associated initiatives to meet such interims. Another major negative is *cost*; a third, that the Lisbon programme looked to many as a *déjà vu* in empty EU promises.

Companies which studied its implementation generally found that the costs of changes in their way of doing business would be far higher than originally expected. This is partly a direct consequence of a lack of political integration in the EU, and therefore of the prerequisites discussed in previous sections. For instance, Europe's regulatory regimes are:

- very different from one another; and

- difficult to tackle without waking the sleeping dogs of embedded interests.

As an example, the British code of market conduct had to be changed to take account of the EU's market *abuse directive*. In London, experts suggested that insurance mediation, an integral part of the EU directive, is the worst example of a measure that has imposed huge costs on British insurers and brokers for highly uncertain benefits. That's EU planning.

Additionally, the proverbial long hard look has been absent. In the hands of the European Commission, what began as a liberalizing initiative turned into a mess of 42 different directives and regulations, some of which are contradictory. Rather than being a road map, these are full of impenetrable detail. In its defence, the Commission says such contradictions became unavoidable as there has been a shift:

- away from an approach based on mutual recognition of each other's regimes;

- to a platform of harmonization, which could better serve all the EU regimes *if* it were fully developed and implemented.

Critics answer that too much effort has been devoted to harmonizing small retail markets and this simply does not make sense. Another reason for disillusionment with FSAP is the continuing parochial behaviour of many EU governments and their central bankers. In his days at the helm of the Bank of Italy, Dr Antonio Fazio stood in the way of European banking consolidation by ruling out takeovers of Italian banks.

- Fazio's roadblocks, and those of other economic nationalists, are symbols of obstacles to the creation of pan-European financial institutions.

- Yet few people doubt that pan-European institutions are likely to have far greater impact in creating a more competitive financial market in the EU than bureaucratic details of FSAP.

Financial integration, social issues, the knowledge society and other plans looking for a home became collectively known as the *Lisbon Strategy*, aimed to make the old continent 'the most competitive and dynamic knowledge-based economy in the world'. This sounds like a *folie des grandeur* at a time when the Lisbon Agenda has found it difficult to lift off.

In 2005 the EU Council of Ministers adopted a package of Integrated Guidelines for Growth and Jobs, bringing together broad economic policy and employment guidelines. In 2006 these Integrated Guidelines were updated following the submission (in autumn 2005) of the Member States' National Reform Program (NRPs) and of the European Commission's Community Lisbon Program.

That's the stuff one can expect from unwilling and unable politicians. In October 2006 Member States submitted updated NRPs, which were assessed by the Commission in its 2007 Annual Progress Report. Then, in March 2007, the European Council endorsed a second update of the Integrated Guidelines, which still needed to be formally adopted by the EU Council of Ministers. With many members applying the brakes, it is not surprising the Lisbon Strategy cannot succeed.

Another pipe dream is the Lisbon Strategy of ambitious budgetary consolidation. Achieving a sound budgetary position is a 'must' but it is unpopular because it means budget cuts. Associated to this is the goal of improving the quality of public finances, which over the years has been answered through steady and growing deficits. It would take a couple of miracles to respond to the Lisbon Agenda's calls for redirecting public spending towards more productive uses.

4. Markets in Financial Instruments Directive by EU Commission

People looking for a sudden 'big bang' change in the financial world of the European Union, something like Thatcher's *Big Bang* which altered the British securities regulation, will be disappointed with the Markets in Financial Instruments Directive (MiFID). The general opinion is that, with many countries and companies behind in its implementation schedule, it will take years for the real impact to be seen.

'The biggest thing now is the need for institutions to complete their plans, stabilize their infrastructure and get a sense of business as normal,' said Stephen Christie, lead partner for regulatory and risk management at Ernst & Young. 'Next is figuring out how to work in a MiFIsD world.' 'If you go to a classic MiFID conference, everyone is giving nice presentations about what it means, but we're not seeing much in the way of big strategic thinking,' suggested Nader Farahati, a consultant at Oliver Wyman.[9]

The European Union's Markets in Financial Instruments Directive, which replaces the Investment Services Directive, aimed to streamline the regulation

---

9   *The Economist*, 26 November 2005.

of the EU's banking industry, increase transparency and reduce costs for users of financial instruments such as equities, bonds and derivatives. According to supporters, MiFID was going to have a profound impact on the organization and business strategies of:

- investment firms;

- stock exchanges;

- asset management firms; and

- other financial services intermediaries.

Critics doubt these claims, as well as the claim that it would lead to more integrated European capital markets, and bring greater competition because it abolished some existing obstacles to competition between trading venues (for instance, by ruling out the provision mandating execution of share trades on the national stock exchange as a requirement for the best execution of transactions by investment intermediaries.)

According to the MiFID, a transferable security that has been listed on a regulated EU market can subsequently be admitted to trading on other regulated markets, even without the consent of the issuer. Accompanied by the exemption from obligation to publish a prospectus in line with conditions specified by the Prospectus Directive (which is a mistake), this aims to provide more competition by regulating the markets' cross-border level (which is positive).

Critics, however, comment that this will lead to *regulatory arbitrage*, with financial institutions being attracted by national markets known to be lightly supervised. Besides that, it will require large amounts of new information technology and a clear decision on who pays the implementation cost of financial companies.

Bankers reckon that MiFID's bill for the average European investment firm would be 30 million euro ($45 million). Another estimate puts the cost of technology implementation in Britain alone at £1.5 billion ($3.0 billion). Notice that these are optimistic statements based on the hope there would be no stop-and-go due to rearguard actions by EU governments aimed at protecting *their* investment banks from mergers and acquisitions.

'This is probably the biggest piece of financial-services legislation ever passed in the world,' said Bob Fuller, head of Information Technology at Dresdner Kleinwort Wasserstein who co-chaired a working group on the directive. 'Its aim is to completely reshape the financial markets in Europe.'[10] In this regard, the failure of FSAP is a bad omen for MiFID.

The integration of financial infrastructures (see section 2), monetary policies, financial markets and accounting standards, as well as the golden horde of different financial players implies significant redistributions of tasks, involves unknown risks and requires a reconfiguration of checks and balances as well as barriers to contagion. This means that public authorities should establish EU-wide mechanisms allowing for:

- monitoring;

- analysis; and

- stress testing of developments in credit, market, liquidity and operational risks.[11]

Within the perspective of an integrated financial system, an integral responsibility of EU-wide action is the development of appropriate legislative and regulatory frameworks, which enable both the broadening of business opportunities and proactive risk control – while delivering market freedom and assuring financial stability. Market forces may only succeed where a legal and regulatory frameworks have paved the way, the judiciary is not corrupt and nepotism or occult interests are not calling the shots – as so often happens.

Indeed, many experts have suggested that, while McCreevy's MiFID initiative is in the right direction, in the jungle of European Union regulations and of highly heterogeneous legislations by jurisdiction it will go nowhere. To reach its goals, it must manage to change the banking laws in different member countries and this is a Herculean task particularly in regard to:

- embedded interest; and

- opacity of financial reporting.

10 *The Economist*, 26 November , 2005.
11 D.N. Chorafas *Stress Testing for Risk Control Under Basel II*, Elsevier, Oxford and Boston, 2007.

The London Stock Exchange (LSE) provides an example. Before Thatcher's *Big Bang* of the mid-1980s, the LSE was run by an 'old boys' network which kept the business closed to outsiders – opaque and inefficient. They raised hell when the government deregulated the financial markets in 1986 but Thatcher stuck to her guns. Measured by results spanning LSE's prosperity of over more than two decades, it is clear that an:

- open;

- transparent; and

- efficient market

has greatly assisted London's City in its reign as global financial hub, but it was beneficial not just to the LSE itself as it became the object of takeovers. The prediction now is that *if* MiFID is successful, *then* the EU stands a good chance of moving towards a single market in financial services in which firms can, at least in theory, do business seamlessly across national borders. What will happen in practice is the theme not of today but of 10 or more years later.

* * *

On 23 May 2008 it was announced that the European Commission would drop proposals that would have made it easier for asset managers to sell funds on a pan-European basis. Charlie McCreevy blamed outstanding supervisory issues for this change in policy, stating that: 'When I bring forward my proposals to the Commission of the UCITS [undertakings for collective investment in transferable securities] framework in the coming weeks, it will not contain management company passport provisions.'[12]

McCreevy added that no such provisions will be advanced unless and until member state security market regulators develop, under the auspices of CESR (Committee of European securities regulators), robust and effective solutions to the supervisory challenges that have been identified in respect of the securities passport proposal. The reader should know that attempts to reform the directive on UCITS have been bogged down in disputes over how far the overhaul of the different fund management rules in EU member countries should go.[13]

---

12 *Financial Times*, 24/25 May 2008.
13 The securities passport idea was supported by Britain, France, and Germany, but was opposed by Luxembourg and Ireland, which have built up large fund administration industries under

5. Current Issues Relating to Trans-Border Integration

Three subjects are outstanding, over and above what the European Commission says: governments must bury their economic nationalism; regulators must work very closely together, abdicating some of their present-day prerogatives; and financial firms must put up skill, dedication, plenty of money and a clear strategic plan to which trans-border market integration is centrepiece. That's a tough call.

At present there is too little by way of evidence that these prerequisites will be fulfilled. Tough timetables don't permit stonewalling, hesitation and delays – yet there are plenty of them. MiFID affects a great number of institutions, investment banks, brokers, exchanges and plenty of other financial firms across the EU which many governments consider to be their national jewels. Experts suggest the overall task is colossal because the new EU directive has a bewildering array of aims:

- to harmonize securities trading;

- to provide protection to investors;

- to remove stockmarket monopolies; and

- in financial terms, to help firms operate seamlessly across the European Union.

In fact, MiFID's effects will be more far-reaching than those of Thatcher's *Big Bang*, if for no other reason than that they will affect not one but 27 countries. The supporters say that it does not matter because the implementation of the aims will be gradual. But the earliest effect is also the one where embedded interests run high. The pressure is on financial exchanges to become more efficient or consolidate; this is in fact happening, but through mergers and acquisitions not by means of Brussels directives.

In counting support for MiFID, experts ask 'who will benefit?', and the answer is not positive for bankers. In a way similar to the Year 2000 (Y2K) problem of the late 1990s, the main beneficiaries will be information technology consultancies, software developers, data providers and outsourcing services. Many investment bankers and asset managers will also profit because of cross-

prevailing arrangements.

border business to be opened up by MiFID, *if* it is successful – but the majority of bankers will probably lose, as only the fittest will survive.

Institutional investors, retail investors, private banks and alternative trading systems might benefit too, albeit much less than the classes identified in the preceding paragraphs. But people knowledgeable in financial markets think that classical stock exchanges, retail stockbrokers and, most importantly, big commercial banks will be losers. Hence, they will:

- present resistance;

- soft-pedal; and

- continue having complaints.

Moreover, there is a widening body of opinion that current complaints from different classes of practitioners are more than just a response due to vested interests. The argument goes like this: apart from specific points about MiFID and the fact that directives from Brussels are washing over Europe's financial centres, there exists a growing *regulatory fatigue*.

The way a senior banker put it, exacerbating the costs of compliance are the enduring uncertainties about MiFID's details which are still rather vague. Additionally, because of striving for rules that are politically acceptable across Europe – which is its usual practice of compromise – the EU has not crafted a precise document. Critics add that no matter what its merits might be, its wording leaves many uncertainties, even after MiFID has taken effect.

Supporters answer that this is most unfortunately unavoidable, because the EU works through inverse delegation. Therefore, national regulators were expected to transpose the EU directive into their own laws by January 2007, well before the November 2007 implementation target; and it is regrettable that this work is still half-finished. They were also supposed to settle different ambiguities by agreeing on definitions.

- That they have not yet done so, the pros add, is not Brussels' fault.

- But admittedly, until they do so MiFID will remain an unstable structure.

Officials at the EU executive add that they have been wary of dictating more detail on MiFID before the initiative was approved not only by the European Parliament , but also by each of the 27 member country parliaments. The other side of the coin is that parliaments, governments and regulators in each European Union state must be put to task because, apart from other issues, investor-protection rules have to be harmonized to provide a consistent standard in areas such as:

- investment advice;

- order-handling procedures; and

- completion of securities trades in a way known as *best execution*.

These three points have much to do with share trading and they are very relevant because MiFID wants to change the nature of competition in equity trades. This may prove complex and controversial. While most shares in Europe are still traded on exchanges, there is growing interest in off-exchange trading between investment banks. MiFID could accelerate this trend, giving investment banks advantage over exchanges.

Financial industry lobby groups have mounted a fierce assault on parts of MiFID they consider vague or objectionable. For their part, established exchanges stonewall because they see that Brussels' new directive will end equity trading monopolies. That raises resistance because existing rules force all share trades through local *bourses* and stock exchanges have their friends in parliaments and in governments.

Active or passive resistance might also develop, country by country, in respect of another goal of MiFID: increased transparency. Investors must be able to subscribe to information services that let them see the whole market in certain shares, not only what is on offer at a local stock exchange.

In Britain, the Financial Services Authority (FSA) has proposed *benchmarking* by disclosing the range of available prices, to ensure that buyers are indeed getting best prices. Last but not least, another major roadblock exists in the transportation of MiFID rules into national laws across the EU.

National differences in legislation, not just in interpretation and practice, are likely to be significant. In theory it's the same rules for all member states, but as we well know from myriad other cases, in the EU it doesn't work that way. Everybody wants to have their cake and eat it too.

6. The Lack of Integration in Euroland's Banking Industry

In an article published in its *Monthly Bulletin*, the European Central Bank made the point that properly integrated financial markets and portfolio diversification opportunities, available with a single currency, provide an important mechanism to counteract the differential impact of asymmetric shocks. This reduces the dependence of firms' and households' saving and borrowing decisions on predominantly national economic and financial developments.[14]

Oriented to Euroland members which share a currency union, this message accurately describes one of *expected* major benefits. In the background lies the fact that company spending and household consumption should not need to follow movements in output because it is possible to borrow abroad. But has this happened since the introduction of the euro?

Recent work confirms that the impact of country-specific output fluctuations on national consumption has decreased since the start of monetary union, which is positive. But at the same time there is no evidence to support any claims that monetary union has really prompted trans-border banking operations, while the challenge of home-host supervision remains (see section 7).

Rather than promoting trans-border operations in the original 12 euro-area countries, strong volume growth in lending between 2004 and 2006, allowed Euroland banks to raise their income and pour money into the new EU accession countries of Eastern Europe. This rush of capital:

- added fuel to that region's economic development;

- but also raised concerns that their consumers were loading up on credit too fast.

Before the July/August 2007 financial crisis, which changed the focal point of attention, a general opinion was that the way in which banks navigated the credit boom in Eastern and Western Europe would determine not just how

---

14   ECB, *Monthly Bulletin*, April 2007.

their investments panned out, but also how new money would shape the fate
of the new accession countries.

Up to 2007, the eight formerly communist regime East European nations
that entered the EU in 2004 had been growing at an annual rate of more than 5
per cent, compared with 1 to 2 per cent in Germany and France and practically
0 per cent in Italy. The expectation that these economies would be an important
contributor to the EU's economic strength must, however, be tempered by the
fact that, with the exception of Poland, these are relatively small economies.

Some economists suggest that easy credit in Eastern European was the effect
rather than the cause of lowered credit standards, since lower credit standards
had been the rule in the 2004 to 2007 timeframe. A positive factor in Eastern
Europe's development was that it had a young, well-educated population
attractive for companies looking for:

- low-cost labour; and

- access to rapidly developing markets.

At the same time, however, intense competition among Western European
credit institutions, particularly in mortgage markets, contributed to a narrowing
of margins and a gradual easing of their lending standards. This was true not
only in Eastern Europe but also in several Euroland countries, building up
future vulnerabilities for banks, especially as lending standards had been too
easy.

Another domain where Euroland's financial services industry left much
to be wanted was in lowering the cost of banking in a trans-border sense. A
2005 study by Netherlands' ING Bank and Capgemini, the French software
company, found huge variations in the price of core banking services, ranging
from:

- an average of 252 euro a year in Italy;

- to 34 euro in Holland, making the difference nearly 1:8.

Is it that Italian banks are so much more greedy? The most likely answer
is that Dutch banks are both better organized and smarter. They make more
money than Italian banks do from selling customers extra services like wealth

management, mortgages, personal loans and ancillary products, rather than turning their clients off with high safekeeping fees for current accounts. Being better organized helps to keep costs lower.

Cost-effectiveness is not a widespread concept among Euroland banks. A study carried out by Mercer Oliver Wyman at about the same time as those previously mentioned, for the Italian Banking Association compared the average cost of keeping a current account in various European countries. In this case cost were found to be:

- 133 euro in Italy;

- 94 euro in France;

- 86 euro in Spain; and

- 68 euro in Germany; here the ratio is 1:2.[15]

Where practically all Euroland banks follow a more or less similar policy is in overcharging on credit card fees. This happens in the US too, where Wal-Mart, a big retailer, led a class action against Visa and MasterCard, the world's two giant credit-card companies, whose members include most of the world's major banks.

Visa and MasterCard, this action said, prevent merchants from steering customers towards using debit cards, which have much lower transaction cost than credit cards. (A big issue is the so-called *interchange fee*, or percentage banks charge merchants at point of sale for processing a credit card payment with another bank. Morgan Stanley, an investment bank, estimates American banks earn around $24 billion a year from interchange fees.)

Every jurisdiction has a different approach to the question of credit card costs. To their credit, French regulators moved against the country's big banks for unreasonable pricing on payments with the *carte bancaire*. In other European countries, too, supervisors intervened to force banks to slash interchange fees on credit cards, on the ground that payments are an area to which banks, customers and regulators must pay a good deal of attention.

---

15 *The Economist*, 21 May 2005.

Another case involving fees in Euroland is the cost of cross-border payments. Since July 2003 a European Union regulation has required banks to apply the same charges for small euro cross-border payments (of up to 12,500 euro) as for domestic payments. But banks found a way to circumvent this directive.

Unless the international bank code number and account number are supplied in exactly the right format, most banks charge an extra handling fee to send a payment outside this network. Moreover, the bank usually needs an arrangment with a correspondent bank in the receiving country, which then uses its own national payment network to send the money to its destination. Hence the double charges, which are extravagant.

This double charges argument forgets that the failure to integrate payment networks is not the client's fault and they should not be made to pay for it. To its credit, the European Central Bank has taken the lead in establishing *Target*, a cross-border network which facilitates Euroland's payment and settlement system.

7. Banking Regulation and the Home-Host Challenge

According to an A.T. Kearney survey of American CEOs, 21 per cent of respondents cited terrorism as the top risk, while 72 per cent said government regulation was the biggest risk when making new investments abroad.[16] One should not expect that the situation in the European Union is any better. As Table 9.2 shows, the EU's supervisory authorities are overflowing with regulatory and supervisory committees of all sorts – but as Henry Ford once said, a committee cannot drive a business just as it cannot drive a car.

Urwick, a well-known British consultant of the 1930s, put his thoughts in a way which hit to the very heart of the problem: a committee has neither a soul to blame, nor a body to kick. In the last analysis, regulatory miscoordination boils down to two background problems facing the globalization and regulation of banking at large, and most specifically a common currency region like Euroland, which aims to integrate its banking industry:

1.   differences in legal mandates; and

2.   authority kept under national jurisdiction.

---

16   *The Economist*, 24 January 2004.

Table 9.2   European Union Regulatory and Supervisory Committees

Committee	Participants
Regulatory Committees	
Banking Advisory Committee (BAC)	Member states' ministries of finance, banking supervisors, central banks, and European Commission (EC)
European Securities Committee (ESC)	Representatives from member states' ministries of finance, European Central Bank (ECB), securities regulators and EC
Insurance Committee	Member states' ministries of finance/economic affairs, insurance supervisory authorities, and EC
Supervisory Committees	
Banking Supervision Committee (BSC)	Member states' central banks, banking supervisors, ECB, EC, and Group of Contact (GoC)
Group of Contact (GoC)	Member states' banking supervisors and EC (Middle Level)
Committee of European Securities Regulators (CESR)	Securities supervisors from EU member states, and EC. The ECB can be invited to participate
Conference of Insurance Supervisory Authorities (CIS)	Member states' insurance supervisors, European Commission
Cross-Sector Committees	
Cross-Sector Roundtables of Regulators (CRR)	Chairperson and secretaries of the BAC, ESC, BSC, GoC, CESR, ands CIS
Mixed Technical Group (MTG)	Member states' regulatory and supervisory authorities for banking, securities, and insurance, and EC. ECB participates as an observer

Pillar 2 of Basel II,[17] the new capital adequacy framework for commercial banks,[18] emphasizes home banking supervision; yet the global financial fabric, too, needs a sheriff as George Soros aptly suggested.[19] Today, host supervisors are more interested in matters concerning depositors at-home protection, while on other issues like bank illiquidity and overleveraging there is a curious laxity on supervisory side. Global supervision is weak if not altogether nonexistent. Yet,

- Citibank operates in 101 countries;

---

17   Pillar 1 is concerned with capital adequacy (and it has been subject to regulatory arbitrage); Pillar 3 is market discipline.

18   D.N. Chorafas, *Economic Capital Allocation with Basle II. Cost and Benefit Analysis,* Butterworth-Heinemann, London and Boston, 2004.

19   In the course of the World Economic Forum of 2008 in Davos, Switzerland.

- Royal Bank of Scotland operates in 80 countries;

- ABN-Amro operated in 60 countries, and had three hosts: Netherlands, US and Brazil;

- Crédit Suisse operates in nearly 100 countries and it also has three hosts: Switzerland, US and Britain.

The issue raised between the lines of these statistics can be expressed in one short question: who is *the* supervisor of these banks? One of the crucial factors determining home-host relationships is the degree of reliance a supervisor can place on assessments of regulatory authorities in other jurisdictions, particularly with respect to:

- validation; and

- ongoing monitoring of capital adequacy, liquidity and risk control.

The way an old proverb has it, who has ten fathers has none. Parties in banking industry transactions worry about counterparty credit risk, and for good reasons as the 2007–2009 banking crisis proves. For their part, large multinational banks with offices in dozens of countries worry that the latitude given to national regulators could lead to a patchwork of incompatible rules.

Not to be left behind, some of the major regulatory authorities are afraid that several national regulators are incapable of supervising adequately the huge multinational financial organizations operating under their jurisdiction. They are also concerned about many unanswered questions on home-host definition. Such arguments are just as valid in Euroland as in the global financial market. For instance, how is the second and third home country defined: is it by:

- being listed in the local exchange?

- Having a large operation? How large?

- Other conditions such as the stature of the local head in the global management framework?

The fact that Basel II's Pillar 2 places a great deal of supervisory responsibility on a mammoth institution's national authority raises the question how large the differences can be in supervisory directives between host country and home country and among the different hosts. Do they have any common criteria? How great is their divergence? Will Pillar 3, that is *market discipline*, iron out differences by jurisdiction? Or will Pillar 3 also be at the discretion of national supervisors?

Other unanswered home-host challenges have been particularly brought into perspective by the subprime crisis of July/August 2007. Which *credit risk* issues should be treated the same way globally? Does it make sense to have different credit risk rules and thresholds by jurisdiction? Similar questions exist for market and operational risks. Should there be global, or at least EU-wide, rules on how often a multinational financial institution must hold meetings with home and host regulators, to discuss:

- credit risk and market risk problems?

- Jurisdictional differences?

- Specific subjects on home-host challenges? Is such accord feasible?

- In which way its effectiveness can be judged?

The home-host issue is in the early stages of being addressed. This, however, is not true of model control (see). 'This [home-host] is a very important issue,' suggested Anders Bredhe of Finansinspektionen, 'We have started discussing it with German and Scandinavian supervisors.'[20] Eventually a written document will stipulate which authority will have responsibility for which part of the bank's book.

The aforementioned regional trans-border effort on home-host coordination is also examining Basel II's IRB models and operational risk models. The principle is shared responsibility. For instance, Swedish supervisors will rely on Norwegian authorities for inspection purposes, but:

- *if* the models and method (M&M) used by the bank's Norwegian subsidiaries were developed in Sweden;

---

20 Notes taken in a personal meeting.

- •   *then* this M&M becomes the responsibility of Swedish supervisors, although they will invite their Norwegian colleagues to participate in the bank's M&M examination.

'The criteria governing home-host relationships are a function not only of type of operations but also of size, and of materiality,' said Joar Langeland, of Skandinaviska Enskilda Banken (SEB) during out meeting in Stockholm. 'We have dialog with Swedish and German supervisors to establish common definitions.'

Since October 1996 BIS released an international directive on supervision of cross-border banking. But these rules were primarily designed to close regulatory loopholes under which some banks have been able to undertake prohibited banking activities, by constructing complex networks of affiliates in offshores, as well as to:

- •   prevent future BCCI risk; and

- •   control systemic dangers.

The goal of the BIS directive has not been to resolve the myriad of day-to-day home-host problems which, given their dynamic nature, cannot be achieved once and for all. Cross-border challenges with models provides another example of the need for steady observation, experimentation and actualization. As the mid-2007 subprime crisis demonstrated, king-sized model risk exists.

8. Beware of Model Risk

In one of the research meetings I held, the question was asked: 'Would you buy the statement that once an internal model for credit risk or market risk is approved at banking group level by home country supervisors, host country supervisors should accept this for all subsidiaries?' My answer was definitely no!, asking the counterparty 'What do you suggest may be the aftermath of cross country differences in:

- •   level of activity;

- •   underlying risk factors;

- market non-linearities;

- fat tails[21] of returns;

- unexpected extreme events;

- level of confidence which has been chosen?'

What about models whose basic assumptions are turned on their head after major events like the July/August 2007 credit crash and those which preceded it? Who should be responsible for auditing the banks models after a major financial adversity: the home supervisor, a group of host supervisors, each of them individually, or all of them together?

From the time of the Market Risk Amendment of 1996[22] until the July/August 2007 major banking crisis, mathematical models were considered to be the upcoming modern way for risk management. However, when their results were put to test by the banking and credit crisis, the confidence placed in them waned. As an article in *The Economist* put it: 'The people at Goldman Sachs lost a packet when something happened that their computers told them should occur only once every 100 millennia.'[23]

All of a sudden the financial industry and its regulators discovered that financial model-making was in its infancy and when confronted with the facts of business life, the assumption underpinning different models did not pan out. Therefore, it is impossible to estimate through artifacts the gains and losses engineered by events like:

- risk embedded in complex instruments;

- asymmetric market behaviour;

- switches in market sentiment;

- tisk concentrations among major players;

---

21 Also known as Hurst exponent, after the British engineer who studied the floods of the Nile, fat tails reflect the fact that certain events (like floods) repeat themselves year after year, rather than being normally distributed.

22 D.N. Chorafas, *The 1996 Market Risk Amendment. Understanding the Marking-to-Model and Value-at-Risk*, McGraw-Hill, Burr Ridge, IL, 1998.

23 *The Economist*, 18 August 2007.

- how long liquidity will last; and

- whether the central bank will be taken hostage.

Even the results provided by the regulators' beloved *value-at-risk* (VAR) proved to be nearer to myth than to reality. Year-end 2007, at Merrill Lynch (excluding CDOs and residual securities) VAR said that the investment bank's exposure was equal to $65 million, but in real life the losses were equal to $8.4 billion.

- The error between model-based and real life exposure to risk, was equal to 12.923 per cent. If subprime and residual securities positions were included, then VAR-based losses were $157 million. In contrast, at end of 2007 real life losses hit $24.5 billion.

- In the aftermath, the difference between marking-to-myth and real life became equal to 15.605 per cent.

Mistakes of that order of magnitude can have catastrophic effects, because when the system is broken somebody has to fix it – and that costs big money. In the early 1980s loose rules and decision delays brought the bailout of Argentina's banking to 55 per cent of GDP. Bailouts and restructuring of Japan's banking system (1991–2007) have cost a stunning 130 per cent of GDP.

(By contrast, in the early 1990s the bill for fixing Sweden's and Norway's banking system – including bailouts – was 3 per cent of GDP. Both countries kept costs low by acting swiftly. Denmark's costs were even lower, because of strict capital rules. Finland's costs were somewhat higher, at 8 per cent of GDP, but way below those of Japan and Argentina.)

The lack of control over financial models closely correlates with the difficulty of providing a homogeneous regulatory home-host environment. One of the stumbling blocks is organizational: coordinating the longer-term view of banking business and shorter-term focus on annual results. Another is defining the exact nature of threats posed by cross-border regulatory uncertainty:

- to the financial industry at large; and

- to financial institutions which find themselves in difficulty when facing contradictory rules and resulting obligations.

The main background reasons of such difficulties can be found in heterogeneous ways of handling different types of risk transfer among jurisdictions; different regulatory rules affecting credit institutions and their use of capital; and the increasingly complex and demanding environment due to high leverage and growing use of derivative instruments.

10

The Euro: Curse or Blessing for the EU Economy?

1. The Euro's Tenth Anniversary and Ireland's Debacle

The euro is unique among the main currencies in that it is the product of a monetary union that followed a common market agreement, but has not been accompanied by political union. This asymmetric approach to economics and politics has raised a long list of questions about the common currency's future prospects, particularly in the longer term.

The pros say that in its first decade of life, up to January 2009, from the standpoint of economic stability the euro has been a success. But at the same time economists admit that, contrary to the hope when it was launched, with a few exceptions such as Ireland and Spain,[1] the common currency has not fostered fast economic growth. What it did was strip off the licence to print money. This should have forced Euroland's member countries to put their house in order: they didn't.

Will the second decade of the euro's life be different from the first? In February 2009 one of Euroland's finance ministers conceded what matters for him is 'the markets, not Maastricht'.[2] Other government officials said that several countries are finding that they are too disorderly to follow a strict monetary policy; still others have pointed out that the Maastricht criteria for the euro have been rendered irrelevant by the excesses of some of Euroland's members.

Critics of the process which instituted a common currency without a political union bring up Ireland as an example. The Irish government's late

---

1   Which now are in trouble because of their excesses.
2   Meaning the accords which led to the common currency (see section 3).

2008 wholesale guarantee of the country's overleveraged banking sector, in terms of deposits and debt, has damaged the euro. Such a move would have been threadbare if Ireland had still managed its own currency:

- investors would have taken fright at the scale of the Irish banks' excesses and obligations, compared with the country's GDP;

- only the fact of being part of Euroland has made a currency run far less likely, while it increased the likelihood of the European Central Bank and Deutsche Bundesbank intervention.

Indeed, on 23 February 2009 the wires carried the news that Nouriel Roubini, professor of economics at New York University, had spoken of an unnamed country which might default because of overexposure to guarantees provided to its banks. Another piece of market information (in fact, a rumour) was that ECB and Bundesbank were preparing a plan of support in case it became necessary – though Euroland's rules forbid this intervention. With all this, the eyes of many market specialists turned towards the island nation.

At the same time, the share price of Irish banks tumbled as investors fretted that the government's nationalization of the Anglo Irish Bank would not be the last; and economists stated the obvious: that the fallout of this particular crisis would have been much worse were Ireland not part of Euroland. Not only would the market reaction have emulated that of Iceland in 2008, but also Ireland would never have been a financial centre without Euro membership.

Ireland, of course, has by no means been a lonely contributor to Euroland's tremors. Belgium, with its big banks and huge public debt, has also benefited handsomely from being a Euroland member. Outside the euro, Spain would have struggled to fund its current account deficit, the world's second largest. And Italy would have seen a run on its currency if it were still the lira (see section 10).

The bad news for the euro came to the foreground in the big way, as in January 2009 prices of credit default swaps on certain Euroland sovereign debts rose sharply. This suggested that investors had started to become concerned about risk of default. Examples are risk premiums for indebted governments such as Greece, Italy and Spain.

- Investors fretted about the three countries' demand for cash; and

- their fears reflected uncertainty about how those governments debts would be financed.

It is not only Ireland, Greece, Portugal and Spain who are expected to see their debt-to-GDP ratios rise by 10 per cent or more in 2009, but also Austria may be joining the downbeat club. By February 2009 Greece was paying 5.6 per cent for 10-year debt, which is 250 basis points (2.5 percentage points) more than Germany and two-fifths of a point more than Poland, which is not even in Euroland. (The Greek government debt is set to pass 100 per cent of GDP in 2009, joining Italy, the only other Euroland member that has such a high ratio.)

All this is happening because fiscal discipline has taken a holiday and wages have been allowed to race forward. As an average in Euroland, between 1999 and 2007 unit labour costs rose by 14 per cent, but in Greece, Italy, Portugal and Spain they rose by 26 per cent or more – and they went up by 33 per cent in Ireland – versus 2.5 per cent in Germany. No wonder Ireland is no more competitive.

Moreover, housing slumps in Ireland and Spain have crushed domestic demand. With unemployment rising, public finances are worsening as tax receipts continue to deteriorate. As a result of past mistakes, and governments' failure to reform, some euro members are struggling with the rigour of a currency union. After they profited handsomely, they now they have to foot the bill. All this is bad news for Euroland at large, and not only for the aforementioned countries.

Because they are in Euroland, Spain, Portugal, Greece, Italy and Ireland know (or at least should know) that devaluation is not an option – unless they leave the euro, which would be incredibly disruptive and would push up their financing costs even further. At the end of the day the governments of these five countries have only two options:

- get out of Euroland;

- or choose a long, hard tightening of the belt.

Notice that France, too, and even Germany and Holland must be very careful in their policies and labour costs as well as of guaranteeing banking and other debts. The example of Ireland is startling. Bank debts have been estimated at 230 per cent of GDP – which means that the financial decadence of the banking system may well overwhelm the resources of the country that stands behind it.

- Keeping in mind these facts and figures, the reader should not be surprised that financial analysts have become negative towards the euro.

- The way a February 2009 Bank of America/Merrill Lynch study has it, the outlook for the euro is for depreciation as it faces several specific negative factors.

One of the most important of these factors is that the ongoing deleveraging of the European banking industry is likely to generate demand for US dollars. Also likely to weigh on the euro are the negative implications for credit provision. This, the aforementioned study says, leads to still another observation: that the market is yet to fully price the forecast of a 1 per cent terminal value of the ECB's minimum bid rate.[3] Other reasons negatively weighing on the euro as global currency are:

- the reserve managers re-balancing by selling off euro, as forex reserves fall (and this seems set to continue);

- widening of government debt spreads, which is likely to resume as risk appetite deteriorates;

- the fact the fiscal challenges facing some Euroland member states are mounting; and

- ongoing deterioration of Euroland's basic balance, given the combination of current account deficit and longer term capital outflows.

A February 2009 study by Crédit Suisse ranks Greece (credit rating A-), Italy (A+), Spain (AA+) and Ireland (AAA with negative outlook) at the top of the list of Euroland members whose sovereign risk has risen.[4] In fact, these ratings are far too optimistic and out of touch with reality. If Italy's is A+, Ireland's should

---

3   Bank of America/Merrill Lynch, *Forex Focus*, 17 February 2009.
4   Crédit Suisse, Research Monthly/Fixed Income, February 10 2009.

be more like A- if not outright BBB- (because of the meltdown in its financial industry) and Spain's should be A+ at best.

Indeed, in the January 2009 Bank of America/Merrill Lynch classification of banking systems by proportion of foreign claims,[5] Ireland stands just a hair shorter of bankrupt Iceland, at about 160 per cent – versus 91 per cent for Britain (which is itself much too high), 79 per cent for Greece and just 21 per cent for Russia. The latter is followed by the United States at 20 per cent. (The best of all states in this classification is Israel with about 4 per cent.)

Like it or not, these are the facts, for which there exist more than one reason. The way an article in the *Economist* had it, according to a current joke the difference between Ireland and Iceland is one letter and six months. More precisely, however, the real difference lies in a four-letter word: euro.

Peter Sutherland, a former European commissioner from Ireland, thinks that Europe's single currency has kept Ireland afloat.[6] That has been true so far, but in 2009 the country's GDP is expected to contract by 5 per cent and the unemployment rate to rise over 9 per cent. That's bad news both for Ireland and for the euro.

2. Establishing a Sustainable and Credible Common Currency

Globalization has made national currencies more vulnerable to volatility and shocks. By contrast, at least theoretically, a monetary union should have made them more stable. Practically, this did not happen because of the lack of political union and therefore of common purpose and a common direction. The policy of trying to stand taller by stepping on the shoulders of others has also played a role. It is therefore instructive to:

- turn back the clock; and

- try to establish whether the euro has been a fertile or a fragile idea.

Politics may make a great deal of difference. One of the euro's challenges has been political and social tensions in countries like Italy and France stemming

---

5   Bank of America/Merrill Lynch, *RIC Monthly Investment Overview*, 13 January 2009.
6   *The Economist*, 7 February 2009.

from an underperforming economy and the fact that politicians find nothing
better than blaming the European Central Bank for their own inability to:

- revive exports;

- swamp unemployment; and

- balance the current account.

Evidently, such attitudes don't help the euro's prospects, even if the
currency shines because of a very weak dollar. Ill-conceived attacks against the
independence of the European Central Bank come from both the left and the
right. In January 2007, speaking against the European Central Bank's monetary
policy for purely populist reasons, the French Socialist presidential candidate
Segolène Royal said that the ECB thought too much of the euro and not enough
'of the people'. This is a nonsense statement, which disregards basic facts of
economic life:

- the real enemy of the people is *inflation*; and

- all the European Central Bank is doing is to try to guard financial
  stability, avoiding inflationary risk.

Royal was not elected, but here is what a feature article in *The Economist*
had to say about the elected French president 'Mr Sarkozy has already moved
to liberalize the rigid French labor market, for example by reducing taxation on
overtime hours… But his credibility as a reformer has been marred by attacks
on the independence of the European Central Bank. He needs to stop blaming
France's economic problems on the strong euro.'[7]

The Economist comment is not so much a critique of Nicolas Sarkozy, but
evidence that politicking in the EU works against the euro. What *The Economist*
did not say is that, short of political union – which is not in the cards – the EU
resembles most closely what Alexei Tolstoy wrote about a family: a group of
enemies under the same roof. Indeed, in its commentary the British weekly
might have added the thoughts:

- after all, what is left of the 'European Union', other than the euro?

---

7   *The Economist*, 1 September 2000.

- Is the notion of financial discipline incomprehensible or is it that the importance of monetary stability is not really appreciated?

The cavalier attitude of some EU governments (and of the American government as well) towards financial stability, budgetary deficits and national debt typically characterizes not just one but all political parties. Under the presidency of Jacques Chirac, the governments of Raffarin and de Villepin pushed the French national debt from 55 per cent to 66 per cent of gross national product (GNP). This represents a more than 2 per cent per year increase in red ink

Notice that France is no exception in Euroland, or for that matter in Europe and the other continents. The Bush Administration, which got into the habit of huge budget deficits, increased the US debt by 43 per cent in its first seven years in office. Japan, formerly the rock of monetary stability, also went overboard in its national debt, while unsuccessfully trying to pull itself up by its bootstraps.

- The American people and the Japanese people are paying for these deficits with their standard of living;

- but in the case of Euroland, who are the people who will be called on for the deficits of the French and Italian governments?

Confronted with this query, many of the economists who had welcomed the euro, over the then prevailing flexible currency exchange rates for the 12 EU members originally joining the common currency, now question their own judgement. The fault, these economists say, is that several countries in Euroland made small game of the *Stability and Growth Pact* (Chapter 11).

Financial discipline makes the difference. Malta provides an example of beneficial effects of meeting the euro's entry criteria. In 2004, its public debt was almost 75 per cent of GDP and its budget deficit nearly 5 per cent. To qualify for membership, Lawrence Gonzi's centre-right government imposed austerity measures that would have been unthinkable without the lure of euro entry. But would they last?

Fiscal discipline and redimensioning of entitlements to a level each Euroland economy can afford is the answer. This, however, seems easier to do prior to entering the euro to qualify for membership than in subsequent years. 'Every finance minister knows what to do. But then no one knows how to win the next election,' says Jean-Claude Juncker, formerly Luxembourg's prime minister and currently chairman of Euroland's Financial Ministers' Committee.[8]

Individually, the different members of Euroland know that for the common good – and for their own benefit – it is important to continue on a sustainable and credible path of fiscal consolidation based on structural measures; also, to improve fiscal performance by tangibly reducing the country's debt ratio. Many governments also appreciate the importance of maintaining moderate wage increases that take into account:

- growth in labour productivity;

- Euroland vs globalized labour market conditions; and

- developments in the most important competitor countries, which is synonymous to saying 'China' (Part I).

The message conveyed by these three points is that of urgency regarding structural reforms of labour markets, along with a government policy which reduces risk associated with inflation inertia. Along with redimensioning of entitlements, a true labour market reform will not only make Euroland's economies more resilient to shocks but also create the best conditions for sustainable economic expansion *and* growth in employment.

A similar statement is valid about the need for Euroland's governments to provide a credible, well-documented path for being in charge of their current accounts. It might not be easily apparent, but there is a correlation between the requirement for increasing productivity and maintaining moderate wage growth in the public and private sectors, on one hand, and that of rebalancing the current account of those member states which are in the red, on the other.

3. The Birth of European Monetary Union and Advent of the Euro

An opinion often heard among economists is that *if* monetary union was an objective of the original Common Market (in 1957) and of the EU which followed it *then* rules and timetables should have been spelt out since the start. This has not been the case, probably because the theme of the founding fathers was political integration, not just a wider market with or without a common

---

8   *The Economist*, 14 July 2007.

currency. It was only in 1970 that the Werner Plan set a timetable for monetary union, but:

- it failed to clearly describe its characteristics, targets, and constraints; and

- it never got an unconditional agreement by all EU governments that they would make their national economic interests subservient to the supranational, common monetary unit.

The lack of such an agreement proved to be fatal. What has happened since 1970 confirms the experience with many other projects: Any plan which leaves plenty of uncertainties and ambiguities in its interpretation, and whose implementation depends on goodwill by different parties, is not really worth its salt.

Sometime after the Werner Plan was established the European Monetary System (EMS) and its Exchange Rate Mechanism (ERM) were introduced. These featured some limited objectives in terms of a common monetary policy by focusing on a stable currency zone (more on this later). This was a separate initiative from the European Currency Unit (ECU), which represented a basket of all currencies within the EU.

Several arguments were put forward in the 1980s, first heating then cooling the debate about a European Monetary Union (EMU). Behind them could be found two strong wills. Jacques Delors, then president of the EU Commission, pushed hard for monetary union and a single European central bank. By contrast, Margaret Thatcher, then British Prime Minister, was holding back just as hard, recognizing the loss of sovereignty that monetary union involves.[9]

In December 1989 a European summit overrode Thatcher's objections and set a timetable for negotiations for a common EU currency. The prevailing view was that of building an economic bloc that could stand up to America. This met with resistance from Thatcher, as she expressed plenty of reserves about economic and financial controls to be exercised by:

- the Brussels bureaucracy; and

---

9   In retrospect, there was practically no loss of national sovereignty because the politicians of
    Euroland shot down key clauses of the Stability Pact.

- a European Central Bank.

Critics of the decisions taken in December 1989 say that Thatcher's opposition, and her forceful personality, were not the only reason why what came out of that meeting was half-baked. They contend that all other heads of state were indecisive, because they were unclear in their mind *whether* they wanted a strong EU and even more uncertain about the wisdom of a strong common currency. Everybody seems to have recognized that even the level of monetary policy unification requires an unavoidable loss of independence, as:

- economic rules and interest rate levels would have to be set by one central bank in Europe; and

- political decisions would have to be made by a centralized European Parliament, which has never had much authority and does not look as if it is going to have in the future.

For instance, it was suggested at the time that *if* monetary and economic unification was to become a reality, *then* the European Parliament should have the authority to ensure compliance. This was the right concept, but it did not please many EU members and no decision was taken in its regard. What did happen, however, is that the projected common European currency found François Mitterrand as its Godfather.

As President of France, Mitterrand looked at the euro not so much as a common money but as an intentional political decision binding the Deutschmark to the French franc and other weaker currencies – and, by extension, putting a cap on the independence of German foreign policy. By all the evidence Helmut Kohl went along, which is further confirmation that economic policy decisions taken in the EU:

- are not technical;

- they are political, by more than 90 per cent.

Existing evidence suggests that at the beginning the Germans were reluctant to abandon the Deutschmark (DM). After the fall of the Iron Curtain, however, the Federal Republic had made a leveraged buyout (LBO) for East Germany. It was said at the time that François Mitterrand put the DM's integration into a common EU currency as precondition to Germany's unification, and Helmut Kohl accepted.

It did not take long for the Germans to regret that decision to march in step, but short of opting out of the EU there was no way to revert commitments made at the small Dutch town of Maastricht, where 12 European Union heads of government met on 9/10 December 1991. Political commentators were divided in their opinion regarding the most likely after-effects. Optimists said that what had been at stake was nothing less than the political and economic shape of Europe:

- Maastricht aimed to draw up the rules and timetables for close EC monetary *and* political union; and

- the single currency stipulated by Maastricht's European Monetary Union (EMU), later to be baptized 'euro', was the evidence.

Pessimists answered that the euro was partly a political ploy and partly smoke and mirrors. In retrospect, the evidence is that the euro falls somewhere between these two opinions – but no matter who is right and who is wrong, political union did not see the light. Nor did the EU Commission and European Parliament gain power over defence and foreign policy, which were seen at the time as reasonable sequels to the monetary decision.

Moreover, not everybody was comfortable with the Maastricht's currency rules, but it did not really matter because Mitterrand was determined to have his way, Kohl had agreed to it, and even some of those who doubted the single currency's wisdom knew that EMS discipline had won them gains against inflation and lower interest rates. Additionally, on the business side, many European executives were pushing hard for success at Maastricht. Otherwise, they argued:

- they will still face 12 monetary, fiscal, and legal regimes; and

- they would not be able to compete against Japan and the United States (who are the wrong targets – the country against which they are not able to compete is China).

All told, Maastricht produced an agreement mainly because of the combined weight of France and Germany. With the exception of Britain and the

Scandinavian countries, the rest of the EU had little choice but to follow. Years down the line, however, those who doubted that a single currency was a sort of financial penicillin had their day. In the 2003–2008 timeframe:

- five out of 12 Euroland members were in breach of the original Stability and Growth Pact, and

- France, Germany, Italy, Portugal and Greece, who broke the rules, did not face any biting penalties.

Nor did the free riders care for the damage they were doing to a pact they had signed. When Francis Mer, French Finance Minister under Chirac, was challenged to explain to colleagues why he was *not* bringing his country's deficit into line, he said he had 'other priorities'. This cavalier attitude to accommodating internal political aims left everybody who wanted the euro to succeed seriously concerned.

4. The Euro is a Currency without a Country

When the common currency was still on the drafting board, a few economists expressed doubts about its future because, as they put it, the euro was a currency without a country. Today many experts share this opinion, which was at the time both a critique and a prognostication of peril. The supporters answer that the euro gained weight, if for no other reason because of common interests linking the countries of Euroland to one another.

1.   Is the strategy of Euroland's members based on common interests?

2.   What's the weight of Euroland countries in economic terms? and

3.   What kind of results have their often quoted 'convergence of interests' provided so far?

Rather than betting on common interests and going forward, some of Euroland's member states have so far demonstrated an imperfect understanding of the modern economy's dynamics. Those who criticize the original 'convergence of interests' argument of the common currency, suggest that exactly the opposite has taken place. Under euro's umbrella governments are more likely to overspend *if* they, and the markets, assume they will be spared the consequences.

The fate of a currency without a country could not be described in more lucid terms. Critics say that because of their budget deficits over several years the governments of Italy, Germany, and France, the three bigger Euroland countries, have interfered a great deal with the job of the European Central Bank – and they have shown total disrespect for the Stability Pact. So did Portugal.

Yet, the politicians in charge of these Euroland countries' fortunes are old enough to understand that at the end of the day one must pay for loose budgetary policies which increase the monetary base and create inflation. Economic theory teaches that, as is the case with every asset:

- the value of a currency comes from the fact that it is *limited in supply*;

- the euro's original Stability and Growth Pact (Chapter 11) focused on maintaining smooth functioning, through checks and balances on money supply.

Through a snapshot of nominal GDP of European Union's original six member states, which are also the pillars of Euroland, Table 10.1 provides the answer to the second question regarding the weight of countries in economic terms. Another objective of a sound monetary policy based on financial stability is that of upholding the economy's strength, which helps in facilitating and supporting the production factors' efficient performance.

This is also the sense of convergence of interests among Euroland's member states. As the European Central Bank has suggested on several occasions, to achieve financial stability it is necessary to have in place mechanisms and controls that are designed:

- 'To prevent financial problems from becoming systemic and/or threatening the stability of the financial and economic system, and

- [are able to do so] without undermining the economy's ability to sustain growth and perform its other important functions.'[10]

---

10 European Central Bank, *Financial Stability Review*, Frankfurt, June 2005.

Table 10.1   Nominal GDP of Euroland (in US$, 2005)

Original 6 of EU	$ Trillion
Germany	2.79
France	2.11
Italy	1.77
Netherlands	0.63
Belgium	0.37
Luxembourg	<u>trivial</u>
Total	**say 7.67**

With the other countries of euroland (Spain represents $1.13 trillion), in mid-2007 the nominal GDP has been above $10 trillion, roughly representing:

- 75 percent of US GDP, and
- 200 percent of Japan's

But Euroland also featured about 300 percent of Japan's inflation

In July 2007, the *Monthly Bulletin* of ECB pressed again the point that upside risks to price stability arise from increases in administered prices and indirect taxes, as well as the potentially pro-cyclical stance of fiscal policy in some countries and further oil price rises. Based on these premises, the Monthly Bulletin concluded that:

> *The monetary analysis confirms the prevailing upside risks to price stability at medium to longer horizons. ... The ongoing strength of monetary expansion is reflected in the continued rapid growth of M3, which increased at an annual rate of 10.7 percent in May (2007), as well as the still high level of credit growth.*[11]

These were wise words, written some time ahead of the explosion of the credit bubble because of the US subprimes, as well as a great laxity in extending credits and in prudential supervision.

Other dangers, too, confronted the currency without a country. According to one body of opinion, even had the rules of the original Stability and Growth Pact not been downgraded by Euroland's governments, a way to get round them through the current accounts loophole would have been found.

In the globalized economy, imports and exports form a structure which can be easily subverted. Growing imbalances in current accounts is by no means a phenomenon limited to Euroland. America provides the best long-term

---

11   ECB, *Monthly Bulletin*, July 2007.

example. Because this is a flaw to a currency's well-being, as well as to that of international commercial and financial exchanges, some economists have contemplated going back to a Bretton Woods model, while others have stated that floating currencies could work smoothly only if:

- there were many more controls on capital flows, which could be counterproductive;

- a global sheriff penalizes countries which, by design or negligence allow their currencies to steadily depreciate;[12] and

- a new guarantor of last resort is found, to assume the role the US played under Bretton Woods, particularly in terms of convertibility.

The world's economy is too large for any single party to carry it on its shoulders – whether that party is the United States, the European Union, China with its 1.4 trillion dollars cash, or some sort of a common purse. Countries are unwilling to assume that role, because global regulation of Bretton Woods type, can be:

- costly;

- demanding; and

- very complex.

Just like the euro, a new Bretton Woods would be a pact without a country – contrary to the original which was based on *direct delegation* to the United States of the mission to establish a centralized currency exchange rate system, with the US dollar as the pivot point. In the immediate post-World War II years up to 1971, the American government acted as guarantor, explicitly assuming such obligation with the gold at Fort Knox as assets.

In contrast to that dollar-based model, the euro system works by *inverse delegation*. However, Euroland's member states have delegated to the European Central Bank *only* monetary policy and from time to time, when government

---

12 The steady depreciation of an important currency like the US dollar strongly recalls the cheat thy neighbour policy of the 1920s, which led to the Great Depression.

budgets are stretched, even that is questioned by different heads of Euroland states.

One might argue that the role of a *virtual guarantor* has been played by the rules of a sound economic behaviour described in *Euroland's Stability and Growth Pact*. But as we will see in Chapter 11, since Day 1 the original notion of a Stability Pact was watered down at the insistence of France's Jacques Chirac. Then, in 2005 the Stability Pact was send to the gallows by several of Euroland's member states, including Germany, which until then had been a model of financial stability in Euroland, the EU and the world at large.

5. Challenges of a Single Currency

The true challenge of a single currency is not necessarily to prevent all financial problems from arising; in fact, it is unwise to expect that a dynamic and effective financial system could avoid instances of market volatility and turbulence. Nor is it rational to postulate that all governments would exercise fiscal responsibility, or all financial institutions would be capable of perfectly managing:

- risks they assume; and

- uncertainties they are confronted with.

The *real challenge* lies in the ability to maintain a balancing act which meets both stability and growth targets, as well as being able to give in advance signals about the likelihood of systemic problems and thus putting central bankers in a position to face them. Such problems have to be managed by means of alert and concerted action, using a system of rules and regulations that:

- if necessary, restrict financial activities;

- can pre-empt peaks of market turbulence; and

- make it possible to contain the systemic risk that individual bank failures could create.

If this is *not* done, then we talk of *financial instability* rather than of stability, with the result that it becomes difficult to manage systemic risk as well as to maintain and safeguard financial assets. Under these conditions, a single currency is a hindrance rather than a help for the economy of a group of nations which lack political integration.

All this is written in the understanding that, as the 76th Annual Report of the Bank for International Settlements (BIS) pointed out well ahead of the banking crisis if 2007: 'Overall, the coming years are likely to be more challenging for the financial sector than the recent past. This puts a premium on proper risk management and on preparation to deal with expected and unexpected sources of strain.'[13] What BIS writes about financial institutions applies equally to governments.

- Since the introduction of the euro, they have been lousy in managing their finances; and

- they have simply capitalized on very low interest rates which they used to increase their deficits.

BIS also aptly notes: 'Neither the reasons behind historically low real interest rates, nor the macro-economic implications of a sharp increase after a long period of low rates, are will understood.' In other terms, the Fed's post-crisis sharp cut in interest rates has been tantamount to navigating in uncharted waters.

Based on BIS statistics, the upper half of Figure 10.1 shows that, starting in late 2002 all the way through to early 2005, the US Federal Funds rate was so low that, given inflation, the real interest rate was negative. This:

- cheated bondholders and depositors; and

- led pension funds as well as other institutional investors to take extraordinary risks by putting their money into hedge funds and alternative investments.[14]

As for the euro, in the lower half of Figure 10.1 the reader can see that real interest rate has been practically zero over 2003 and 2004, also due to fact that the prevailing inflation was running high in 2004, 2005 and 2006. Table 10.2 suggests

---

13 Bank for International Settlements, '76th Annual Report, 1 April 2005–31 March 2006', Basel.
14 D.N. Chorafas, *Alternative Investments and the Mismanagement of Risk*, Macmillan/Palgrave, London, 2003.

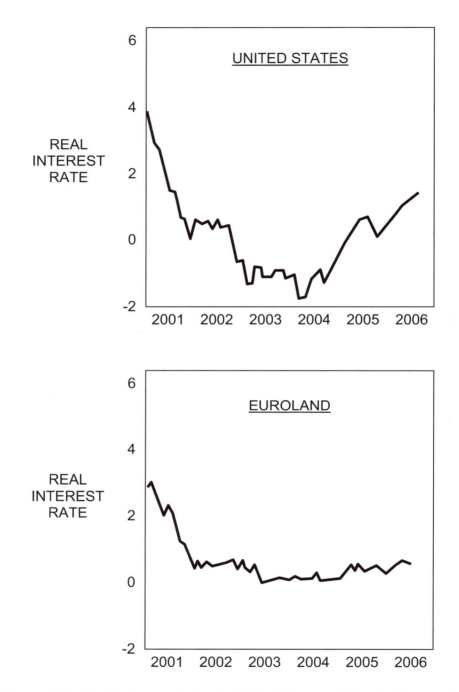

Figure 10.1 **Real interest rates in the United States and Euroland, 2001–2006**

Table 10.2 Annual Percentage Changes of HICP Inflation in Euroland 2004–2006*

Overall index of which:	2004	2005	2005 Dec.	2006 Jan.	2006 Feb.	2006 Mar.	2006 Apr.
Energy	4.5	10.1	11.2	13.6	12.5	10.5	11.0
Services	2.6	2.3	2.1	2.0	2.0	1.9	2.2

* ECB, *Monthly Bulletin*, June 2006

that rock bottom interest rates were just a small fraction of inflation in energy, and no better than inflation in services. This was the interest rate policy, but the prognostication about inflation was right. ECB's June 2006 *Monthly Bulletin* states:

> In the view of the Governing Council, risks to the outlook for price developments remain on the upside and include further increases in oil prices, a stronger pass-through of past oil price rises into consumer prices than currently anticipated, additional increases in administered prices and indirect taxes, and – more fundamentally – stronger than expected wage developments due to second-round effects of past oil price increases.

Consumers who can read the numbers and understand what very low interest rates mean to their savings, see quite clearly that such rock bottom interest rates have been a cheat. In fact, they have cheated all investors – from small savers to institutional ones. Over and above the issue that the dollar had a negative interest rate and the euro's real interest rate was maintained too long at zero, European Union governments decided to tax bondholders and depositors, *as if* their plan was to discourage savings.

Big budget deficits by Euroland's member states made the picture bleaker. Several experts suggested that the abuse of the euro and the associated controversy about Europe's experiment in monetary union, should have been foreseen and taken into account when the common currency was contemplated; but it was not. Supporters responded that there had at least been some agreement among sovereign governments about where costs and benefits lay from their viewpoint:

- the benefits were microeconomic, consisting of *potential* gains in trade and growth by doing away with costs of changing currencies and with exchange rate uncertainty;

- the costs were macro-economic, caused by money supply and the fact of foregoing the right to set interest rates, to suit specific economic conditions of a member state.

Another dichotomy dividing supporters and critics of the euro has been its significant appreciation against the US dollar and British pound as well as its performance against some other major currencies – a very heterogeneous one indeed. From mid-2007 to mid-2008, the euro posted:

- considerable gains against the Korean won (17.5 per cent) and the Canadian dollar (7 per cent) and a 1 per cent gain against the Chinese yuan;

- by contrast, it slipped further against the Czech krona (-5 per cent) and Polish zloty (-5.5 per cent), as well as Hungarian forint (nearly 2 per cent), Swiss franc, Swedish krona and yen.

On average the euro appreciated against the 22 major currencies contained in the exchange rate index and reached a new historic high in mid-April 2008. The effective exchange rate[15] was 3 per cent above its level at the beginning of 2008 and around 12 per cent higher than at the start of Euroland's monetary union.[16]

As is to be expected, the euro's strength was and remains the subject of on-and-off meetings of the *Eurogroup*, the club that brings together Euroland's finance ministers with Jean-Claude Trichet, president of the European Central Bank and Joaquin Almunia from the European Commission. Publicly, France is always pressing for depreciation of the euro, but rumour has it that what France says outside is a lot stronger than what it says inside the Eurogroup.

Without being invited to express an opinion, in an interview with *Le Monde*, the Paris daily, Dominique Strauss-Kahn, a former French finance minister who now runs the International Monetary Fund, said the euro was overvalued and blamed the excessive power of the ECB. At the same time, Strauss-Kahn said the ECB had done well in controlling inflation, which is its mandate inherited from the Bundesbank.

---

15 Taking account of inflation differentials.
16 Statistics by Deutsche Bundesbank, Monthly Report, May 2008.

Contrary to the French, who suffer from archaic labour laws that no politicians so far have been brave enough to restructure, Germans love the strong euro. The news was that the euro's appreciation dampened the strong inflation impulses acting on the domestic Euroland economy, because of the dollar-denominated international commodity and agricultural markets. Another challenge for the euro is the inflation from the housing market, particularly in Spain and Ireland, which over the past decade has been greater than in America.

Thomas Meyer of Deutsche Bank reckons that in the past five years, Spain accounted for more than one-third of Euroland's growth in consumer spending, more than half of the increase in investment and nearly two-thirds of the job gains of the euro area's bigger four economies.[17] Spain's boom has been built on a ready supply of loans. But the credit squeeze means that borrowed funds are now harder to come by, which leaves its economy vulnerable. Germany does not want imported inflation because of a weaker euro and Spain simply cannot afford it.

6. A Positive Example: Germany Thrives with the Euro

The message the preceding sections gave the reader is that Euroland's different member states are doing as they please in terms of fiscal policy and the budget, including, quite evidently, big budgetary deficits. One of the frequently-heard reasons for lack of coordination and EU-wide discipline is that national governments don't like to relinquish domestic monetary control. But at the same time, with lack of budgetary discipline and with frictions amplified by economic nationalism,

- today the EU is nothing more than an extensive free trade area; and

- in this landscape, everybody looks after their own interests.

Many economists worry that the manner in which Euroland's member states treat their common currency resembles a great deal the competitive devaluations of the late 1920s and they warn that such a practice can have disastrous consequences. This is, however, true only for those Euroland

---

17 *The Economist*, 5 January 2008.

countries which don't care to put their house in order. Germany, Holland, Finland and Ireland have prospered with the common currency.

In 2007, German exporters benefited from growth in world trade despite an expensive euro, with its current account from foreign trade being positive and fears that the stronger euro might have a highly adverse effect on German business activity dissipated. There was a sharp increase of 8.5 per cent in export sales of German goods, even if the appreciation of the euro had led to:

- a deterioration in German enterprises' price competitiveness in sales markets outside Euroland; and

- pricing and profits from exports to the Southeast Asian emerging markets and to China had to adjust to the new realities of currency exchange.

The quality of German goods as well as greater attention to costs kept the increase in the price of exports manageable. A more expensive euro softened the increase in oil prices, and altogether Germany's current account surplus rose by 1.5 percentage points to 7.5 per cent of gross domestic product.

The interest of these references lies in the fact that Germany and the other countries which prospered with an appreciating euro provide a good example of how to handle shifts in relative prices effectively. The first step in understanding the underlying policy is to read the fine print on how specific markets for exports and imports affect foreign trade, and thus economic growth, via their impact on competitiveness.

Another integral part of such a study is to analyze the effects which result from purchasing power related income gains or losses, known as *terms of trade effects*. These generally tend to counteract the competition effects. Then comes elaboration of invoicing practices and enterprises' hedging activities designed to cushion the effects of currency appreciation.

No doubt over the longer term, volume effects may be expected to occur, as exporters and importers will not be able to completely factor lasting exchange rate shifts into their prices. Germany, for example, provides empirical evidence that the exchange rate elasticity of its foreign trade, especially exports, has declined over the past few years. Longer-terms strategies therefore have to be elaborated, which accounts for this change.

The lesson to be learned from Germany's experience with the euro's appreciation against key currencies is that, to a significant extent, the impact of exchange rate movements on real exports depends both on hedging and on the time horizon of a strategic plan. Over the short term, an important role is played by the choice of invoicing currency and degree of cross-currency hedges.

- *If* it has been agreed that the delivery contracts for German exports will be invoiced in euros;

- *then* the foreign buyer bears the exchange rate risk of an appreciating euro.

On the other hand, exporters whose sales are invoiced in dollars will hold their position if they hedge their anticipated foreign currency denominated revenue flows. Otherwise, a bilateral appreciation of the euro causes their export revenues to fall when they settle already concluded transactions.[18]

Based on statistics by the Deutsche Bundesbank, Figure 10.2 provides a snapshot of Germany's imports and exports in 2007. The No. 1 export items, at nearly 44 per cent, have been capital goods. Germany imported and exported about the same amount of intermediate goods (in value) and was a net importer of oil and of consumer goods.

It needs no explanation that not every country in Euroland has the same foreign trade pattern or has made a strategic plan able to capitalize on a stronger euro. Moreover, new Euroland members (Slovenia since 1 January 2007;[19] Malta and Cyprus since 1 January 2008) are very small economies in comparison to Germany and France. Consequently, the statistical and macro-economic features of Euroland did not change following the latest enlargement; it is, however, interesting to review their characteristics briefly.

To start with, the labour markets in Cyprus and Malta differ from those in the rest of Euroland. The labour market in Cyprus is relatively flexible with a

---

18 According to surveys conducted by the German Ifo Institute, 80 per cent of the country's exports are currently invoiced in euro and only 13 per cent in dollars.

19 The Slovenian currency entered the Exchange Rate Mechanism II (ERM II) in June 2004. Because the Slovenian currency's central rate against the euro has not been devalued within ERM II and the *tolar-euro* exchange rate has stayed close to central rate, the ECB supported Slovenia as first country to enter Euroland, other than its original 12 members. A similar argument prevailed with the currencies of Cyprus and Malta.

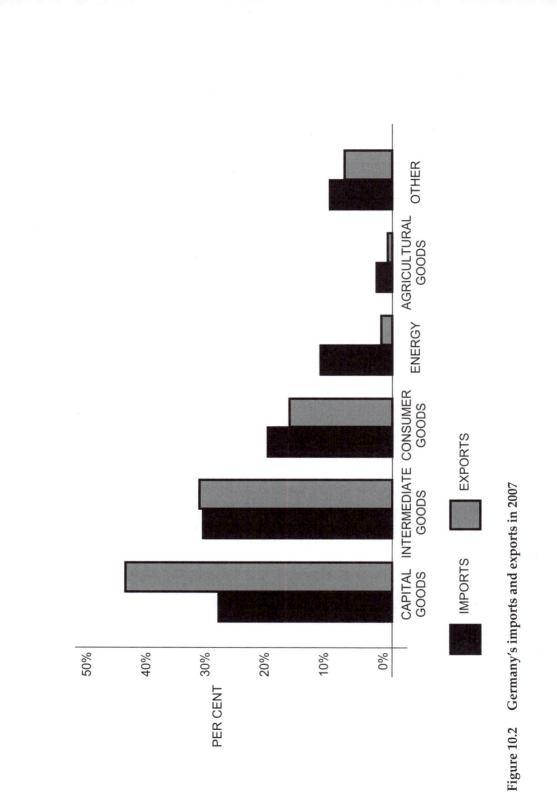

Figure 10.2   Germany's imports and exports in 2007

low unemployment rate, high labour participation and a higher employment rate than Euroland's average.

The labour market in Malta is characterized by low participation and a low employment rate. Therefore, attention must be paid to overcoming structural constraints on economic growth and job creation, notably by fostering labour participation. Key elements of further progress are:

- the strengthening of competition in product markets; and

- improvements in the functioning of the labour market.

Cyprus has a relatively high dependence on tourism and financial services, while that of industry is lower. In Cyprus the financial sector is fairly well developed, reflecting the contribution of outstanding credit to the private sector and stock market capitalization, as share of GDP. By contrast, in Malta both of these financial indicators are less developed, diminishing the importance of the financial sector.

To put its house in order Malta would be well advised to study the mistakes made by other Euroland member countries like France, Greece, Italy and Portugal, which stayed put in terms of reforms in spite of having joined the euro. In this way, they have managed to lose between 35 and 45 per cent of international competitiveness to Germany – a fact exerting a serious toll on their growth and overall performance – while, like Germany, Ireland and Finland prospered with the euro.

It is indeed irrational that, instead of fiscal discipline, Euroland member states with run-away budgets have invented new terms for old concepts, like the *monetary shield* typically used with currencies at the edge of precipice. 'What will a weak euro bring?' asks Patrik Artus, research director at Natixis, the French investment bank. His answer is: 'Nothing or nearly so because an estimated 0.6 percent of additional development, if the euro's value drops 10 percent, will be counterbalanced by a 0.4 percent reduction in consumption due to loss of buying power and inflation.'[20]

New member countries of the EU, and most particularly of Euroland, should appreciate that recriminations against the ECB, rather than hard work to put the balances straight at home, are so much more damaging because they

---

20 *Challenges* No. 58, 30 November 2006.

distract the public's attention from the real problem expressed so nicely by an old proverb: the time to fix your roof is in good weather.

From 2004 to early 2007 there was an unusually favourable global environment which ,instead of roof-fixing, was used to paper over the cracks in Euroland's weak economies. Financial history, however, cautions that it is a grave mistake to assume that supportive conditions will continue indefinitely. The global crisis which started July/August 2007 has further shaken the foundation of the single currency, obliging the ECB to postpone a needed interest rate increase. It is to its credit that its top management stood firm and did not cut interest rates.

7. Italy's and the Euro's Years of Crisis are Not Over

Mid-2005 *Global Research Highlights*, a Merrill Lynch publication, had this to say on Euroland's common currency: 'Many market participants are very concerned about what's ahead for the euro in light of the *widespread uncertainty surrounding the outlook for the EU*,[21] now that voters in France and the Netherlands have rejected that organization's proposed constitution.'[22] While the analyst whose opinion this quotation reflects thought that pessimism about the euro was overdone, others believed that:

•   there were serious reasons for being pessimistic; and

•   troubles connected to the euro would mount in the longer run.

Someone with a negative opinion about the euro was Ken Clarke, former British Chancellor of the Exchequer, prominent Conservative Party member, and (rare bird) a pro-EU Tory. Clarke was quoted as saying: 'I thought [the euro] would lead to increased productivity, efficiency and living standard, and stimulate policy reforms,'[23] before going on to predict that Britain would not join the single currency for at least ten years.

Ken Clarke's comments are particularly interesting because he is experienced enough to have a qualifying opinion. Also, and most importantly, only four years earlier Clarke's pro-EU and *pro-euro* standing is thought to have cost him

---

21   Emphasis added.
22   Merrill Lynch, 'Global Research Highlights', 17 June 2005.
23   *The Economist*, 27 August 2005.

his chance of becoming leader of the Tory Party. Predominantly Euro-sceptic Tory Party members picked Iain Duncan Smith rather than voting for the much more forthcoming Clarke.

But having seen the euro's run, Clarke's opinion changed. In an August 2005 article in *Central Banking*, he described the euro *as a failure* because it had not had the expected effect on promoting economic efficiency and improving living standards in Euroland. He went on to claim that the economic conditions to take Britain into the euro had never been ideal. Other euro-critics added that conditions for joining the euro have not been ideal for plenty of other countries – for instance, Italy.

First-class central bankers at ECB have done their best to keep the euro on course. The value of a currency, however, does not depend only on monetary policies – but also on budgetary, investment and taxation policies, which are exclusive domains of individual EU governments. These three, plus monetary policy, constitute the four wheels of the economy and, like the four wheels of a vehicle, they must work in unison.

- The economy is like a tramway in San Francisco going up- or downhill.

- *If* the conductor puts the brakes on only one of the wheels, *then* the vehicle will derail.

The fact the European Central Bank watches the euro's behaviour carefully is the only good news that I know about this currency. In September 2006 the ECB's *Monthly Bulletin* pressed this point: '…strong vigilance remains of the essence so as to ensure that upside risks to price stability are contained.'[24] In reality, however, they are not, because Euroland's governments don't care to control them.

When, in 2006, Romano Prodi and his centre-left coalition came to power in Italy, the former boss of the EU Commission promised to contain the huge deficits left by his predecessor to the tune of 4.6 per cent of GDP; or, 160 per cent over what the Stability Pact allowed as an extreme case. This would have needed budget cuts of the order of 80 to 100 billion euro ($120 to $150 billion), or somewhat more.

---

24 ECB, *Monthly Bulletin*, September 2006.

Tommaso Padoa-Schioppa, Italy's Economics Minister, prepared the austerity budget which was due, but leftist political pressures within the coalition government overturned it. The Italian Prime Minister and his ministers suddenly found that 'enhanced growth' – a pure fantasy – would feed into higher tax revenues. The windfall would have been so much that Prodi announced he was jettisoning €5 billion euro ($7 billion) of the spending cuts that he had planned for 2007. He did not, he said, 'want to make Italians weep.'[25]

The government justified another cut of 10 billion euro because of expected higher revenues by 'being tough on tax evasion, which is endemic in Italy. Adding all pipe dreams together left 'only' €60 billion euro in budgetary cuts for the government to make to stabilize economic factors and try to bring in some growth. Right? Wrong!

In September 2006, Prodi was quoted by the financial global networks as saying that he did not know where to find these €60 billion euro in cuts. He did not heed the advice of André Tardieu, French radical socialist prime minister in the early 1930s and World War I French High Commissioner in Washington, who, while in office, said: 'We must tax the poor, they are the most numerous.'

Caught between contradictory demands for raising and lowering taxes Padoa-Schioppa reminded people that Italy had vast debt whose interest soaks up cash that could be spent on infrastructure and welfare. Those Italians who pay their due complained that their country of residence was an onerous place. What is more, taxpayers got llittle value for money. Public spending in Italy was higher than in Germany (though lower than in France), but:

- public sector pay was high; and

- the quality of public services was among the worst in Europe.

An article in *The Economist* pointed out that such an imbalance fuels growing impatience with the politicians.[26] Mid-2007 Umberto Bossi, leader of the Northern League, proposed a tax strike – a sign of exasperation, notably in Italy's industrial north. To make matters worse, mid-2007 there were signs that the economy was losing speed. It grew by only 0.1 per cent in the second

---

25 *The Economist*, 16 September 2006.
26 *The Economist*, 15 September 2007.

quarter of that year, obliging Prodi to eat his words about filling the government coffers from great revenue coming from economic growth.

For all the reasons already explained, voices were raised in Italy that the country should opt out of the euro, which its economy was not ready to join when it did. Italy, euro-critics said, should return to the country's former currency, the lira – as well as to the policy of slow devaluation. This, however, is more easily said than done. In June 2005, then Justice minister Robert Castelli (of the second Berlusconi government) was quoted in the *Financial Times* as saying that he doubted whether there was an automatic benefit from the euro. In Castelli's words:

- Does sterling have no economic foundation, because it is outside the euro?

- Is Denmark living in absolute poverty, because it is outside the euro?

Not to be left behind, also in the Berlusconi government of mid-2005, then Social Welfare minister Roberto Maroni made several public statements suggesting that Italy should return to the lira. When reporters said to Maroni that Italy could end up with an Argentina-style crisis if it were to leave the euro, Maroni answered: 'We're already heading towards an Argentina style crisis, that's why we have to change direction.'

Beyond such suggestions, however, lies the fact that although Berlusconi and Prodi were at odds in a political sense, as prime ministers they followed very similar policies in terms of wanting budget discipline. It is all a matter of musical chairs: Berlusconi's government followed Prodi's government, then came another Berlusconi government, still another Prodi government and, following the mid-April 2008 election, Berlusconi is again prime minister.

What remains invariable is the policy of the easier way out: continuing to live by overspending at the expense of better-managed Euroland economies like Finland, Holland, Ireland and a resurgent Germany. Politicians don't heed the advice of cool heads, which have repeatedly warned of looming danger if this cheat thy Euroland neighbour policy continues.

In late 2006, a study published by the Centre for European Reform (CER), a London thinktank, pointed out that Italy needed to run a primary budget *surplus* of 2 per cent to 3 per cent to prevent the ratio of public debt to GDP from rising further. Instead, in 2006 there was a 4.6 per cent *deficit* – or, a gap of more than 7 per cent of GDP between:

- what Italy can afford to spend; and

- what its government actually spends.

No wonder that the number of experts fretting gloomily about the sustainability of Europe's single currency increased. How the market thinks about the euro's standing country by country,is demonstrated by the premium of German government bonds. In the first week of March 2008, for 10-year government bonds by Germany and Italy the so-called *Italian Premium* (a term with negative connotations) was 70 basis points (bp). As for the French government, to sell its debt to investors it had to pay 29 bp over those of Germany.[27]

8. Exit the Euro: A Simulation by Standard & Poor's

The missed opportunity of political union, at least among the original six founding members of the EU, is in itself a demonstration of lack of political resolve. It is also a documentation that monetary unions which lean into the prevailing political wind find it difficult to stand up. The careful investor ought therefore to consider how likely it is that each of Euroland's member countries (and public companies) would repay their debt in hard currency, should the government leave the euro.

- Will all current Euroland states remain members in one, two, or three decades?

- What is the future of 30- and 50-year bonds now issued, which ask investors to trust the euro because it will still be around. Will it?

Otmar Issing, formerly the European Central Bank's chief economist, said that a return to the lira would be 'economic suicide'. But in early August 2005, Christian Noyer, governor of the Banque de France stated that, 'Of course, European Monetary Union member states may, if they so please, leave the

---

27   *Figaro*, 8/9 March 2008.

euro system.'[28] For its part, HSBC has published studies that conclude the euro system is about to break up. We shall see; but we must also be prudent.

Whether coming into or going out of a monetary union, the law of unexpected consequences is always at work. For instance, the lira's reintroduction could add to Italy's troubles rather than relieve them. Buyers of Italian government bonds would surely demand insurance in the form of higher bond yields against the risk of devaluation (see section 5). About a decade ago, before the euro, spreads on Italian gilts had reached 650 basis points compared to German debt. Investors are well aware that Italy's public debt is over 106 per cent of GDP, and growing.

These are far from being academic questions. They are core issues in economic and financial terms. Standard & Poor's (S&P), the independent rating agency, has made a simulation which practically suggests that repercussions of *exit* would depend on the reasons for leaving. In S&P's simulation, a country or two suddenly announce that they leave Euroland:

- Italy and Greece might want to regain their own currency, only to devalue it.

- both lost competitiveness since the 1990s. Though they benefited from the euro, *their* inflation eroded the advantage of staying in Euroland.

In S&P's simulation Italy makes a surprise exit from the euro and promptly devalues the new lira by 27 per cent.[29] leaving investors to lick their wounds. (This 27 per cent is not theoretical. At the time of the simulation it roughly corresponded to the inflationary policies of the Italian government since joining the euro.)

Most, but not all, politicians in Rome refuse to think about leaving the euro, yet this might well become necessary – even if it is going to be quite costly, as Argentina found when it was forced off its currency peg to the dollar in 2001. But what else can Italy do, if its politicians are unable or unwilling to put the economy straight?

---

28 *EIR*, 12 August 2005.
29 *The Economist*, 26 November 2005.

A better possibility, of course, is to follow the German example and endure years of wage restraint. Italy, France and other Euroland countries should shatter their two-tier labour market, which has become common in Europe, with insiders on permanent contracts insulated from the fears of unemployment afflicting temporary workers. In 2007, Nicolas Sarkozy had the guts to start demolishing such privileges by attacking the special retirement contracts, which featherbed a small part of the population at the expense of everybody else.

Change is evidently not easy, and this comes into the hypotheses underpinning the S&P and other models. In a properly-done simulation the hypotheses on which it is based must realistically reflect current and projected economic and financial conditions, within the environment under investigation. For instance, the reason for the simulation may be to study:

- the processes underlying or expected to underlie a crisis; or

- changes in technical and operational procedures and infrastructures; or

- conflicting incentives among authorities participating to a common goal, like financial stability.

All three bullets identify legitimate research issues. Dr Wilhelm Hankel, professor of Economics at Frankfurt University, was a board member and chief economist at Kreditanstalt für Wiederaufbau (KfW), a major state-owned German financial institution, in the 1960s. Later he was president of Hessische Landesbank. (A Landesbank acts as the state-controlled treasury of savings banks and bank of the local government.) In an interview he gave to the *Executive Intelligence Review* (*EIR*), Dr Hankel had this to say about euro's future, most particularly the likelihood of:

- quitting the Maastricht Treaty, in accordance with international law; and

- returning to national currencies, such as the Deutschmark for Germany.

In Hankel's opinion, currency reconversion is no technical problem, nor are there problems from a strictly economic standpoint. But there will be a very expensive process in exiting the euro, costing as much as it did to join the euro: roughly 80 billion DM (more than 40 billion euro) for Germany alone.[30] Dr Hankel added that:

- at the time of joining the euro, the German government did not foot the bill, as it was picked up, in the main, by the private sector at about 500 euro for every German citizen;

- by contrast, the German federal government would have to pay 40 billion euro or more to untangle the Gordian knot of belonging to the euro.

There would also be other costs in an exit drive. In the case of Italy and Greece, for example, legally speaking their debts would still be payable in euros. According to the S&P study, Italy's public debt would jump at a stroke, from a little over 106 per cent of GDP to 138 per cent and Greece's from 107 per cent to 161 per cent of GDP. Neither government could service these debts without strain. Moreover:

- Italy's credit rating would drop from AA- to A-;

- Greece's would drop from A to BBB, next to the lowest level of investment grade.

Many experts also believe that exiting the euro would lead to a spark of inflation, particularly if the 2001 conversion policies prevail. As Dr Hankel stated in his interview with *EIR*, in Germany with the DM to euro conversion, only the exchange ratio for incomes was fixed. What happened to prices was left to private businesses with the outcome being inflation.

Sometimes, Dr Hankel says, a restaurant will charge the same price in euro for a bottle of wine that it charged for the same bottle in DM. With that, the real price has doubled! The same result, some analysts suggest, would be repeated a second time with the *exit*. Price increases, sometimes significant,were the wrong dynamics of the euro – but with the exception of the Dutch, no Euroland government cared to control the price spiral.

What the preceding paragraphs bring to the reader's attention is further evidence that *planning* is a fundamental process, albeit one which is held in

---

30 *EIR*, 12 August 2005.

low esteem by the European Union's politicians; and *control* has an even lower standing in their priorities. *If* at the end, the common currency for politically divided countries proves to be strategically questionable, and *if* Euroland's member states start abandoning ship, which is not unlikely, *then* the euro will turn into the twenty-first century's big financial fiasco.

11

Euroland's Missed Opportunities

1. Political Union Would Have Been the Better Solution

Chapter 10 brought to the reader's attention the reasons why the euro's prospects are anything but bright. Such facts do not discourage its supporters from believing the euro will still make it. Their main two arguments are that strains in Euroland are not very large; and both intra- and inter-European economic cycles have recently become more synchronized, which is interpreted as meaning economic convergence

The answer to these arguments is that, lower interest rates[1] aside, most of the benefits the euro was expected to present to Euroland's member states remain might-have-beens. Nor can one expect that this will change radically, because EU's politicians, chiefs of state, prime ministers and finance ministers put their country's interests way ahead of the common good. The so-called 'good news' that comes out of their interminable summits and conferences:

- are only promises about the future; and

- the deliverables are steadily pushed further out.

George Clemenceau, French Prime Minister at end of World War I and master politician, used to ask: Do you know why the Socialists talk always in future tense?, answering his own query with the statement: Because they can deliver nothing today! To take just one example, Jacques Chirac, Tony Blair and the other political CEOs who gathered in Brussels 23/24 March 2006 for an 'Energy Summit', produced a communiqué which promised a great solution to

---

1 Contrary to what the pros say, very low interest rates mandated by the central bank, are set to help the government(s) which is (are) overleveraged and still continue(s) to borrow. They are not made to help consumers while they severely penalize savers and pension funds.

the European Union's energy problem by *2050*, while they know very well that four and a half decades down the line:

- none of them will probably be in this world; and

- therefore none could be held responsible for his 'promises' to the EU citizens.

Promises engage only those who listen to them, said Charles Pasqua, a French politician. Apart from meaningless promises, however, the other issue revealed by that late March 2006 EU 'summit' has been that no participating politician took a stand against the rising economic nationalism in the European Union, and its negative impact.

Otmar Issing, former member of the Governing Council of ECB and former chief economist of Deutsche Bundesbank, is right when he says that the single currency needed greater political union.[2] The Maastricht criteria reflected in the Stability and Growth Pact put limits to budget deficits (to less than 3 per cent of GDP) and guarantee the European Central Bank's independence. All this makes good reading on paper, but governments have the nasty habit of putting the agreements they have signed in a time closet.

Economic nationalism in the EU is a touchy subject, and therefore it dropped out of the communiqué. Also kept off the radar screen was the fact that, as all chiefs of state and finance ministers knew very well, the accounts of Euroland's member states, and of the EU's at large, quite simply cannot be balanced. There is too much of a discrepancy between:

- total revenue; and

- total expenditure.

As a percentage of GDP, the *average* gap was 2.6 per cent in 2002, 3.1 per cent in 2003, 2.8 per cent in 2004, 2.4 per cent in 2005 and 2.4 per cent in 2006 (and about the same in 2007). In other terms, year after year there is always a deficit, which is much bigger in some of the major EU countries whose governments have classically been the big spenders. 'Do you know what creates inflation?', Dr Arthur Burns, former Fed chairman, asked his students at Columbia

---

2   Otmar Issing, *The Birth of the Euro*, Cambridge University Press, Cambridge, 2009.

University, answering his own question with the statement: 'Government deficits create inflation.'

What might have been different if, in 1957, instead of a 'common market' the six had opted for outright political union? The most evident answer is *unity of command*, which is fundamental to the success of every organization – whether a company or a state. *If* there had unity of command and *if* the EU's single government had had first-class politicians, economists and social experts, then we might have seen a European renaissance.

This did not happen. As Abraham Lincoln once said, a house divided among itself cannot stand. The 'house divided' is precisely the reason why the reference to the March 2006 'summit' is important. What was said and what was not (but should have been) said documented a policy of *avoiding* to talk about the essential by spending one's time beating around the bush.

The same policy of avoidance of tackling the essential problems, particularly some governments big spending plans, prevailed in 1991 while laying the foundations for a European Monetary Union; the Maastricht agreements. Because they were made without attention to salient issues, and less than necessary care for detail, these EMU plans ran into serious difficulties in the crises of 1992 and 1993.

Additionally, one of the least discussed but most damaging failures of Maastricht is that it did not ask, let alone answer, the question of what is a 'too large' Euroland membership (as well as EU membership). Nor did it ask where the limits lie in a landscape of diverse collection of countries under a varying degree of economic development. Is this a mockery of a 'union'? Nor did Maastricht elaborate on who could benefit from monetary union and *why*. In principle, states and their citizen can benefit from a monetary union *if*:

- they trade a lot with each other (France and Germany, for instance, fulfill this criterion);

- the economic shocks they face are correlated. As we saw, the case of Italy is not that of Ireland, Holland, or Finland;

- there is a high degree of labour mobility among them. This is what the EU's Bolkenstein[3] Directive tried to achieve, but it was shot down; and

- there exists political union, as well as a fiscal system able to transfer funds to regions or sectors of the economy that suffer adverse shocks.

It would be superfluous to explain that (with minor exceptions here and there) none of these criteria characterize the collection of Euroland's member states, or for that matter the European Union as an integral entity. What is widespread is infighting about who gets the bigger part of the cake, as exemplified by the case of the costly and distortionary Common Agricultural Policy (CAP) which has become an example of pork barrel politics.[4]

Could all this have been different *were* there a political union of EU member states? This is a tough question to answer, because the response one gives will be based on hypotheses and assumptions – both being tentative statements until provided with proof. The safest bet, however, is that a political union would have developed homogeneous directives, rules and regulations for all member states – as well as a more open economic landscape than the current Euroland, in terms of:

- fiscal policies;

- taxation;

- labour mobility;

- endowments; and

- decisions affecting financial stability.

Another domain where a political union would have given commendable results is in regard to criteria for EU enlargement. By expanding the perimeter

---

3   EU Commissioner Bolkenstein has been accused by several EU states as trying to destabilize *their* labour market allowing free movement of labour among member countries. In reality what he did was to apply (not change) the clauses of the EU charter.

4   'Pork barrel', an American expression, is often used to describe an ongoing practice in the US Congress. It graphically tells how everybody tries to help himself or herself out of the common purse – or out of a barrel where goodies like pork fat are stored.

of the EU into totally asymmetric situations, such as the projected inclusion of Turkey – heaven forbid – the current EU mismanagers don't only move *against* public opinion and public will, but they also distort Europe's competitive setting. Membership by relatively poor economies taxes the more advanced economies in an inordinate way, damages their competitiveness and lowers their standard of living.

2. Clash of Dirigisme and of Free Economy

An EU political union would not have altered the clash between state planning and liberalism in any significant way. *Dirigisme* is a French word which stands for an economy directed 'from above', by autocrats and bureaucrats who supposedly know everything better than the market. The practice of *dirigisme* has not only characterized socialist and communist regimes but also right-wing governments whose decisions weigh heavily in the market because of:

- state control;

- huge subsidies;

- the practice of economic nationalism and more.

There is plenty of evidence that *dirigisme* has failed miserably, but it is still practiced because it inflates egos. This is anathema to economists and policymakers who prize enterprise and, as does Milton Friedman, give priority to sound monetary policy. Dr Friedman, who has been credited with ending the post-WWII Keynesian consensus, urged governments to cut spending and privatize state services, but gave warning that 'Hell hath no fury like a bureaucrat scorned.'[5]

In a book published in 1962, Milton Friedman advanced the thesis that capitalism and freedom are definitely intertwined, with the one supporting the other. Without capitalism and the economic freedom it brings, there could be no political freedom. The state's role, he argued, should be little more than to:

- promote competition;

- enforce contracts; and

---

5   *The Economist*, 25 November 2006.

- provide a monetary framework which keeps a brake on inflation.

Dirigisme works in exactly the opposite way. It tries to arbitrate unemployment and inflation (often with disastrous results), applies price controls for farming and industrial products, increases tariffs and import quotas to protect 'national' industries; establishes minimum wages and also as taxes heavily and overspends by increasing the national debt. Plenty of economists now argue that the main culprit of a dull economy is the heavily indebted state which, for instance, in France:

- takes nearly 40 per cent of GDP in taxes;

- spends for interest payments all money collected from personal taxes;

- imposes burdensome and capricious regulations on enterprises;

- fails to liberalize the labour market;

- puts economic nationalism ahead of free competition; and

- becomes the superfixer of all problems, without knowing what it is doing.

On 14 November 2006, on the occasion of his visit to troubled EADS/Airbus, the beleaguered Franco-German aircraft manufacturer, Dominique de Villepin, then French centre-right prime minister, said that the European Central Bank could no more fix the exchange rate of the euro all by itself. 'The governments' – and evidently above all his government – 'must play a role in it', de Villepin stated, essentially demolishing the central bank's independent status.

The statement that 'we cannot allow the European Central Bank to act alone in rates,'[6] shows both *dirigisme* and economic illiteracy because, as the careful reader will recall from Chapter 7, in a globalized economy no central bank truly 'fixes' exchange rates. It only decides on interest rates and even that is a conditional statement, because the shape of the yield curve is decided by the market and not by the central bankers.

---

6   *The Economist*, 18 November 2006.

Critics of socialist-inspired *dirigisme* say that a key reason why both French centre-right and centre-left governments blame the ECB is that an expensive euro hurts not only Airbus but other French exporters too. Since 2004, France's exports have sold less well abroad, while there has been strong demand for imported consumer goods, swallowing the current account deficit. The United States, too, runs a long-standing huge current account deficit. as we have already seen.

Much could be learned from other countries' mistakes but past experience is of no interest to *dirigisme*. What is important is that cheap populist statements can be made for public consumption and as excuses for unfortunate initiatives taken by bureaucrats and politicians. Contrary to easy remedies, to redress themselves and their fortunes EADS (and its subsidiary Airbus) must:

- restructure;

- reorganize; and

- cut costs with a sharp knife.

In practical terms, this means major layoffs (hence unemployment), as well as radical downsizing of the number of suppliers from about 3,500 to 500. Any EU president or prime minister who thinks that *dirigisme* produces miracles would benefit by reading the works of Milton Friedman, who said that if governments try to push unemployment below its natural rate they would succeed in pushing inflation even higher.

Dr Friedman could also have added that a mixture of *dirigisme* and *populism* can lead to funny business. After blasting the euro's high exchange rate versus the dollar (airliners are negotiated in US dollars), to ease the pain of downsizing de Villepin offered EADS/Airbus government subsidies and guarantees. This downplayed the fact that the airframer's problem:

- was much deeper than could be solved by throwing money at it; and

- had very much to do with competitiveness in the global economy.

Within the EU, one of the reasons why *dirigisme* did not deliver is that French industry lost competitiveness within Euroland, ceding market share to freshly competitive German companies. Additionally, even in its internal market it could not match the very low-cost Chinese products, because when choosing suppliers French companies and consumers were increasingly looking abroad for:

- lower prices; and

- better service.

Several French economists blame that loss of competitiveness on a high minimum wage (up by 40 per cent between 1997 and 2007) and to the impact of the 35-hour working week. Both had a negative effect on companies' ability to staff back offices and customer service centres. Another trigger for pessimism was that household debt threatened consumer spending. In 2007 the savings rate of French households fell below its lowest historical level.

It was a deliberate decision to bring these facts into perspective, to avoid a misunderstanding that, had there been a political union in the EU, this would have solved all of the problems. It would have solved some of the problems, but others, like the clash between *dirigisme* and a liberal economy, would have continued to divide public opinion and government policy.

3. Treaty of Lisbon and ECB

It took a couple of years, and a great many arguments and counter-arguments, to develop a draft of a European Union Constitution that took account the (most illogical) steady increase in member states. After French and Dutch voters rejected it by a comfortable majority, the EU's decision-making mechanism found itself at an impasse. The way forward was a mini-constitution, better known as *The Treaty of Lisbon*:

- signed in Lisbon, Portugal on December 2007 by the heads of state or government of the 27 EU member states;

- but awaiting ratification by each member state on an individual basis.

Known as the Treaty on the Functioning of the European Union, the Lisbon agreement is far-reaching because it amends the Treaty on European Union and the Treaty that originally established the European Community. One of its clauses is that all stages leading to ratification have to be completed before it can enter into force on 1 January 2009.

- Ratification can be made through a vote in parliament.

- It is not mandatory to have a referendum as *should* have been the case to protect the interests of the sovereign people.

Several of the clauses contained in the Treaty of Lisbon regard changes in economic and monetary policy procedures. One of the most important specifies that the European Central Bank will become an institution of the European Union. The ECB has so far been listed in Article 9, along with other institutions:

- European Parliament;

- European Council;

- European Commission;

- Court of Justice of the EU; and

- Court of Auditors.

There is also the Euro Group, established as an informal committee at the Luxembourg European Council in December 1997, which is now specialized in protocol. It will continue to be a forum for informal exchange of opinions, consisting of meetings of ministers of the member states whose currency is the euro and the participation of the European Commission as well as of the ECB.

The European Central Bank differs from the other institutions whose status is elaborated in the Treaty of Lisbon in that it has its own legal personality and its capital belongs to the national central banks of Euroland's members.[7] As a result, it is financially independent and not part of the Community budget. The Treaty also specifies that in the case of institutional changes in the monetary area, the ECB must be consulted.

---

7   Nevertheless, the May 1998 EU summit which launched the euro had degenerated into a 12-hour squabble among heads of state over who should be ECB's boss.

The president, vice-president and other members of the Executive Board of the ECB will be selected and appointed by the European Council, acting by a qualified majority. This contrasts to current law which specifies that they are appointed by common accord of governments of member states, at the level of the heads of state or government: in other words, through compromises.

A new Chapter 3a of the Treaty of Lisbon, 'Provisions specific to member states whose currency is the euro', addresses the rules governing external representation. At present this has been laid down in Article 111 (4) of the EC Treaty. A significant change in comparison with current law is the mention of:

- common positions; and

- unified representation.

This provides the ECB with more clout than the simple mention of positions and representation in the EC Treaty. Additionally, Article 115c does not include the new provision which states that the allocation of responsibilities set forth in Articles 99 and 105 of the EC Treaty must be complied with in the area of external representation.

Other articles, however, are not to everyone's liking. For instance, several people have asked for cancellation, or at least suspension, of Article 56 of the Treaty of Lisbon which forbids all member states imposing restrictions on the free movement of capital. According to some opinions, raising borders to financial flows will limit dislocations like those originated in July/August 2008 and subsequent months from the US subprime mortgage market, including its:

- liquidity tensions; and

- spread of turbulence beyond country borders.

In terms of economic policy coordination and policing action within Euroland, the Treaty of Lisbon specifies that the European Commission may address a warning to member states concerned if it finds that their economic policy is not consistent with the broad economic policy guidelines adopted by the Council. This early warning right did not exist up to the present time.

(Under current EU law, the Council may address a recommendation to a member state if it is established that its economic policy is not consistent with guidelines. The amendment made by the Treaty of Lisbon will allow the Council to make a decision without taking into account the vote of the member state concerned. Member states that are not part of Euroland are excluded from decisions concerning the euro.)

In all likelihood – after having taken note of the fact that in 1557, in Spain, the Genovese bankers' indulgence of Philip II warfare and budget deficits caused the world's first sovereign bankruptcy – the Treaty of Lisbon will give a member state no say in the decision on the existence of an excessive deficit. Furthermore, to accelerate and simplify the taking of decisions, the two-thirds majority presently envisaged for further procedural steps will be replaced by a qualified majority – an issue which has led to plenty of compromises since the early discussions on the EU's Constitution.

'Fiscal sustainability is a precondition for stability and growth,' says the European Central Bank. 'The perception that public finances are on an unsustainable path would create uncertainty in the economy and lead agents to take into account in their decisions the consequences of a persistent deterioration of public finances, i.e. either major policy reversals or disruptive market reactions.'[8]

The respected former chairman of the Federal Reserve has said something similar about the American economy. On 9 April 2008,[9] Dr Paul Volcker stated that financial crises don't usually happen unless there are other underlying problems in the economy. 'You cannot go on forever spending more than you are producing. You have to rely on unorthodox finance to sustain it,' Volcker said, adding that lack of stability in the dollar is likely to hurt the world economy. The same is true of an eventual lack of stability in the euro.

4. The EU President's Accountability

Who should be the topmost fiscal sustainability watchdog in the EU? The evident answer is the European Commission (which is the EU's executive branch) and most particularly its president. That position must be held by a person qualified enough to appreciate that longer-term uncertainty leads to

---

8   ECB, *Monthly Bulletin*, February 2007.
9   In an event sponsored by the Harvard Club.

short-term decisions, while politicians are inclined to run larger longer-term deficits. Two problems make themselves felt:

1. Members of the EU Commission and *its* president (as distinct from the EU president, a position projected by the Treaty of Lisbon) are appointed by the governments of member states.

They are not elected by the people, therefore they can hardly afford to rein in the governments appointing them, if and when the latter violate EU rules including those of fiscal discipline. Should it then be some other EU president rather than the president of the Commission who exercises control authority? Or, more precisely, should there be *one, two* or *three* presidents?

Any rational person would answer the last question by saying that *one* is plenty, while two is counterproductive and three is chaoic, as each one will step on the other's toes, arguments will be interminable, conflicts of interest will become mountains and in the end nothing will be done. Yes, but this is the EU and there are going to be three presidents – all of them selected by horse-trading politicians. That's enough to make the Treaty of Lisbon a non-event.

If the EU president were to have any authority at all, *then* he or she should have been elected by the pan-European public, becoming the boss of both the European Commission and the European Council – the latter being the body that brings together all 27 heads of EU governments. He or she should also have been invested with the authority to ask for clear decisions by the European Council, putting them into execution by the European Commission under his authority.

The fact that this is not the case speaks volumes about the inefficiency of EU organization and structure. Even more hilarious is the fact that not only do the Commission and the Council remain two quite separate bodies, but also the European Council is going to have two presidents whose functions are and remain fuzzy.[10]

2. Up to now, the EU presidency has been a six-month merry-go-round among heads of member states, not a firm platform from

---

10 Under Lisbon there is also a half-baked post for 'EU foreign minister', who would double up as Commissioner of External Affairs. That's a figurehead job, since 51 years of EU history document that its members – whether six, 10, 15 or 27 – never agree on a common foreign policy. A recent example is whether or not to participate in the opening ceremony of China's 2008 Olympic Games, given the events in Tibet.

which the president can lead the union. This changes with the new Lisbon mini-treaty, and it becomes worse.

Tony Blair (who pushed for the post's creation) is a candidate and so are Juncker, Schüssel, Rasmussen, Ahern and many others. That's normal. Less so is the fact that plenty of EU heads of state want to carry on rotating the EU presidency, and it is quite probable that they will have their way. Like too many generals, too many presidents make the EU look like a banana republic.

This in no way means that the rotating presidency was a success story. Take as an example the 1 July 2007 rotation in the EU's presidency. On 2 July 2007 – a day after being invested with presidential credentials – José Socratés, Portugal's socialist prime minister, launched his six-month tenure by immediately flying to Africa for preparatory talks for an awkward summit of the two continents. (Socratés' initiative capsized when, to his credit, Gordon Brown refused to join the chorus.)

To put it mildly, an African summit is far from being the EU's top priority. If anything, Socratés first concern should have been to get the EU's economy moving again, particularly that of countries like his own, whose growth of gross domestic product lags the EU's average (since 2002). Some experts even questioned Portugal's credentials for leading the relaunching of the EU economy, since it had plenty to do at home in order to catch up.

Here are a couple of examples. Reading and maths skills among 15-year-old Portuguese are among the weakest in Europe, with between 22 and 30 per cent performing at or below the level of 'very basic', according to the OECD. 'This level of performance is clearly incompatible with the demands of modern European economy,' said a senior western diplomat in Lisbon.[11] Correctly, Socratés had made education a priority, but then he put the plan on the back burner.

Not is Portugal a model of fiscal policy and this makes it an unlikely reformer of EU finances. Yet, this is an urgent mission. Known as 'the EU budget', the financing package for 2007 to 2013 agreed on in December 2005, in one of the many 'summits', includes a clause promising a through budgetary review in 2008. This was a concession to the British, who had to give up part of their budget rebate to get that deal – but, concession or no concession, once it has been decided it must be done.

---

11 *Financial Times*, 3 July 2007.

When the 2005 negotiations took place, Tony Blair had demanded further reform of the Common Agricultural Policy (CAP) as his price for negotiating on the British rebate. That request was blocked by Chirac's intransigence. Subsequently, the promise of a review became a face-saving device for Blair, but other EU governments were not in accord and therefore did nothing to honour their signature. What is the EU president's position on the budgetary issue? Does he have any?

It is equally important to know the EU president's position on the French request for broader dialogue on closer economic coordination across the eurozone, and on the ECB's interest rate policy – increasingly and incorrectly presented to the electorate as an exchange rate policy. Behind these critiques lies a thinly veiled attack on the ECB's independence. Is the president of the EU in accord, or is he against them? The issues treated in preceding paragraphs are and remain valid for the new EU president and his/her successors.

- Who else has more authority over the EU's fiscal sustainability than its president?

- Who else is better positioned to analyze and criticize the links between fiscal policies and domestic as well as external imbalances?

- Who else is expected to guide in the reduction of the member states public debt, in the establishment of financial stability, growth and employment decisions?

The EU president must also be in charge of the framework for policy coordination, taking account of the need of an institutional mechanism to counteract the risks to fiscal sustainability. His, rather than the Council's, is the duty to call to order countries with fiscal problems which favour a loose implementation of the EU's rules, thereby eroding public confidence in the conduct of sound economic policies. No doubt one of the EU president's priorities should be a relaunch of the ailing Lisbon Agenda (Chapter 10).

In June 2007, the French president said his government would only balance its budget by the end of his term in 2012, rather than by 2010 as agreed by the previous French government. *What if* every government in Euroland does the same? The European public is entitled to know the position the EU president takes in that regard, as well as his reasons for the decision he makes.

Other issues, too, demand clear answers from the European Union's CEO. Is the EU president for or against Euroland's Stability and Growth Pact (section 5)? Does he support ambitious structural reforms, which would further contribute to the smooth functioning of monetary union, or does he prefer the status quo of uncontrollable budgetary deficits no matter their negative impact on growth and on job creation?

No EU president, or for that matter EU Commission, can pretend ignorance of the fact that deficits and big debt figures are an anathema to the spirit of the Maastricht Treaty, which was ratified by all of Euroland's member states. (This is also the reason why government deficit and debt are also known as 'Maastricht deficit and debt.') But are the EU president, the president of the EU Commission and the latter's members able to act against the violators?

5. Euroland's Stability and Growth Pact

As the careful reader will remember from Chapter 10, the decision to go ahead with the euro was political, not financial; a weak alternative to political union. François Mitterrand asked that West Germany deposited the Deutschmark as collateral *if* it wanted to see its leveraged buyout (LBO) for East Germany succeed (Like many leveraged buyouts, this one proved to be a disaster.) In exchange, the Germans required a plan that assured that future monetary policy is exercised in a:

- sound; and

- prudent way.

This had to be none other than the excellent monetary policy followed after World War II by the Deutsche Bundesbank. Financial stability, however, is an alien term to other EU members and as should have been expected from Day 1 the projected *Stability and Growth Pact* became the subject of interminable negotiations. Jacques Chirac, who in the meantime succeeded Mitterand as French president, lead the opposition to strict financial policy measures, his influence being wrong for two reasons:

1. at the time Stability and Growth Pact negotiations took place, the French franc had stabilized and represented good value; and

2.   the president of a country is expected to know that loose rules of financial discipline incite every member of Euroland to gamble on the new currency to its advantage.

Years of loose monetary policy are not erased from peoples memories because a new pact is signed. It therefore came as a surprise that, when the euro began life, several economists from countries where monetary discipline is little known directed their fire at the Stability and Growth Pact. They criticized it as attempting to set rigid limits on budget deficits run by euro members and threatened big fines if those limits were breached.

If these were the economists fears, they did not need to worry, least of all about them coming true. Predictably, the Stability Pact was swiftly broken by France, Italy, Portugal, Greece *and* Germany. Then, in March 2005 it was renegotiated, watered down and fitted with extra loopholes (more on this later).

In fact, even in its first version the Stability Pact was not the ironclad agreement originally projected, because long negotiation saw to it that many of its rules were less rigorous than they should have been. Because of this, a strict interpretation was needed to avoid unsound public finances in Euroland's member states. Emphasis should have been placed on *common* fiscal policies, which did not happen.

In February 2005, as first application of the stability provisions the excessive deficit procedure was put in motion against *Greece*, owing to that country's failure to implement the recommended corrective measures. Additionally, in 2005 the European Commission initiated excessive deficit procedures against *Italy* and *Portugal* owing to breaches of the 3 per cent limit of budgetary deficit. But nothing was done against similar events in *France* – although in mid-March 2006 *Germany*, too, was given notice under the excessive deficit procedure.

Needless to say, all this was cosmetic. Mid-July 2006 headlines announced: 'The EU and Germany make peace over budgets.' As had been widely expected, in a way quite similar to the lack of penalties against huge deficits by Rome, Lisbon and Paris, the European Commission froze any action against Berlin over its excessive budget deficit. Joaquin Almunia, the EU Monetary Affairs Commissioner, simply said on 19 July that Angela Merkel's government 'is on track' to meet its deficit to below 3 per cent of GDP.

The Commission considered that no further steps in the excessive deficit procedure for Germany were needed at present, added Almunia. But Daniel Gros, director of the Brussels-based Centre for European Policy Studies, admitted that neither France nor Germany was likely to be a credible advocate for enforcing the revamped (and downgraded) Stability Pact, since Paris and Berlin would continue to require considerable public borrowing for the foreseeable future.[12]

A weak and toothless European Commission, whose membership depends on patronage and goodwill of heads of member states, could do nothing other than look the other way – even with violations of a watered down Stability Pact, which had in the meantime come into existence. Indeed, at its 20 March 2005, meeting, the Council of Euroland's ministers had adopted a report to heads of state whose title, 'Improving the Implementation of the Stability and Growth Pact', was highly misleading; but:

- *if* instead of 'Improving' they had written 'Diluting';

- *Then*, the report's title would have been correct.

This Stability Pact dilution of clauses was approved by the European Council at its meeting in Brussels on 22/23 March 2005. Some matters, however, had been left undecided – such as the technical implementation of decisions dwelling within a member state's fiscal framework. Left to be settled later on or (more likely) never, these undecided issues continue to provide plenty of loopholes for old and new violators of the Stability Pact.

6. Fireworks with Financial Stability

On 20 April 2007, Euroland's ministers of finance and the economy did not miss the opportunity to verbally reaffirm their adherence to the sound fiscal policy principles of the revised Stability and Growth Pact. But while Euroland was still experiencing economic good times, they fell well short of making full use of the current economic growth and better tax revenues to pursue sound fiscal policies. Deficits were still rampant and they evidently became much worse in 2008 as growth ebbed.

---

12 *Financial Times*, 17 July 2006.

Yet assuring progress towards sustainable fiscal positions has been a key priority, in line with the preventive principle established by the Stability Pact which, among other goals, aims to prepare for the impending budgetary impact of ageing European populations. Working against the euro's stability is the fact that member countries don't bother to:

- speed up the pace of deficit and debt reduction; or

- pursue an annual adjustment in cyclical terms, net of one-off and temporary measures.

Quite to the contrary, *as if* the goal was to promote irresponsible fiscal deficit procedures, Article 104 (2a) of the revised Stability Treaty formally allowed the reference value for governments red ink deficit to be exceeded under two totally subjective conditions:

- *if* the excess was only 'exceptional' and 'temporary'; and

- *if* the ratio of the government deficit to GDP remained close to the reference value (of 60 per cent).[13]

One of the more risky loopholes created by the badly massaged version of Euroland's Stability and Growth Pact is that governments can have high deficits in 'bad years', provided they make up for them in 'good years'. Even in *Alice in Wonderland* such a clause would not have worked. Indeed, in June 2006, a little over a year after the downgraded Stability Pact came into effect, the European Commission gave a toothless warning that:

- Euroland countries were failing to use the cyclical upturn to cut their budget deficits;[14] and

- while the average deficit in the euro area has been 2.4 per cent of GDP, in the first half of 2006 several countries were well over the 3 per cent ceiling.

---

13 In a TV show several years ago, Groucho Marx, the comedian, was asked how old he was. He answered: 'I am approaching 60.' 'Come on,' said the moderator, 'you are older than that.' 'Yes,' answered Marx, 'but I didn't say from which side I'm approaching it.'
14 *The Economist*, 17 June 2006.

The new risks added to Euroland's and the euro's financial stability don't end there. In contrast to the original Stability arrangement, post-March 2005 exceptional economic circumstances have been loosely defined as a negative growth rate (Italy being a steady on/off example), or a considerable accumulated loss of output during periods of below-average growth (try to guess what this means).

The diluted Stability Pact, for example, would have considered Japan, which experienced negative growth practically every year since 1990 and annual budget deficits of incredible proportions, as being a paradigm of correct economic policies. Japan ran these deficits for reasons of reflating its financial industry and other sectors of the economy, with disastrous results. Their cost was the doubling of the country's national debt and this should be a warning to other countries not to repeat Japan's experience.

By giving *carte blanche* for deficits, the 'new' Stability and Growth Pact leaves the door open to more *dirigisme* (see section 2), and from there to a rampant bad management of state finances. For instance, the downsized Pact of 2005 foresaw that in case of *special circumstances* the deadline for correcting the deficit may be extended to two years following its identification.

It is, moreover, hilarious that the arbiters of these bad steps are none other than the states which violated the stability clauses in the first place. A long list of aberrations consists of the many other subjective reasons for avoiding fiscal discipline, such as:

- growth rates below potential growth (!);

- the salutary effect of earlier budgetary consolidation in 'good times'(!!);

- burdens resulting from financial contributions to fostering international solidarity (!!!);

- implementation of the Lisbon strategy (the defunct one, see Chapter 10);

- expenditures on research, development and innovation;

- public investment (Hitler had a similar policy);

- quality of public finances (no kidding);

- pension reform (a vast, expansive and expensive issue).

In the original Stability Pact, special conditions included only three chapters: natural disasters, GDP decline of at least 2 per cent and GDP decline of between 0.75 per cent and 2 per cent per year at the Council's discretion. The horde of lightweight conditions added in March 2005 is ludicrous at best. Practically, all of them work *against* economic progress and financial stability.

Critics are vocal. They say that, apart from specific clauses, which are simply excuses for red ink, the overall reason for changes to the original Stability and Growth Pact is that governments running big deficits want to have their hands free to add red ink as they please. This reference includes the concept of taking account of *country-specific* circumstances – a very subjective issue indeed.

The 2007–2009 economic and banking crisis provides an example on how subjective this can be. Quoting from ECB's Financial Stability Review: 'Following a period of buoyant activity, which was also associated with the build-up of some financial imbalances, macroeconomic conditions in many new EU Member States deteriorated in the first half of 2008, albeit with marked differences across individual countries. Furthermore, in October 2008 financial markets in some central and eastern European (CEE) countries also suffered from heightened risk aversion....'[15]

In other terms, investors got the message that it is not enough to be a member of the EU in order to be taken as a financially sound country. A further important point that this European Central Bank study makes is that established financial links between different parts of the EU become channels for potential contagion between:

- the banking industry in Euroland; and

- the banking industry in the new EU accession countries.

This can conceivably result in severe and prolonged macro-economic stress which could give rise to risks to Euroland's financial stability. Nor are monetary dangers faced by the EU's new members the only reason for worries about the euro's future. Ireland, Spain, Portugal, Greece, Ireland and Italy are, so to

---

15 ECB, *Financial Stability Review*, December 2008.

speak, part of the 'old EU' but, as we saw in Chapter 10 they might also turn
into reasons for Euroland's destabilization. One should not forget the role the
French may play. In November 2008:

- Nicolas Sarkozy, the French president, called for suspension of the
  Stability and Growth Pact;

- to her credit, Angela Merkel, the German chancellor, immediately
  rejected *that* idea.

As if all this was not enough, the very sense of risk management has gone
missing. Milton Friedman had good reasons when, in an interview with the
Financial Times in late June 2003, he made the claim that the euro 'won't last'. In
the background of Dr Friedman's bold statement was his belief that the eurozone
will split apart within 'the next 10 to 15 years'. Though the Nobel Laureate was
careful to offer the proviso that he has sometimes been wrong, he followed his
statement with bold advice to the British government to stay out of the euro.

Because the criticism of careless management of risks associated with
Euroland's financial stability has been severe, the bigger member countries have
sought to find some sort of justification for all these mishaps. The justification
given by the EU Council was the *heterogeneity of the Community* following the
recent EU enlargement. In other words, first the bureaucrats and heads of state
destroy the original EU's homogeneity through super-enlargement; then they
kill financial stability through huge fiscal deficits.

Aristophanes, the ancient Greek playwright, could not have written a
better comedy than the one the different EU heads of state are writing among
themselves and on the back of EU citizens. Every day a new funny act is added.
On 16 June 2006, the Finnish prime minister who headed the EU Council,
publicly stated that enlargement would continue because it is 'so successful'.
Probably he forgot that in 2005 he had signed the 'heterogeneity' clause of the
watered down Stability Pact.

7. Risk Management: The Way to Come Up from Under

It will not be long before the citizens of Euroland wake up to discover that
none of the politicians at the helm of its member states has an inkling of the
science of risk management, whose spirit has been superbly phrased centuries

ago by Roger of Hourdon. Changing only one word, it reads: 'If not practiced beforehand, the science of risk management[16] cannot be gained when it becomes necessary. Nor indeed can the athlete bring high spirits to the contest, who never has been trained to practice it.'

Judging by the lack of financial discipline in budgets and current accounts, a general drift towards deficits and accumulation of national debt, the athletes of Euroland's political, social, and economic policies and decisions have not been practicing the risk management skills demanded by their jobs. Sometimes, however, they decide to be frank about it. Here is something you don't hear a head of state or prime minister saying every day:

> 'We screwed up. Not just a bit. Big time... It was perfectly clear that
> what we were saying wasn't true... You cannot mention a single major
> government measure we can be proud of... I almost died when I had to
> pretend that we were actually governing. We lied morning, noon and
> night.'[17]

This is what Ferenc Gyurcsany, Hungary's Prime Minister, said to members of his own Socialist Party at a meeting after he won the highly contested election in April 2006. When a tape of his comments was leaked, this admission of *mea culpa* brought thousands onto the streets besieging the state broadcasting station and burning cars – probably taking a leaf out of the book of the Maghrebians in permanent revolt in the Paris suburbs.

Hungary is not the only European Union country needing shock therapy to redress its battered finances, but its example provides food for thought on the risks big spending countries are taking (including, of course, the United States). Waking up after its prime minister's admission of having lied about the state of the economy, and of the nation, the Hungarian government said that it was going to administer a shock therapy to make up for lost time. We shall see.

The austerity plan being contemplated would cut a total of 8 per cent of GDP over the next three years. Supposedly, this would be done the way it should: 6 per cent from spending cuts and only 2 per cent from tax increases (Italy take note). The public payroll, said a spokesman for the Hungarian government, would be trimmed by 20 per cent and the number of top officials cut by 40 per cent. Next in line would be health reforms, ending universal health care free

---

16   Roger of Hourdon spoke of 'the science of war'.
17   *The Economist*, 23 September 2006.

for all at the point of delivery. There would also be increases in tuition fees for higher education, lower petrol subsidies, a property tax and cuts in pensions.

These are risk management measures every government should take, but will they be *truly* applied? 'Sooner or later,' said Hungarian Socialist Party leader Gyurcsany, 'things have to change, and sooner is better.' This plan is bold, and therefore impressive. The same is true of the Hungarian prime minister's statement that it is much easier to raise taxes than to cut spending – which is precisely what the centre-left Romano Prodi government did in Italy in 2006, despite its pre-election promises.

Since the end of World War II, Italy and Hungary have had much in common, even if they belonged to two different blocks. Then, from the fall of the Iron Curtain onwards, successive Hungarian governments from the left and the right behaved in a fully populist manner, and they did so with spectacular irresponsibility. They:

- increased public sector salaries;

- doubled the minimum wage; and

- pushed up the nominal incomes by almost 30 per cent in two years.

Finally, reality caught up with both the government and the ordinary citizen. Because, the Hungarian economy had been dangerously overheating, to cool it the central bank raised interest rates. To overcome the handicap of more expensive credit, Hungarians borrowed abroad at lower rates. By summer 2006, most new loans were in Swiss francs through the carry trade, while the country's current-account deficit hit *9 per cent of GDP* and the budget deficit *10 per cent*.

As usually happens, fireworks were part of the show. With disaster around the corner Hungarians declared themselves 'ready' to come into Euroland, taking as example neighbouring Italy, which also joined Euroland before having brought fiscal indiscipline under control.

One of the best handicaps to economic and financial stability that has been invented is misinformation about the state of the nation and of its citizen. There is always the easy excuse that the government needs 'more time' to balance its budget and comply with fiscal rules; for instance, those underpinning the euro. But in these statements one can find a contradiction between:

- pleading for greater leniency in implementing existing commitments; and

- advocating closer economic cooperation in domains which require plenty of financing.

This is not the way in which risk management works. Let's face it, the governments of the European Union don't want to have a definition of what is meant by rigorous financial discipline. Their focus is not on developing new wealth by liberalizing product and labour markets, restructuring their balance sheets and deleveraging their economies. Rather, they want to distribute the money which they don't have through red ink policies.

To make ends meet, governments are raising funds through taxes and they leverage themselves by means of inflation – including inflation in labour costs by upping minimum wages, which makes a country's products and services uncompetitive in both the global marketplace and a regional one, like Euroland's. In 10 years, from 1998 to 2007:

- Portugal's unit labour costs increased by over 40 per cent;

- those of Greece by 35 per cent;

- Italy and Spain followed, each by 32 per cent;

- by contrast, Germany's unit labour costs *shrank* by about 1 per cent.

The difference between Portugal, Ireland, Italy, Greece and Spain (the PIIGS) on one side, and Germany on the other is discipline and restructuring, as well as the will of to go through the unavoidable uncertainties of transformational change. These qualities of change and restructuring are anathema to the politicians running the fortunes of the majority of Euroland's members. Their excuse for lack of financial discipline is that voters, and the country as a whole, are not ready to face up to unpleasant truths. Voters, however, have to be led, not just followed up the wrong path.

Index

If you have found this resource useful you may be interested in other titles from Gower Applied Research

The Business of Europe is Politics
Dimitris N Chorafas
978-0-566-09151-3

Looking Beyond Profit
Peggy Chiu
978-0-7546-7337-8

The Durable Corporation
Güler Aras and David Crowther
978-0-566-08819-3

Spirituality and Corporate Social Responsibility
David Buna-Litic
978-0-7546-4763-8

Transformation Management
Ronnie Lessem and Alexander Schieffer
978-0-566-08896-4

Integral Research and Innovation
Ronnie Lessem and Alexander Schieffer
978-0-566-08918-3

Wealth, Welfare and the Global Free Market
Ibrahim Ozer Ertuna
978-0-566-08905-3

GOWER